MENTAL CONFLICT

Mental conflict is the condition of a divided mind consciously torn between contrary desires or beliefs. For Greek philosophers it is a puzzle provocative of theory; they accommodate it differently within different structurings of the mind's operations.

Socrates focuses all a man's desires upon a single goal taken to constitute the human good. This permits vacillation between varying conceptions of the end or devisings of the means, and consequent regret; but judgement, or misjudgement, is always in control. Plato comes instead to find a disunity in desire, which means that reason may fail to be master within its own house. Unity is to be worked for in the convergence of all desires through the persuasions of reason.

Aristotle assents to rather the same view but supposes that, when reason fails to win out in action, it also loses out in judgement, ceasing to perceive the demands of the situation. Plato's practical reason is a child of heaven, whose voice is not stilled by being unheeded, while Aristotle's is a creature of earth, emergent out of desire and eclipsed by desires in effective revolt.

The Stoics return to a Socratic insistence that my decision is the decision of my reason. Emotion may still intrude, but as a perversion of reason. Thus they can maintain that the person remains single as the subject of decision, the agent of action, and the bearer of responsibility.

This book is the first detailed analysis of the treatment of mental conflict within Greek philosophy. It will be important reading for all students and teachers of ancient and moral philosophy.

A.W. Price is Reader in Philosophy at the University of York. In 1989/90 he was a Junior Fellow at the Center for Hellenic Studies, Washington DC. He has taught at Wadham College Oxford, the University of Hong Kong, Brown University and the Graduate School of the Chinese Academy of Social Sciences. He is the author of *Love and Friendship in Plato and Aristotle* (1989).

ISSUES IN ANCIENT PHILOSOPHY
General editor: Malcolm Schofield

GOD AND GREEK PHILOSOPHY
L.P. Gerson

ANCIENT CONCEPTS OF PHILOSOPHY
William Jordan

LANGUAGE, THOUGHT AND FALSEHOOD
Nicholas Denyer

MENTAL CONFLICT

A. W. Price

London and New York

First published 1995
by Routledge
11 New Fetter Lane, London EC4P 4EE

Simultaneously published in the USA and Canada
by Routledge
29 West 35th Street, New York, NY 10001

© 1995 A.W. Price

Typeset in Garamond by
Ponting–Green Publishing Services,
Chesham, Buckinghamshire
Printed and bound in Great Britain by
T.J. Press (Padstow) Ltd, Padstow, Cornwall

British Library Cataloguing in Publication Data
A catalogue record for this book is available from
the British Library

Library of Congress Cataloging in Publication Data
Mental conflict/A.W. Price
p.   cm. – (Issues in ancient philosophy)
Includes bibliographical references (p.   ) and indexes.
1. Philosophy of mind. 2. Philosophy, Ancient.
I. Title. II. Series.
B105.M55P75   1994
128'.2'0938–dc20   94–3935

ISBN 0–415–04151–1 (hbk)
ISBN 0–415–11557–4 (pbk)

FOR DOLORES

But once in a while the odd thing happens,
Once in a while the moon turns blue.

W.H. Auden, *Paul Bunyan*

CONTENTS

Preface   ix
Hors-d'œuvre   xii

INTRODUCTION   1

1 SOCRATES   8
   Socrates and Diotima: an appendix   27

2 PLATO   30

3 ARISTOTLE   104

4 THE STOICS   145
   Between Plato and the Stoa: appendix on Posidonius   175

   Notes   179
   Primary sources   205
   Note on translations   209
   Secondary citations   211
   Index   215

PREFACE

This volume owes its existence to two pieces of good fortune, an invitation from Malcolm Schofield on behalf of Routledge, and an appointment to the Center for Hellenic Studies in Washington, DC for 1989–90. Together, they provided me with the stimulus and opportunity to explore a perennial topic about which we should still be able to learn much from a reflective study of Greek philosophy.

I know no scholar for whom a year at the Center was not a period in paradise. I was further lucky that my time there fell within the ideally beneficent and sagacious reign of Zeph and Diana Stewart, whose kindness and conversation were relished by everyone. Otherwise my happiness owed most to two friends: Andrei Lebedev, whose spontaneity, warmth, and intensity introduced me to a new and un-English style of friendship, and Peter Cockhill, who made a virtue of absence by a constant and stylish correspondence in which a unique personality was always present. Of course America is a land of companionship: old and new friends whom I made or met there included Henry and Hazel Dicum, John and Kate Ferrari, Dick and Catherine Hare, Ian Ker, Tony Long, David Mabberley, Paige Newmark, Martha Nussbaum, Tom and Peg Olshewsky, Michael Pakaluk and his family, Andrei Rossius, Chris Shields, Tatyana Tolstaya, and Stephen White. As for my dedication, 'What would bechance at Lyonnesse / While I should sojourn there / No prophet durst declare.'

I am indebted to Malcolm Schofield not only for inviting this book, and then awaiting it patiently, but for improving it all materially. I am also grateful for written comments on parts of it from John Ferrari, Chris Shields, and Christopher Taylor. Some late revisions were prompted by the kind loan of two papers by John Cooper; a summary of his reconstrual of Posidonius in Annas (1992)

ix

had already awakened me from dogmatic slumber. The unnecessary deficiencies that remain, and do not derive from sheer oversight, may be blamed on lack of stamina: as E.M. Cioran has written,

> A work is finished when we can no longer improve it, though we know it to be inadequate and incomplete. We are so overtaxed by it that we no longer have the power to add a single comma, however indispensable.

I fear that I may be found ungenerous to the living, if not over-scrupulous towards the dead, in making so much reference to primary texts, but often rather little to secondary literature. In fact, I have been continually educated by contributors to the present renaissance in the philosophical study of the Greeks. I gained from my old tutor Anthony Kenny a first realization that reading texts can be, like death, well, a biggish adventure. That lesson has been refreshed by the example of Martha Nussbaum, who inimitably displays how to live dangerously; anyone who infers from our livelier differences of opinion that I am ungrateful for the enlivening is ignorant of the rules of the game. My understanding of Aristotle's moral psychology owes most to Loening (1903), a lucid and self-effacing work that is transparent to a cornucopia of citations (which is why I shall not refer to it again). It will be more evident how much I have learnt about the Stoics from Inwood (1985). Were I intending to make a direct contribution to modern philosophy, I would be hard put to it to match the virtues of Pears (1984) and Gardner (1993). As it is, it is work enough to aspire towards the high standards of Gregory Vlastos, a great scholar and good man whom we all miss; 'No matter. Further and further still / Through the world's vaporous vitiate air / His words wing on – as live words will.'

I am aware that readers and reviewers in a hurry would prefer a book less densely written than this one. As Chabrier remarked of his opera *Gwendoline*, it needs to be taken in dilution. I hope that the patient student, using what I write as a commentary upon the texts and not as a substitute for them, will come to attend to them more keenly, whether in the Greek or in translation. Philosophical exegesis is a dialectic of attending to texts and having ideas, but interpreters' ideas that are not ways of reading or explaining or assessing particular points in a text inhabit a limbo between interpretation and free invention which is usually (though not always) a habitat of second-rate philosophizing. I have less hope, or desire, that my conclusions should be generally accepted; for I have to confess that, despite the good fortune of the invitation and the appointment, I would have hesitated to embark upon this topic if I had been able to predict how difficult it would turn out to be.

HORS-D'ŒUVRE

All that you have said seems spoken after my own mind,
Yet still the heart in me swells up in anger.

Homer, Iliad

I am aware of these things you warn me of,
But, though I have understanding, my nature compels me.

Euripides, Chrysippus

I begin to speak, but my lips deny passage to my words;
A great force sends out my voice, and a greater holds it back.
Heavenly gods, you can all witness that this thing that I desire,
I do not desire.

Seneca, Phaedra

Though with their high wrongs I am struck to th'quick,
Yet with my nobler reason 'gainst my fury
Do I take part.

Shakespeare, The Tempest

Since thy original lapse, true Liberty
Is lost, which always with right Reason dwells
Twinn'd, and from her hath no dividual being:
Reason in man obscur'd, or not obeyd,
Immediately inordinate desires
And upstart Passions catch the Government
From Reason, and to servitude reduce
Man till then free.

Milton, Paradise Lost

HORS-D'ŒUVRE

When the court of the mind is ruled by Reason,
  I know it is wiser for us to part;
But Love is a spy who is plotting treason,
  In league with that warm, red rebel, the Heart.
            Ella Wheeler Wilcox, 'Communism'

What are we but sedition? like this poor France, faction against faction, within ourselves, every piece playing every moment its own game, with as much difference between us and ourselves as between ourselves and others. Whoever will look narrowly into his own bosom will hardly find himself twice in the same condition. I give to myself sometimes one face and sometimes another, according to the side I turn to. I have nothing to say of myself, entirely and without qualification.

            (Montaigne, in Walter Pater, *Gaston de Latour*)

'Does my vain spirit ever tell me I am wrong?' 'Not your vain spirit, but your serious spirit. – If one leads you wrong, I am sure the other tells you of it.'

            (Jane Austen, *Emma*)

'You see,' said Billy Smallbury, 'the man's will was to do right, sure enough, but his heart didn't chime in.'

            (Thomas Hardy, *Far from the Madding Crowd*)

His reason and his propensities had seldom any reciprocating influence, having separated by mutual consent long ago: thence it sometimes happened that, while his intentions were as honourable as could be wished, any particular deed formed a dark background which threw them into fine relief. The sergeant's vicious phases being the offspring of impulse, and his virtuous phases of cool meditation, the latter had a modest tendency to be oftener heard of than seen.

            (ibid.)

For her good intentions and her firm will to decency were something that she did not for an instant lose even during such states; only, then they stood outside, waiting, and simply had no say in this world so changed by desires.

            (Robert Musil, *The Man without Qualities*)

xiii

And even now, though his intellect told him that the message probably meant death – still, that was not what he believed, and the unreasonable hope persisted, and his heart banged.

(George Orwell, *1984*)

I have never had much trouble simultaneously entertaining diametrically opposed propositions, and welcome the possibility that this is not because I have one mind and am out of it, but because I have lots of them, all beavering away on their own. I know perfectly well that magpies are powerless to influence our fate or foreshadow misfortune and I also know with certainty that they jolly well can.

(Alice Thomas Ellis, *Home Life Three*)

INTRODUCTION

In social conflict one person opposes another. They may differ in belief (say about the various consequences of different economic policies), or in preference (say about whether to go to war, or where to build a new road), or, most often, in both. Frequently they will differ in their evaluations, that is, in their views of what is good or best, of what matters or matters most and how it matters. Here their divergence is indissolubly both in belief, since they disagree about what is true and false, and in desire if not in preference, since the presence of appropriate desire is a mark of sincerity in an evaluation. (I can find a proposal ingenious without favouring it, but not without being attracted in a way by the thought of its adoption or implementation.) It is further necessary, if the difference is to amount to a conflict, that the parties should not merely contradict each other, but confront one another as adversaries. When Chairman Mao proclaimed 'Let a hundred flowers bloom, and a hundred schools of thought contend', he was (ostensibly) welcoming a variety of opinions and predilections that might co-exist and compete in a free market of ideas within a society of comrades. In situations of conflict, views that are not one's own appear threatening or damaging: they present themselves not as sources of refreshing variety or of healthy competition, but as objects of hostility. One can enjoy contradiction, and benefit from competition, but the parties to a conflict are not just rivals but antagonists. Conflict is always uncomfortable.

In mental conflict a mind is divided against itself, and becomes a battleground of opposing beliefs or desires. The conflicted mind is characterized by relations not just of difference and divergence, but of contention and confrontation. It feels itself not so much attracted from outside by incompatible alternatives between which it has to make a choice, as torn within itself by hostile forces between which it cannot make peace. It is aware not just of contrasting considerations that need to be brought together in an exercise of judgement, but of colliding tendencies that refuse to co-exist within a single perspective. One may perceive an external figure ambivalently as a friend and as an enemy, with something like a gestalt switch between the two aspects as one's attitude alternates between love and hate. Even if both responses are perceptive and not simply projective, one may fail to form or maintain a unified grasp of a complex reality, vacillating instead between simple views that resist reconciliation within a conspectus. What hinders the achievement of a single viewpoint is not the complexity of the object but the ambivalence of the subject: his attitudes are mutually antithetical, and hold out against one another instead of co-operating in a durable synthesis. At heart his enmity is self-directed, so that he feels partly alien to himself. The external object may become the occasion of his internal conflict, but he is himself its cause. Most hatred contains an element of self-hatred; as E.M. Cioran has put it, 'Two enemies – the same man *divided*.'[1]

It is inevitable that we should speak of mental conflict in social language. There is no easy demarcation here between metaphor and reality: the mind constitutes itself according to a model in our language that is also its own, so that our ways of speaking are its ways of being. Its modes of differentiating itself from the world become modes of differentiation within itself. Interpersonal relations are reflected internally by intrapersonal ones, so that the mind becomes the scene of a quasi-social drama. It is no accident that already in antiquity the classic source for what I have been describing should have been a dramatic monologue in which a single character engages in an argument with herself as strenuous as any that she conducts with others. Medea is being betrayed by her husband Jason who proposes to discard her in pursuit of a marriage of social advancement. She once killed a brother to save him, and has already set in train the death of his wife-to-be; so her standards of decisive action are high. She now feels that full revenge demands the lives of their two children; but is she capable of that sacrifice? Euripides represents her mental conflict in a long speech (*Medea*, 1021–80) marked by abrupt transitions. Preserving and signalling these, one may reduce her train of thought to the following spare summary:

A My children, you have a home to inhabit for ever [that is,

Hades], while I shall depart in exile for a foreign land, losing you for ever. How unhappy I am in my wilfulness! (1021–39)

B Alas, why do you look and smile at me? My heart fails me. Farewell my previous plans – I shall take my children away (1040–8).

C Yet do I want to become ridiculous by leaving my enemies unpunished? What a coward I am to open my mind to feeble words! Enter the house, children (1049–55).

D No, my heart, do not act so. Spare my children. Living with us there they will gladden you (1056–8).

E But I shall never hand over my children to be abused by my enemies. I am taking the most wretched path, and sending these on a more wretched still. I wish to address my children. How I love them! I can no longer look at them, but am defeated by my ills. I understand what ills I am about to dare, but my heart is master of my deliberations (1059–80).[2]

The passage became famous, and fuelled many theories. Integral to the conflict from which Medea suffers is that her emotions pull not only in different directions but against one another: she feels divided not only within but against herself. Her feelings as a mother show up the 'wilfulness' of her desire for revenge (1028), while her desire for revenge shows up her feelings as a mother as 'feeble' (1052). So much is clear, but much else is open: there would seem to be three broad lines of interpretation, which I shall label concisely, if not quite appositely, 'oscillation', 'vacillation', and 'lack of self-control'. (It is not my task to arbitrate between them; the passage suits my purposes because it can be read variously.)

(i) *Oscillation* involves a clear purpose that is certain to prevail, but shifting thoughts. Medea has long made her decision (at least by 791–7), from which the chorus could not shake her (812–19); in the words of Mrs Thatcher, 'The lady's not for turning.' (This could explain her most troubling illogicality, that within a few lines, 1058–61, she takes the alternative to killing her children to be taking them with her, and leaving them behind: if she is already committed to killing them, she need not decide what she would do otherwise.) Hugh Lloyd-Jones puts it well:

> The fate of the children has long since been decided; Medea has never seriously contemplated renouncing her revenge, for if she did so, she would not be Medea. The poet is not

3

showing us how Medea makes her decision; that decision
has been taken, swiftly and silently, long before; rather, he
is showing us the full extent of the agony which the
prospect of the decision's execution causes.

(1980: 59)

Medea oscillates between restating her irrevocable decision, and
dwelling upon its cost to herself. (Egocentricity is a feature of
her reflections even at their most motherly.) As the moment of
execution approaches, she takes refuge in expressions of affection that she can allow herself just because they are futile. Her
mind is determined but conflicted: the imminence of action
intensifies compunction that decision could not silence. She
realizes that what she is planning is 'ill' in the sense not that it
is wrong, but that its costs are high. When she says 'My heart is
master of my deliberations', she may intend either – and
Euripides may intend both – of two constructions: she may
mean that her tender reflections are powerless against her
passionate purpose ('is master of' meaning *defeats*), or that her
passion dictates her plans ('is master of' meaning *directs*).
Revenge is her overriding goal, and nothing can impede it. She
is the reluctant but resolute victim of her own strength of will.

(ii) *Vacillation* excludes any fixed purpose. As the time draws near,
even Medea becomes indecisive. When she twice switches, first
rapidly then abruptly, to thoughts of sparing her children (B,
D), she means what she says, and is not indulging in idle
temptations. She realizes simultaneously that now is the time to
act on her decision, and that no decision is binding; she suffers
from an awareness of her own freedom. As befits a barbarian
woman, her rationality is limited: she is able to entertain
conflicting considerations in turn, but not to integrate them
within a single process of deliberation that could yield a decision
all things considered. She comes closer to an all-in view towards
the end (within E); but even there she can only register the 'ills'
from which she suffers and those which she intends (1077–8),
with no ability to weigh costs and benefits against one another.
Hence she can only switch between different perspectives, until
ultimately, if only through exhaustion, she feels ready to act
within one that prevails. Her vacillation comes to an end,
without achieving resolution, when she senses – or lets herself
suppose – that she no longer has the strength to endure the pain

that comes of dwelling on the drawbacks. She does not make up her mind: her mind gives up. She declares that she knows what she is up to at the moment when she can no longer face up to it (1076–8). She will be acting on an abdication of decision.

(iii) *Lack of self-control* is a failure to maintain one's autonomy in action or judgement. The abruptness of Medea's shifts and turns can be understood in another way. A speaker can only, without ambiguity, express one thought at a time, but the state of mind that Medea is displaying may be one not of change but of division; transitions may be lacking because her thoughts are not evolving, but locked in a wrestler's hold. Whether or not there is any uncertainty about the outcome, she is conscious of a play of opposing forces that holds her mind in tension. Her own identity relates uncertainly to the powers within her. She can address her heart (*thymos*) as if it were a distinct person whom she may entreat to act otherwise, and hope to persuade by reminder of a possible benefit *to itself* (D). She seems half puppet and half puppeteer; she can say 'I am overcome by ills' (1077), but often seems the impresario of her own passionate repertory. When she concludes, as I rendered it, 'I understand what ills I am about to perform, but my heart is master of my deliberations' (1078–9), she can be understood in two ways. She may mean that her heart defeats her reflections in action, so that she considers the murder to be wrong all things considered but is carried away by an overpowering passion; if so, she remains reasonable in reflection, and is led into action by forces with which she refuses to identify.[3] Alternatively, her reason may have been taken over by a dominant passion that wins out not just in action but also in deliberation: passion suborns reason and drives out reason-ableness, with or without the subject's connivance. Either way, there can arise a complex mix of autonomy and heteronomy: the subject may allow one set of motivations to become dominant, though aware that what is once given may be regretted and yet not easily taken back. The ambiguity need not be resolved: we may understand Medea as alternately listening to reason's own voice, which opposes anger, and lending that voice to the cause of anger to become its mouthpiece.

Greek philosophers offer accounts of mental conflict that connect with these interpretations of Euripides. They must accommodate some common property if it is indeed of mental conflict that each is offering an account, but within different articulations of the mind's structure:

(a) All human purposes are the offspring of reason, which assesses options as subserving a single long-term goal that is the ultimate target of all desire. Rational judgement is the focus of our thinking and the stimulus of our desiring. It does not follow that we always succeed in being sensible and reasonable. (ii) is still possible: a man may fail to maintain a constant conception of the end, or may keep changing his mind about how to achieve it. This may fill his mind with ruefulness, so that he feels conflicted between thoughts and second thoughts. (i) is less possible: if all desire shares a single long-term goal, then decision may still be difficult, but not in the manner of causing agonizing about the costs even if it is right. (iii) is impossible: reason is always in control, and can be neither suborned nor overridden by passion.

(b) Reason is not one part of the soul among others, if that means that reason can decide one way and the subject consciously act in another. The decision of reason is the final word of the individual, whose nature is rational – if also fallible. As within (iii), reason may succumb to passion, losing its capacity to reach a reflective decision, and lapsing into passionate resolves. Yet these are still simply the subject's (cf. Gill 1987: 30 on *Medea* 1079); and passion cannot produce action contrary to actual rational choice. Mental conflict is still possible, and it can take two forms. Firstly, as in (i), a man may, in an idiomatic sense, not *want* to act as reason prescribes. Irrational inclinations (in Stoic jargon, attractions towards irrational presentations) may remain as an undertow, dragging against the dominant current of reason. Secondly, as in (ii), reason may itself be torn, so that it teeters between different possibilities satisfying conflicting considerations (again in Stoic jargon, havering between assents to opposed presentations). It rebounds from its own decisions, so that it backs and fills to a shifting wind. Thus a man may know what to do but not feel like doing it, or he may be in two or more minds about what to do.

(c) Reason is one part of the soul among others, each deriving from different sources in the psyche characteristically different desires and goals. Man is a composite, and the fault-lines show. No part is privileged in that its decisions are bound to be of effect, nor does the subject enjoy the privilege of being able to make a decision independently of his composite psychology. How I act depends on the relative strengths of the interested parts; *I* do not stand regal and apart, bestowing efficacy according to my will. Judgement ideally expresses a united mind, but reason has no magic to impose unity or to make disunity of no effect. However, the various parts do interact: the irrational soul may be subordinate to reason, so that rational judgement is echoed through the soul; or, as within (iii), it may suborn reason, so that the capacities of reason come to serve the ends of unreason. Acting with and upon the parts of his soul, an individual can to an extent modify their repertory. Though the subject cannot transcend his own psychology, we should not view him as passive: the parts of his soul are *his* parts, and what *they* do *he* does. Yet not all that he does is done freely. Mental life is a complicated mixture of self-manifestation and self-creation. The divided mind is a mind that has failed fully to re-create itself according to some ideal of how it should become united.

Within Greek philosophy, we find Socrates championing (a), while the mature Plato elaborates (c), and the Stoics (b). Aristotle is hard to place. In many ways he appears to follow Plato, though with scruples about the language of 'parts' and the lines of partition. However, he agrees with Socrates that no man can consciously act contrary to rational judgement. Somehow he must be preserving features of Plato's account while so relating practical reason to the rest of the soul that Socrates turns out in one way to have been right. (a) seems individual, and indeed idiosyncratic, but to examine (b) and (c) is at the same time to reconsider whether they must really be theoretical rivals, or might just constitute different pictures or ways of speaking. Often in philosophy disagreements need less to be resolved than dissolved. Studying in turn the treatments of mental conflict in Socrates, Plato, Aristotle, and the Stoics, we should learn much about the difficulties that come of our being human; also about those that come when we are doing philosophy.

1

SOCRATES

1

Plato's early dialogues contain a moral psychology very different from that which emerges in the *Gorgias* and *Phaedo* and is elaborated in the *Republic*. We need not decide here whether they present the mature views of the historical Socrates or the early views of Plato himself; they may, of course, do both. Their conception of the nature and goal of desire appears at once attractive and alien: *we*, surely, cannot be quite like that. It has the corollary that most forms of mental conflict become an impossibility. It is thus highly relevant to our topic in an indirect way: we learn how we might be if we were to be less liable to mental conflict than we are. Socrates illumines the reality that he denies.

My primary source for Socrates' general conception of desire will be the *Symposium*. To the informed, this may seem a perverse choice, for it is one of the first dialogues, together with the *Phaedo*, in which Plato ascends far beyond anything that we have reason to take as Socratic into the empyrean of his own theory of transcendent Forms. However, while the *Symposium* provides no reliable independent evidence of earlier views, nothing prevents it from combining a psychology that is strictly or loosely Socratic (strictly if it presents Socrates' own views, loosely if it develops them) with a metaphysics that is wholly Platonic; and this is what I believe it to do. Diotima, the mythical priestess whom Socrates cites as his mentor, introduces the ascent-passage which first features the Forms with a sentence that marks off what follows: 'Into these matters of love perhaps you too, Socrates, could be initiated; but I do not know if you would be capable of the rites and revelations for the sake of which even they exist, if anyone pursues them correctly' (209e5–210a2). This indicates

8

SOCRATES

that the so-called 'lesser mysteries' which precede the 'greater' are either Socratic, or at least much more nearly Socratic than the theory of Forms; so there is no sound inference from the Platonism of the ensuing metaphysics against the Socratism of the antecedent psychology.[1] The combination is still unexpected – which may be why it is overlooked. What could explain it? We need to remember that the *Symposium* is not a treatise by Plato on the nature of love, but a series of speeches trying to praise love as beautifully as possible, just as Eryximachus proposed (177d2–3).[2] It is true that Socrates initially agrees with the proposal (d6–e6), but later baulks when it appears that truth is not expected of encomia (198c5–199a6). However, there may be fine authorial irony when he offers instead not a eulogy but the truth told in his own way (199a6–b1): what he will say may be truth from his own point of view, but eulogy from Plato's. By retaining a Socratic psychology Plato can combine what Socrates contrasts: Socrates will tell the truth as he sees it, but in Plato's eyes that will be half-truth too approving of love by half. It is striking that Socrates makes no distinction between good and bad love such as was drawn by Pausanias (who refused simply to eulogize Eros, instead opposing a popular love that is indeed vulgar to a heavenly love that is free of outrage, 180c4–181c4), and will be recurrent in Plato (cf. *Rep* 3.403a4–b3, *Phdr* 265e3–266b1, *Laws* 8.837b2–d1). As we shall see, Socrates remains free of moral error in Plato's eyes, for his vision of love is blind to those aspects that are not proper objects of eulogy. A Socratic conception of love is an expression of innocence.

Agathon threw out the commonplace that love is of beauty (197b5); Socrates wishes to draw the conclusion that its object is one's own happiness (204e6–7). He gets there partly on his own, partly on the authority of Diotima. What takes him there is three quick transitions: Love loves beautiful things to have them for himself (204d5–7), to love beautiful things is to love good things (e1–3), and to have good things is to be happy (204e5–205a1). Thus the lover desires to have beautiful things; so he desires to have good things; so he desires to be happy. Happiness is a final end: we need not ask why anyone wishes to be happy (205a2–3). As so often, Socrates makes his way with a mixture of truisms and surprises; all his steps are presented as obvious, and yet none is simply downhill. The topic of the *Symposium* is specifically erotic love, and this is most plausibly of beauty not because love is an effect of which only beauty can be a cause (*pace* 206d3–7), but because to be in love with someone is to find him beautiful: as we would say, beauty is not always the

9

material, but is always the *intentional*, object or occasion of love. Further, this beauty is specifically erotic: it is the kind of beauty that is correlative to a sexual response or a personal infatuation. It is a different if related matter to identify love's goal or objective, though the concept of desire blurs the distinction: in love, I am said to desire both a person to be won (who is the object), and some end to be achieved (which is my objective). We may presume that the lover wishes to possess the beloved in some way. If he is to think of achieving that goal as itself beautiful, this may derive from his finding the beloved beautiful, but implies a different manner of being beautiful. When Socrates is later reported as refusing to make love to Alcibiades on the ground, as I would paraphrase it, that while *he* was beautiful, *that* would not be (218e2–219a1), his objection was presumably not aesthetic, let alone erotic, but (in some way) moral.[3] It was earlier agreed that good things are also beautiful (201c2–3). This must apply even to health, strength, and wealth (all mentioned at 200c6–d1), which are commonplace examples of goods (cf. *Gorg* 451e3–5, 467e4–5) even if the commonplace is not secure from Socratic questioning elsewhere (cf. the argument around a claim at *Meno* 88d4–5 that they really vary between being good and bad). Beauty here can be nothing specifically and literally sensible. It is rather, metaphorically, the face that goodness wears when it draws or attracts us (cf. Price 1989: 16). This thought can help us to follow the new claim not only that beautiful things are also good (so that beauties and goods coincide actually or materially), but that to desire to have beautiful things is to desire to have good things (so that beauties and goods coincide intentionally): to desire a good is to find it beautiful, and what one finds beautiful, in this sense, is what one desires as good.[4] Socrates is thus depending upon a sleight of hand (shifting from the erotic beauty of love's object to the different beauty of its objective) and an assumption: goodness is the goal of desire. Agathon's commonplace has been translated into Socratic philosophy.

Now it is possible to accept the assumption in a sense that relegates it to tautology: thinking good might reduce to desiring, so that to think something good is simply to desire it; goodness might merely be the *formal* object of desire. That this is not Socrates' meaning is clear when he distinguishes the good from other alleged *substantial* objects of desire: love is only of the half or of the whole if these happen to be good, and only of one's own if one calls goodness 'one's own' (205e1–8); desiring does not constitute thinking good but presupposes it. Socrates adds further substance to the goal of desire in two ways. The shift from 'beautiful' to 'good' is not made for its own sake, but to introduce the thought that the final end of desire is *eudaimonia* or happiness (202c6–11, 204e1–7). Happiness is the state of having acquired goods and beauties (202c10–11, 205a1), and of possessing them still (204e5–7). It is a complex state, requiring the enjoyment of a multiplicity of goods over a long period of time. (As Aristotle was to put it, 'One swallow does not make a summer', *NE* 1.7.1098a18–19.) Next, Socrates advances from the proposition that men always want to have good things (205a7–8) to the yet more striking claim that they want to have them always (206a9–12). Desire is thus identified as a point of view upon a very broad perspective: to desire a thing is to take a wide view of it as it were both spatially, within a broad pattern, and temporally, within an unending sequence, of goods.

We may be happy to accept that there is such desire, but hesitate to claim that all desire is such. Do, and can, all desires always take such long views? This worry increases when Socrates reports Diotima as defining love more specifically and idiomatically as one of the species of desire: though all men love and desire happiness, we call 'lovers' only those who pursue it in one manner among others (205a5–d8). What is the defining goal of love narrowly so called? It is to achieve desire's final end, which includes immortality, through the means of 'generation in beauty' (206e2–207a4). In sexual reproduction or verbal communication the lover passes on his physical or mental life to a child or loved one so that it will continue even after he himself has died. Diotima speaks as if the thesis that generic love is for always possessing the good oneself (206a11–12) *entails* the corollary that specific love pursues the end of immortality through the means of generation in beauty (note the repeated 'necessary', 207a1, a3). Here the Socratic view that all desire is directed towards happiness, and so concerned about one's whole life, is developed into a yet stranger thesis, useful to Plato in defining the specificities of love, that it must be sensitive to the demands of immortality. (We may prefer to distinguish sharply between (a) always desiring to possess the good, (b) desiring to possess it now and ever after, i.e., so long as one is alive, and (c) desiring to exist, and to possess it, for ever – none of which entails, or need involve, the next.) I need not now discuss the details or the difficulties (some of which I treat in Price 1989: 25–35). What we have to notice here is how extraordinary the theory is as an account not just of the project of procreation, but of all erotic desire. In particular, do sexual desires all really derive from so distant a goal? Socrates urges us to accept that they do. He makes out that the pull of generation is evident even in our physiology: it is beauty that causes sexual arousal, and the reason is that conception and procreation cannot take place 'in the ugly' (206c4–d1); further, our metabolism is constantly setting us an example by replacing old 'hair and flesh and bones and blood' by new (207d5–e1). He takes our bodies to be the home of a natural teleology whereby 'mortal nature seeks so far as it can to exist always and be immortal' (d1–2). This nature is evident in our bodily processes, and in the behaviour of unintelligent creatures: we see how keen animals are not only to copulate but to bring up offspring, and even, if necessary, to die so that it can live (207a7–b6). Of course they are dumb, but we share an animal nature with them, and can draw on our own conscious and communicable desires in order to interpret what they are really after. We are aware within ourselves of the pull of immortality in many forms: the ambitious are ready to face any danger for the sake of a lasting reputation (208c4–d2); Alcestis, Achilles, and Codrus, all of whom laid down their lives, can only have thought to leave an undying memory behind them (d1–e1); men who prefer women to boys suppose that by begetting children they will achieve eternal happiness for themselves (e1–5). Thus sexual desires have a double aspect, being children at once of our ultimate ends, and of our physical make-up. The two aspects are wedded by the natural teleology that governs all living creatures: immortality is an end common to unconscious processes and conscious purposes. Sexual desires are at once spontaneous responses (like sexual arousal) and immortal longings.

This conception fits the purposes of eulogy in two ways. Firstly, it marginalizes, if it does not actually exclude, the sterilities of the practising pederast, viewed ambivalently by most Greeks (cf. Pausanias' speech in the *Symposium*) and dismissively by Socrates (who once compared them to piglets' rubbing themselves against stones, Xenophon *Memorabilia* 1.2.29–30). In pursuit of 'immortality together with the good' (206e8–207a1) a man may still pursue transient goods that have a place within a longer sequence, but ephemeral indulgence cuts sexuality off from the roots that bed it so deeply in our biology. It is, in fact, *un*erotic, in that it discards the purpose that marks off eros from other human pursuits. (Here the theory has prescriptive implications that may be motivations.) Secondly, and most relevantly for us, Socrates' conception would

12

appear to exclude any real conflict between sexual desires and moral scruples: if all desires aim at the same long-term goal, achieving it demands judgement and perseverance but not self-control. Now this might be doubted. Borrow a different example, that of thirst, from the *Republic* (4.439b3–c7). Even if Socrates is right, might I still not feel thirsty at a time when I know, say for reasons of etiquette, that I must not drink? And might this not produce a conflict between thirst, urging me towards the happiness of drinking, and other considerations that tell decisively against drinking on behalf of happiness overall? This is plausible but not cogent. If all my desires share the final goal of my overall well-being, and I am of one mind in judging that this requires me not to drink, thirst cannot fuel a conflict of desire. What makes thirst refractory in the *Republic* is that it assigns to appetites a final goal of their own, namely, sensual pleasure (cf. 436a11, 439d8); then thirst may be inhibited (say by visions of a hangover, when the only drink available is gin), but it will tend to be deaf to the dry demands of prudence. If Socrates' view that all desire derives from a single conception of the good is to apply even to sensual desires, he must make the most of a distinction between thirst as a sensation (which has a cause but not a goal), and thirst as a desire (which pursues happiness). Plato will call appetite 'a companion of various repletions and pleasures' (*Rep* 439d8), whose impulses come of 'affections and diseases' (d2). Socrates must liken the thirsty man who knows he must not drink to a man walking uphill with tired feet but a mind fully set on completing his journey: both feel a discomfort that is not a conflict. The discomfort gives him *some reason* to drink; and he may well have *some desire* to drink, but one that, if outweighed, retains no factional power of resistance. Thirst may not be silenced or lose its voice (for relieving discomfort is a special part of happiness), but it will be hushed and no longer demand a hearing: the discomfort may continue to gnaw, but the desire must cease to press.[5] Without final ends of its own, appetite cannot battle against reason.[6]

If the conception of desire in the *Symposium* remains Socratic, it is also precarious, for it is easier to suppose that desires that are rooted in the body have their own ends that are not identical to the goal of reason. In the *Phaedo*, written at about the same time as the *Symposium*, Plato ascribes desires to the body itself (66c7), and aims them at 'the pleasures that are through the body' (65a7). Celebrating the escape of the soul from the body, and not hymning the loves of soul and body, the *Phaedo* takes a less positive view of the body's inclinations. The *Symposium* avoids pointing soul and body in different directions: even if we say (as Socrates in fact does not) that our bodies desire what our 'mortal nature' pursues (207d1), this will still be a single end desired as a result both of rational deliberation (cf. 207b6–7), and of a natural teleology that explains both animal behaviour and physiological processes.[7] Of course the upshot contradicts common sense, and may seem not so much innocent as myopic. Socrates owes us a redescription of the phenomena that we commonly take to constitute mental conflict. For this we must now turn to an earlier and more thoroughly Socratic dialogue, the *Protagoras*.

2

The section of the *Protagoras* that concerns us (351b3–358d4) reaches a statement of a Socratic thesis within the scope of a less expected supposition:

> If what is pleasant is good, no one who either knows or believes that something else is better than what he is doing, and is in his power to do, subsequently does the other, when he can do what is better.

(358b6–c1)

This conjunction of the novel and the familiar raises questions: has Socrates really adopted hedonism? If not, why is he making use of it? What will be implicit in the *Symposium* has been explicitly argued here: knowledge of the good can never be defeated by desire. Yet it is unclear what Socrates is up to.

The Socratic thesis itself is at once reasserted categorically:

> Now surely no one freely goes for bad things or things he believes to be bad; it's not, it seems to me, in human nature to be prepared to go for what you think to be bad in preference to what is good.

(358c6–d2)

I have already noted (in §1) that a statement like this can be saying very little. We read much the same not only in the half-Socratic *Gorgias* ('It is for the sake of the good that those who do these things do them all', 468b7–8), but even in the non-Socratic *Republic* (the good is 'that which every soul pursues and for its sake does all things', 6.505d11–e1), where rational and irrational desires are targeted upon very different objects. What gives the statement substance here in the *Protagoras* is two things. Firstly, a 'bad' action is taken to be one that the agent performs instead of an alternative that is both 'better than what he is doing, and is in his power to do' (358b7–c1). The thought is not merely that all desires aim at goods, but that one must choose to do what one judges to be best. Secondly, it is assumed that the agent is out for his own good. Socrates gets to hedonism through the concept of living well (*eu zên*): no one counts as living well if he lives in pain (351b3–6), and what is good is living a pleasant life to the end (b6–c1). He later argues that the many call some pleasures wrong because they produce eventual and greater pains (353c4–354d3), implicitly for the agent.[8] People do not merely pursue the good, but make their choices after weighing the alternatives, short-term and long-term, as if in the scales (356a8–c1). Pursuing the good in a maximizing mode, they need an art of measurement as a guide (356c8–357d7). Hedonism seems to consort happily with this conception of choice, for the pleasures and pains of a lifetime sound the sorts of thing to be weighed one against another.

What form does the hedonism take? Plato takes us briskly through an ascending sequence of theses: pleasure (or at least no preponderance of pain) is a necessary condition of living well (351b4–6); pleasure is a sufficient condition of living well (b6–c1); things are good in respect of being pleasant (c4–5); things are bad to the extent that they are painful (c5–6), good to the extent that they are pleasant (e1–2); pleasure is good (e2–3); being pleasant is identical to being good (e5–6). This final claim takes a linguistic turn: the terms 'pleasant' and 'good' name one value, not two (355b3–c1, c5–6). Short-term pleasures may turn out badly in the long run, and in this sense pleasant things can be evils (353c8–354c2). Socrates anticipated that from the start (351c5), and it disarms the initial resistance to hedonism that Protagoras shares with the many (c1–d7). It is implied that most people do not observe the maxim 'Know thyself' that Socrates is always quoting (e.g., 343b3); for he argues that they really accept hedonism, and infers that pleasure is all that they pursue (354b5–d1). If we distinguish ethical hedonism as a thesis about values (pleasure is the only good) from psychological hedonism as a thesis about ends (people only pursue pleasure), psychological hedonism must be true of the many since they accept ethical hedonism, and only pursue the good.

Why does Socrates bring hedonism into his argument? It may be that he is sincerely recommending a hedonism that neither overvalues the pleasure of the moment, nor cultivates an excess of appetite (like Callicles in the *Gorgias*), but looks to the long term and still takes overall happiness as the final good and goal. Such a hedonism might be ascribed to the preface to the laws of Plato's eventual republic (*Laws* 5.732e4–734e2): pleasures and pains are especially human, and from them every mortal creature is suspended by the strongest cords (732e4–7); in their number, magnitude, intensity, and equality they determine desire and choice (733b6–c1); we desire a predominance of pleasure over pain, and 'if we say that we desire anything besides these, we say so through ignorance and inexperience of actual life' (d4–6). However, it seems clear that such remarks define not what constitutes the human good, but what motivates us to act well or badly (cf. 2.662b4–663b6). It is only in trivial cases that pleasure, or charm (*charis*), is the criterion of goodness (667b5–e9); though the focus there is upon means rather than ends, we read that both the instrumental and the intrinsic value of learning (*to eu kai to kalôs*) are not pleasure or charm but truth (c5–7, cf. 5.730c1–4). Even in the preface to the laws, an enlightened hedonism provides a specially human motivation for cultivating virtues of mind and body that are already identified: it is not as a tautology, but after argument, that the Stranger adds that a life of virtue, mental as well as physical, is pleasanter than one of vice (734d4–6). Pleasure and pain are crucial in moral education, for pleasure and pain, love and hatred, must be rightly directed (2.653b1–c4, cf. 659d4–e3); there is no statement that they are equally crucial for distinguishing right from wrong. It is rather typical of Plato to argue that the life of virtue, already identified and commended, is also the pleasantest (cf. *Rep* 9.581e6–582a2) than either to try to identify it, or to feel a need to justify it, by appeal to pleasure. In the *Phaedo*, Socrates distinguishes a real virtue which is motivated by wisdom from a vulgar virtue which through 'the exchanging of pleasures for pleasures, pains for pains, and fear for fear, greater for lesser ones, like coins' can only achieve courage through cowardice (as when a man endures death for fear of greater evils), and temperance through intemperance (as when he abstains from present pleasures because he is overcome by future ones, 68c5–69c3). Yet, in the *Protagoras*, he infers from hedonism that our salvation lies in an art of measurement that would save us from the illusions of perspective that magnify the pleasures of the moment (356c5–357d7). This is hardly the Socrates who resisted coercion to join in the arrest of Leon on the ground that he cared nothing about dying and everything about avoiding injustice (*Apol* 32c4–d5, cf. 28b5–9, d6–10), and refused to escape from prison on the ground that the prospect of death or of any other misfortune counted not at all against the danger of acting unjustly (*Crito* 48c6–d5). It is true that the eschatology of the *Gorgias* would permit a hedonistic grounding of the crucial maxim 'It is worse to do than to suffer wrong' (e.g., 473a5), but scorning to let prudence weigh against morality, Socrates cannot wish to rest morality upon prudence. To borrow a metaphor from Aristotle, Socrates and Plato welcome pleasure as a bloom upon the face of virtue (*NE* 10.4.1174b33), but do not accept it as virtue's yardstick; as a criterion of the fitting, it is at most a *parergon* (Plato, *Polit* 286d4–6). It is unlikely that either of them would ever have accepted hedonism as a decision procedure.[9]

At least if we insist on that, we shall be sensitive to indications that Socrates is keeping his own options open. He proposes hedonism first to Protagoras (351b3–e11), and then to the common man (353c4–355a5). His own role is to ask them questions that elicit answers that they may *suppose* him to endorse (e.g., 351e4–6). He comes close to committing himself when he asks the common man, 'Don't you think, as Protagoras and I maintain, that the only reason these things are bad is that they result in pains and deprive one of other pleasures?' (353e5–354a1); however, I think that it is un-ambiguous in context that they are agreeing only about what the common man thinks, for that, and not whether he is right, has been the issue since 353c1 (as 354a1–2, c2–3, d3–4, e2 will confirm) – and Protagoras has not yet himself adopted hedonism either. Socrates presses him to disregard familiar objections, but gives the common man every opportunity to come up with an alternative, if he can. With an irony that is finally transparent, he rounds off his recom-mendation of an art of measurement with an endorsement of sophistic education, for all its expense (357e4–8). What, then, is he about? We may need to remember certain facts about Protagoras: not only that he held that virtue can be taught, which was a theme earlier in the dialogue (318a6–b7), but that he famously maintained 'Man is the measure of all things' (cf. *Theaet* 151e8–152a5). Perhaps Socrates is now developing a Protagorean ethic that identifies the good with something at once subjective in one way (a datum of personal experience) and objective in another (a matter for measure-ment). If so, he is offering a purged Protagoreanism that subjects us neither to 'the power of appearances' (356d4), nor to anything that transcends our common humanity. We are to deny that everything is as it appears (a thesis spelt out for sensible properties at *Theaet* 152a6–c3, but rejected here on the ground that perspectival variations can be corrected instead of accepted, 356c5–e2), while conceding that certain experiences (those of pleasure and pain, immediate and eventual) determine certain realities (those of objective good and evil). It is then an extra gain if hedonism can be put into service to justify a Socratic claim that it suits Protagoras' profession as a sophist to confirm: knowledge is enough to save a man (352c2–d3, cf. *Lach* 194d1–2, *Gorg* 460b6–8). It is this thesis that leads them to the topic of mental conflict.

According to the opinion of the majority, Socrates says, a man may be ruled in action not by his knowledge, but by passion, pleasure, pain, love, or fear (352b3–8); in short, 'They just look at knowledge as a slave who gets dragged about by all the rest' (c1–2). Socrates does not deny that experiences of the kind that people call 'being overcome by pleasure' are real ones, though he considers that phrase a misdescription (352e5–353a6). No one (we may take him to suppose) can be more liable to be overcome by pleasure than a hedonist, and hedonism serves to reduce the common explanations to a single one: if pleasure is the only positive value, and all that people pursue, it is always by pleasure, in the last analysis, that a man is mastered. But if pleasure is identical to the good, Socrates objects, it becomes 'absurd' (*geloios*, from the Greek for laughter) to say that 'a man often does bad things though he knows they are bad and could refrain from doing them, because he is driven and overwhelmed by pleasures' (355a6–b1). To make the absurdity plain, he first names the single value 'good', and then ('So much for that', e4) 'pleasant'. If we use the term 'good', the common view carries the overtly 'absurd' implication that 'somebody should do bad things, though he knows they are bad, and doesn't have to do them, because he is overcome by good things' (d1–3). The upshot is that free action cannot be consciously contrary to practical judgement; as we would say, it cannot be affected by acrasia or, more precisely, 'hard acrasia' (to be distinguished from 'soft' in Chapter 2 §11).

Difficulties have been raised over the validity and force of this argument. In his acute commentary (from which one learns even in dissent), C.C.W. Taylor finds two fallacies in the substitution of 'good' for 'pleasant':

(a) A man is worsted by immediate pleasure, while what he holds to be good is what he thinks contributes towards a life in which pleasure predominates over pain.[10] It is in an extended sense of 'pleasant' (causing a life more pleasure than pain) that he equates 'pleasant' with 'good', while it is in a familiar sense of 'pleasant' (enjoyable in itself) that he is worsted by the pleasant; so he would not agree that he is worsted by the good.

(b) Even if 'pleasant' is equivalent to 'good', and I am worsted by pleasure, it does not follow that I am worsted by the good, for that is implicitly an intentional context ('worsted by' meaning 'worsted by a desire for'). Indeed, even if I accept the equivalence without qualification, I will only be worsted by the good when I am worsted by pleasure if my acceptance of the equivalence is instrumental in causing my action (Taylor 1991: 180–1).

Perhaps neither point is fatal. Against (a), I would rather suppose that, when Socrates has the common man equate 'good' and 'pleasant' (355b4–c1), he is not equivocating between 'pleasant' in its familiar sense (as at 351d7–e1) and 'pleasant' in a new and Pickwickian sense of 'causing a life more pleasure than pain', while staying with a single sense of 'good', but moving from an all-in use of 'good' (in which to be good is to cause a life more pleasure than pain) to a use both simple and intrinsic (in which to be good is to be pleasant), while staying with the only sense that 'pleasant' has. The opposite shift, from the simple and intrinsic to the all-in, has already occurred to the opposite of 'good' within a single sentence:

> So it's pain which you regard as bad, and pleasure as good, since you even call enjoyment itself bad when it deprives you of greater pleasures than it has in itself, or leads to pains which are greater than its own pleasures.
>
> (354c5–d1)

If pain is the only simple intrinsic evil and pleasure the only simple intrinsic good (as I would clarify 354c5–6 and 355a1–2), then what is good overall, within the perspective of a lifetime, can indeed only be what contributes to a life in which pleasure predominates over pain. Less ambiguously expressed, what is rejected as absurd (at 355d1–3) is that someone should freely choose to perform an act, knowing that it will reduce his enjoyment of the good, out of a weakness for enjoying the good. Against (b), one may relativize Socrates' inference to human psychology, which (allegedly) ascribes intrinsic goodness always and only to pleasure, and appeal to a tight internal relation between goodness and desire: if I only desire the pleasant for its own sake, and to desire is to desire as good, then 'desiring as pleasant' and 'desiring as good in itself' name one and the same kind of desire; so to be defeated by a desire for a pleasure is indeed to be defeated by a desire for a good. If the argument is so interpreted and supplemented, the substitutions seem to be valid. What is the force of its conclusion? I suggest that Socrates finds it incredible that anyone should be so inconsistent as to be consciously led by the attraction of things of one kind, namely, 'good things', into choosing to do things of the opposite kind, namely, 'bad things'. Such self-defeating action would invite the impatient question, 'Is goodness what you are after, or isn't it?' We may object (as I shall later in this section) that it can make a difference that the goodness is immediate, and the badness prospective, so that they are not exactly opposite; indeed, it is only this distinction that saves the description from contradicting itself in counting the same actions that are chosen as both good (in themselves) and bad (overall). Yet disambiguation does not seem to help any further: if one's total goal is long term (a life of pleasure), one should not choose an action, knowing it to be bad overall, on the ground that it is good in itself; if one's total goal is short term (the pleasure of the moment), one should not admit that the action is bad overall. The argument appears at least to be free of adventitious fallacy.

What makes the good things by which a man is said to be overcome not worth the bad things that he selects? Socrates can suggest only one answer: the good things are smaller or fewer than the bad ones (355d6–e3). He expands upon this in the parallel argument, which replaces 'good' by 'pleasant': pains that outweigh pleasures must be larger or more numerous or more intense (356a1–5). He dismisses another variable: whether a pleasure is immediate or subsequent can make no difference to what it is worth; supposing that one weighs things up, then one *must* prefer (*lêpteos*, b4) the greater pleasure, and one *must* perform (*prakteos*, b8) the act that brings pleasure to outweigh pain (a5–c1). Is this the 'must' of psychological inevitability (meaning 'is bound to') or of practical necessity (meaning 'needs to')? The former is grammatically improbable (cf. Taylor 1991: 189–90), while the second seems too weak for the conditional: what is necessary in the sense of needed is discovered and not created by reflection, so that it is not only *if* one reflects that one 'must', in the sense of 'needs', do what is needed. Plato's meaning is more likely betwixt and between: where quantitative comparisons can be made, deliberation, in the etymological sense of weighing up, removes all but one of the options, where what is optional depends upon what may indeed be best for all that one knows; one will then attempt the action that deliberation has promoted from a 'may' to a 'must'. What, then, goes wrong on occasions when one prefers the lesser immediate pleasure to the greater but more distant pleasure? How else are we to understand the tendency that most men take for weakness? Socrates blames an illusion of perspective whereby proximity increases apparent magnitude (c5–8). The failure is to calculate correctly, and the cure is an 'art of measurement' (*metrêtikê technê*) to reduce 'the power of appearances' (d4). Without it, we are lost, and vacillate in our acts and choices between resolving and ruing (d4–6); with it, our lives will be saved (356e8–357b3). The experience that looked like one of being weaker than, or overcome by, pleasure turns out, under analysis, to be one of a kind of error that comes of a lack of the knowledge that only measurement can supply. Nothing, after all, is more powerful than knowledge (b4–e2).

Thus mental conflict is accommodated only in the form of a vacillation of judgement, an alternation between contradictory appearances that knowledge alone can resolve. We should not deny that what Socrates is describing is a form of conflict. The power of appearances, he says, 'makes us wander, and choose things and rue them back and forth many times' (356d4–6). The verb *metamelein* (d6), for which 'rue' is archaic, 'regret' weak, and 'repent' religiose, has a resonance that will be sounded in Plato's description of the tyrannical soul in the *Republic*: 'The tyrannized soul – to speak of the soul as a whole – also will least of all do what it wishes, but being always forcibly drawn by a frenzy [literally, 'gadfly'] will be full of turmoil and ruefulness' (9.577e1–3). Compare also Aristotle's characterization of the base man:

> If he cannot at the same time be pained and pleased, still after a short time he is pained because he was pleased, and he could have wished that these things had not been pleasant to him; for bad men are laden with ruefulness.
>
> (*NE* 9.4.1166b22–5)

Yet we miss an awareness of other possibilities, so that it is easy to agree with Taylor when he comments, 'Socrates' reply is disappointing' (1991: 189). Though his main concern in the *Protagoras* is with cases where the agent is free to act otherwise (352d7, 355d2), he also implicitly excludes the defeat of reason by forces that stampede one into action so that one cannot help oneself (as in cases of sudden and irresistible temptation). Even so, he appears to be turning a blind eye to two phenomena. One, which he would only be the first of many to ignore, is that one can be a hedonist without being a maximizer. It is in human nature to be often not too demanding, impatient but quickly contented, idle and inhibited; whatever we are pursuing or practising, a modicum can be enough.[11] While it would be bizarre deliberately to choose a lesser good instead of a greater one that was no less easily and rapidly available, one can opt for one good among others with little or no sense that one owes it to oneself to pursue the greatest good; the best option may yet be optional. (The same is true when one's end is not one's own pleasure but, for example, treating others well; cf. Slote 1986: 45–7.) Such a lack of ambition will usually disincline one for identifying the act that offers the most, but it may also deflect one from performing it even when it has been identified. Out of procrastination, for instance, I may delay turning my mind to a task either because I put off reflecting upon its urgency, or because, while I judge it best to get it done as soon as possible, I am content with the lesser good of 'Better late than never.' There can also be a more painful slippage between judgement and desire: I may have a stronger desire for a salient pleasure although I am consistent in my judgements at the time, and judge not only that it would be better to pursue a presently less appealing one, but that I *ought* to do so – an 'ought' whose emphasis is integral to the content of the thought, expressing a degree of commitment that demands fulfilment. Such conscious *failure* of desire, decision, or act to accord with practical judgement constitutes that weakness which we call hard acrasia: because I am weak, and not because I am undemanding or impatient or easily satisfied, I may consciously fail to desire most, or to decide to do, or to do, what I think I ought to do. Taylor has a good sentence which applies to many of these cases: 'We are frequently more concerned about, and influenced by what is near, both in space and time, than by what is more distant, even though we may know that it is the more distant thing which will have the greater effect on our happiness and misery in the long run' (1991: 188).[12] Often (though not only) for this reason, I may be contented by a good that is salient but not maximal, or I may be robbed of content by a mental conflict that takes not the form, acknowledged by Socrates, of a vacillation over time between deciding and ruing, but of a simultaneous clash between judgement and prevalent desire. These possibilities show that, even where action is known to be possible, we should not equate *thinking best* and *effectively desiring* – that is, desiring in a way that 'moves (or will or would move) a person all the way to action' (Frankfurt 1988b: 14). Socrates infers this equation from a hypothesis of hedonism: as I began by quoting,

> If what is pleasant is good, no one who either knows or believes that something else is better than what he is doing, and is in his power to do, subsequently does the other, when he can do what is better.
>
> (358b6–c1)

As we have seen, he questions how a man can prefer a pleasure to a greater good if he identifies good with pleasure. Yet it now appears that both a lack of commitment to maximization and the lure of the present make this perfectly possible. We may suspect that it is because Socrates is not himself in any doubt about the truth of the equation that he considers too few exceptions to it.[13]

Martha Nussbaum has argued that what shores up the argument of the *Protagoras* is an extreme evaluative monism: Socrates is right to think that acrasia becomes impossible if there is only a single and uniform value by which to assess practical alternatives. An exclusive hedonism fills the bill of making all options commensurable, so that calculation can decide accurately which offers *most*: 'Pleasure enters the argument as an attractive candidate for this role: Socrates adopts it because of the science it promises, rather than for its own intrinsic plausibility' (1986: 110). And commensurability requires not only a single value, but a value that is homogeneous: the attractions of different options must differ only quantitatively, not qualitatively. If this is so, acrasia cannot occur: if I have decided upon some action because it is valuable in a certain way and to a certain degree, what could divert me into a different action which I recognize to be valuable in precisely the same way but to a lesser degree (cf. 1986: 115–16)? Nussbaum takes it for granted that valuing things so goes with a commitment to maximization. This monism, she grants, is foreign to our actual ways of thinking. What Socrates is really doing, she suggests, is inviting us to begin valuing things in the way he describes *in order to become* immune to acrasia: 'Socrates offers us, in the guise of empirical description, a radical proposal for the transformation of our lives' (1986: 117). This is a telling reading, which nicely explains the hedonism as a stand-in for a uniform value still to be identified (cf. 357b5–c1); whether it succeeds in capturing Plato's intentions is more doubtful. Socrates' argument does indeed depend upon a degree of monism (cf. Wiggins 1991b: 257): he finds it particularly implausible that anyone should deliberately sacrifice a greater good to a lesser good of the same salient kind (say, if the goods are both pleasures, and his point of view is hedonistic). What is missing is evidence that he supposes, and would persuade Protagoras, that it matters, both for accuracy of measurement and for the exclusion of acrasia, that goods should be – or be taken to be – not only of the same general but of the same maximally specific kind. Not only here, Socrates and Plato may lack Nussbaum's emphasis upon the concrete rather than the abstract. The thought that commensurability demands homogeneity has its plausibility, once one thinks about the problems of exact comparison, but is hardly a truism. Can it be accepted as the hinge upon which Socrates' argument is meant to turn when it is never stated? His remarks about our need for an art of measurement to correct the illusions of perspective are vague enough (356c8–357d7), and fail to convey clearly that he has in mind anything really extraordinary. He must intend some systematization of procedures and clarification of results, but has no motive, not being a hedonist, to think them through. He calls measurement 'an art and a branch of knowledge' (b4); Taylor renders the phrase 'an art which embodies exact knowledge', but Socrates appears to be insisting not upon its precision but upon its reliability. It is true that the term 'precision' (*akribeia*) is easily associated with 'art' or 'skill' (*technê*, cf. Nussbaum 1986: 96), but it is absent here; we should hesitate to take him to be intending us to share certain thoughts that might arise from reflection upon the prerequisites of precision. His concern is to achieve results that can stand (356d7–e2), and will 'save' or 'preserve' our 'lives' (d3, e2, e6, 356e8–357a1, a6–7), apparently from error and indecision and regret; such talk entails no comparisons very different from the common-sensical examples that he has previously given. When he says that 'making our lives safe' depends upon 'a correct choice of pleasure and pain' (a5–7), he may mean no more than that, if quantitative comparison is the mode of deliberation, things will go badly with us if we cannot rest judgements of the kind that we are used to making upon comparisons that are not mistaken. He urged the common man to agree that, when he refrains from the pleasures of food or drink or sex, it is in order to avoid the pains of later disease or poverty (353c4–e4), and that, when he accepts athletic training or military service or painful medical treatment, it is in order to to enjoy the pleasures of later health or fitness or safety or power or profit

(354a3–b7). He then quickly added that one must take the pains one avoids to be greater than the pleasures one eschews, and the pains one accepts to be smaller than the pleasures one foresees (c6–d1, d5–7). He never indicates that this type of comparison, or some exacter variant upon it, produces a tension that is to be relieved by denying the apparent variety of hedonic values. If his argument is to depend on a postulate that they really only differ quantitatively (with the claim either that this is true, or that believing it is beneficial), he needed to make this plain.

Moreover, Nussbaum fails to bring out the full paradoxicality of the homogeneity on which she rests the exclusion of acrasia. Socrates talks here of weighing not merely pleasures against pleasures and pains against pains, but pleasures against pains. If he accepts that commensurability entails homogeneity, he must hold that pleasures are homogeneous not only among themselves but with pains. The supposition would have to be that the intrinsic differences between pleasures and pains can always be fully captured by placement on a single quantitative scale. How might one begin to make sense of this? Perhaps by comparing sensations of heat and cold: feeling hot and feeling cold seem quite different in kind, but might belong together on a single scale of higher and lower temperatures. But this is confused: what varies in degrees Celsius or Fahrenheit is what thermometers measure, which is not sensations. Even if we keep with the sensory experiences that are commonly thought to suit a simple hedonism best, we shall need to make out that, for example, the pleasure of tasting strawberries only differs from the unpleasantness of tasting aloes in a way that is quantifiable. Well, one can read philosophy in order, like the White Queen, to practise oneself in believing the impossible; but we can expect the premisses that we are intended to supply for ourselves to be less baffling.[14]

I further doubt whether an acceptance of the homogeneity of value would actually exclude acrasia. To adapt an earlier thought, even if one's sole deliberate goal were to enjoy as much as possible of a homogeneous pleasure, one could still succumb acratically to the temptation of the moment, lured by lesser but immediate gratification. If we view pure discounting over time as irrational, we shall say that such an agent has no *reason* to act as he does; yet the proximity of the temptation can still be a sufficient *cause*. Conflict can also be idle: even if I am free of acrasia and disposed to act wisely, I may suffer from desires that continue to press even after judgement has denied them satisfaction. Here too hedonism seems not to help, with or without homogeneity: a voluptuary may well suffer from the pull of a pleasure today that he knows he must sacrifice to the pleasures of tomorrow. (What would save him from discontent would be if he only took long views and were wholly set upon a pleasant *life*.) As a cure for conflict, homogeneous hedonism looks to be more expensive than effective.[15]

How well, then, is hedonism serving Socrates? He is concerned about two forms of weakness: vacillation, and that conscious failure to act upon practical judgement which exemplifies hard acrasia. His argument is that, on the hypothesis of hedonism, there is no possibility of hard acrasia, while the danger of vacillation can be met by an art of measurement. Assuming a tight dependence of desiring upon valuing, he thinks that what should make one most prone to being overcome by pleasure (which is the commonest explanation of acrasia, and can stand in illustratively for the others) would be an acceptance of hedonism as an evaluative thesis. If pleasure is at once the sole intrinsic good and the only object of desire, being unwilling to do what one knows is best because one is overcome by pleasure reduces to loving pleasure so much that one prefers – the lesser to the greater pleasure? Socrates dismisses this as 'absurd'. Thus in his opinion (to which I have objected that it overlooks the lure of the present) vulgar hedonism suits a rejection of hard acrasia as well as philosophical eudaimonism. In the *Symposium* this rejection is an implicit corollary of a theory that all love pursues 'immortality together with the good' (206e8–207a1); here, in the *Protagoras*, it is an explicit (though invalid) inference from a popular postulate that all desire pursues pleasure. Socrates reads his own rationalism into hedonism when he asserts that desire must always prefer what is judged to be the greater pleasure, with no discounting over time. This comes close, and may be equivalent, to a hedonistic eudaimonism to the effect that the sole goal of desire is a pleasant life (or a more, or more nearly, pleasant one).[16] Hence he finds again within hedonism the implausibilities, as they strike us, of his own eudaimonism. He allows that weakness remains possible in the form of vacillation, and advises us to fix the fluctuations of appearance with the cement of knowledge. We need not doubt that he is serious about *this*, but his identification of practical knowledge with an art of measurement is most likely only illustrative. Certainly measurement, when practicable, provides clear and familiar examples of how to achieve reliable results, but it is rather an ideal for the philosopher *in this respect* than a model for moral thinking.[17] Hedonism is a Protagorean system of values that may appear to exemplify the possibility of practical knowledge. In playing along with it Socrates at once suits Protagoras, and brings out the rewards that knowledge would bring. On what values *he* would ground knowledge of right and wrong is a question that can presently remain open.

To understand Socrates more deeply, and to hope to do him more justice, we would need to study not less than the whole of his philosophy. How does what we are offered look at present? His exclusion of most forms of mental conflict seems partly idiosyncratic, in that it depends on the way in which he focuses all desire upon happiness, and partly rationalistic, in that it depends on the assumption that strength of desire must always reflect degree of valuation. His view that all desire derives from an orientation towards one's overall happiness cannot permit simultaneous decision and aversion: if the appeal of an option is outweighed by long-term considerations, I may still have *some* desire for it (if it would help my happiness in a special way), but not one that can cause distress. His attachment of effective desire to practical judgement cannot permit them to be in conscious and simultaneous conflict, if it is impossible to hold consciously conflicting judgements at the same time. Discarding eudaimonism as a thesis about all desire, and accommodating irrationality within a divided mind, Plato was to do fuller justice to the phenomena.

SOCRATES AND DIOTIMA: AN APPENDIX

Malcolm Schofield puts to me a reading of what is going on between Socrates and Diotima in the *Symposium* that usefully challenges my own. As I understand him, he believes that strictly Socratic is only what Socrates puts directly to Agathon (up to 201c9). That serves as a basis for Socrates' presentation of what he was once taught by Diotima (201d1–8), but where this goes beyond what Socrates has agreed with Agathon, it is only loosely Socratic, partly developing Socrates' ideas and partly correcting them. Socrates has accepted from Agathon that love is of beauty (cf. 197b5, 201a5, e5, 204d3), but what he then recounts from Diotima makes a distinction, and doubly corrects him out of his own mouth: *erôs* in the generic sense of 'desire' is of goods, and ultimately of *eudaimonia* or happiness (204e1–205a3); *erôs* in the specific and idiomatic sense of 'love' is not of beauty, but of generation in beauty (206e2–5). Thus beauty is not the goal of love, and has no role to play in defining the object of desire. I would pose a number of points against this. It is the immature Socrates who, purportedly, was once corrected by Diotima (note *pote*, 'once upon a time', 201d2), and a mature Socrates who has just corrected Agathon with arguments similar to those by which Diotima once corrected him (e3–7). I can see no initial plausibility in a claim that the historical Socrates accepted all that Plato's Socrates has put to Agathon, but nothing else that he had learnt from Diotima. At least one point that Socrates did not put to Agathon but now reports from Diotima is evidenced elsewhere as Socratic: Plato's young Socrates needed to be cured of a confusion between opposites and contradictories (201e10–202b2) of which his old one is free (cf. *Lysis* 218a2–b1). Nor can we altogether contrast Diotima as didactic with Socrates as aporetic: Diotima tells Socrates, 'I shall try to teach you that' (204d1–2), a sentence that Schofield finds most *un*-Socratic; yet her initial mode of exposition, through question and answer (cf. 201e2–3), and the confidence of her refutation (cf. e6–7), mirror Socrates' treatment of Agathon. Diotima had certainly to put the young Socrates right about the defining objective of specific *erôs* (he had failed to make any distinction between generic and specific *erôs*, and indeed still only tentatively accepts it at 206e2–6), but she rather explicates than contradicts his conception of the objective of generic *erôs*. When she shifts from 'beautiful' to 'good' in order to win his agreement that the ultimate goal of the latter is happiness, she uses a term 'making a change' (*metaballôn*, 204e1) that in the *Protagoras* signifies switching between equivalent expressions (355e4–7, cf. b3–c1). Though the *Symposium* context is not quite as explicit, all the indications are to the same effect: good things are also beautiful, so that if Love lacks beautiful things, he lacks good ones also (201c2–5); and Socrates can shift indifferently between the phrases 'good things and beautiful things' and 'good and beautiful things' (202c10–d2), which confuses the union of two classes with their intersection *unless* the classes are identical. (For later confirmations of the equivalence of 'good' and 'beautiful', cf. *Rep* 6.505b2–3, *Phil* 64e5–7.) The shift from 'beautiful' to 'good' serves twice, first between Socrates and Agathon (202c6–11), then between Diotima and Socrates (204e1–7), to suit the thought that happiness is the ultimate end of desire, since to be happy is to possess goods and beauties (202c10–11), but more precisely goods (205a1). More purely Socratic dialogues confirm that happiness is the target of all desire: the *Meno* argues for the conclusion that nobody desires what is bad, and everyone wishes for good things, from the premiss that nobody wants to be unhappy

(77b6–78b2); the *Euthydemus* takes it as obvious that we all wish to fare well (*eu prattein*, 278e3–279a2), that is, to be happy (282a2, cf. *Charm* 174b12–c1) – and it may be implicit that this is *all* that we want; it is most likely happiness that is the good which is the first object of love (*prôton philon*) and the final end of all desire in the *Lysis* (219c5–d2, 220b6–7). Even the young Socrates shows no sign, when he emphatically accepts 'Love is for the good to belong to oneself always' (206a11–13), that he is taking anything back; and the wording of a previous exchange (Diotima, 'Or do you think that men [sc., love anything other than the good]?'; Socrates, 'By Zeus, *I* don't' (205e7–206a2)) shows that he did not need Diotima to teach him that. For all these reasons, I stand by my use of the *Symposium* in §1, and cannot believe that the strictly Socratic is over by the end of the exchange with Agathon (201c9).

2

PLATO

1

Wishing to understand Socrates, one finds in the *Symposium*, a mature dialogue of Plato's, an application of a Socratic theory of desire. Proceeding through Plato, one meets in the *Phaedrus*, a later dialogue, an exposition of a different view of desire, familiar and not invented, from which Socrates recoiled and Plato advanced. It is presented in Socrates' first speech (237b7–238c4, 238d8–241d1); his second speech (243e9–257b6) makes use of the mature theory that evolved out of it.

In the *Protagoras*, Socrates recruited Protagoras to stand with him against 'the majority of people' in denying that men may act contrary to knowledge of what is best, defeated by pleasure or pain or by some emotion such as anger, love, or fear (352a9–e4). His discussion at once focused more narrowly on the concept of being defeated by pleasure, I take it for two reasons: first and foremost, to suit the refutation (which proceeds through identifying pleasure with the good); but also, perhaps, to reflect a familiar distinction between desires for pleasure and desires for the good. That was touched on in the *Charmides*, where Socrates takes every desire or appetite (*epithymia*) to be for some pleasure (*hêdonê*), but every wish (*boulêsis*) to be for some good (*agathon*, 167e1–5).[1] However, this distinction should not be pressed into a dichotomy: he proceeds to add, equally casually, that love is of something beautiful, and fear of something fearful (167e7–168a1); and it is left open that desire might be a kind of wish, and pleasure desired as a kind of good. (So Terence Irwin: 'If Socrates believes we desire the pleasant only in so far as it is good . . . , the distinction will be unimportant for him'; 1977: 310 n. 6.) What is clear is that popular thinking tended to pluralism where

30

he insisted upon monism. In the *Gorgias*, which we shall find to be a transitional work, he suddenly talks of 'ruling oneself' (491d7–8); Callicles asks for a gloss, and is offered 'ruling the pleasures and appetites within one' (d9–e1). In the *Republic*, Socrates acknowledges the literal absurdity of the phrase 'master of oneself' (for 'he who is master of himself would also be subject to himself, and vice versa'), and offers a similar interpretation to allay the absurdity: a man is master of himself if a better part within him controls a worse part (4.430e6–431a6).[2] Such language telescopes a wealth of popular philosophy that conceived of yielding to temptation as suffering 'conquest' and 'slavery'.[3] In a conflict between desires, the agent may identify with one side against the other, so that one upshot counts as his victory, the other as his defeat.

This is spelt out in Socrates' first speech in the *Phaedrus*. Here he is speaking not in his own person, but in that of a lover who, pretending not to be in love, is urging his boy to enter into a sexual relationship not with anyone in love with him, but (not that Socrates gets that far) with someone not in love with him, such as himself (237b2–6). We overhear him, therefore, as a lover experienced in love of a kind, but motivated, out of love, to misrepresent love (as Socrates' shame at once betrays, a4–5). The conceptual kernel of his argument is a definition of love that immediately displays it as dangerous. The account of desire that he adopts is doubtless adapted for this purpose, but it also serves Phaedrus, and may serve us, as a popular background to the philosophy to come. It presents each of us as passive in relation to two principles of action that 'lead and rule': an innate desire (*epithymia*) for pleasures, and an acquired opinion (*doxa*) aiming at the best (d6–9). These can agree, or be at variance; when they are at variance, one or the other may prevail (d9–e2). When judgement prevails in leading us rationally towards the best, its mastery is called good sense or moderation (*sôphrosynê*); when desire prevails in dragging us irrationally towards pleasures, its rule is called outrage or excess (*hybris*, 237e2–238a2). Species of excess are then distinguished by the objects of specific ruling desires: gluttony is the prevailing of a desire for food at once over judgement of what is best and over other desires; similarly with a desire for drink, and so on (a2–b5). Excess leads a man along like a 'tyrant' (b2–3). Love is defined as an irrational desire directed at the enjoyment of beauty that has mastered judgement setting off towards the right and is reinforced by related desires (b7–c2). We may take these as desires for the extravagances that make up a lover's life (cf. *Rep* 9.573d2–10): while the drunkard is likely to sacrifice food to drink, so that his thirst for alcohol combats his hunger for food, the libertine is liable to eat and drink, preferably *à deux* in a *chambre séparée*, with a new enthusiasm. Later, Socrates will want to wash the taste from his mouth of such a seaman's view of love (243c6–d5), which 'says nothing healthy or true' (242e5–243a1); finally, he will commend it for identifying, within the genus of madness, a 'left-hand' species of love (266a5). Thus we (who are Plato's readers, not Socrates' auditors) shall be invited to reread his first speech with respect; its psychology deserves attention.

What, more precisely, are the opposed states of mind? To reason is ascribed opinion, but not desire. Irwin infers, 'The rational part is concerned only with the orderly pursuit of non-rational ends, not with the choice of ends' (1977: 238); he thus makes reason the servant of appetite, which is a source of innate desires relating to the needs and habits of the body. However, reason's goal, which is not only 'the best' (237d9) but also 'the right' (238b8), does not sound like a mere sum of goals already given. If it were, there could be conflict between reason and some particular appetite usurping the claims of other appetites (like thirst imprudently eclipsing hunger), but not between reason and appetite in general (*pace* d9–e2). Further, the easy opposition that I have noted between *epithymia* (desire or appetite) and *boulêsis* (wish) makes it unsurprising that *epithymia* should be denied to reason, which is ascribed intentions (it 'aims at' the best, d9), and would surely be allowed wishes. Irrational desires are directed at pleasures (d8), and love is desire of a kind (d3), directed at the enjoyment of beauty (238c1). Such desires are innate (237d7–8), and so precede the acquisition – or else, on Plato's own doctrine of recollection, the recovery – of concepts. Once concepts are acquired, we may imagine desires being accompanied by thoughts of the form 'It would be pleasant to do such-and-such.' What other concepts than that of pleasure attach themselves to desires? Not only in the case of love (d4–5), there is also the concept of beauty. What must the intelligent subject of desire think of as beautiful? Given that the lover will be described as being 'under compulsion to pursue the pleasant in preference to the good' (239c4–5), and that Plato tends to treat the terms 'good' and 'beautiful' as evident equivalents (cf. *Meno* 77b6–7, *Symp* 204d5–e4; Chapter 1, appendix), we should probably not suppose that the lover will think 'It would be beautiful to make love to this boy.' What attracts him is the beauty not of acts but of bodies (238c2), and his thought will rather be 'It would be pleasant to make love to this beautiful boy.' Similarly, in the case of a discriminating thirst, there could be the thought 'It would be pleasant to drink this exquisite claret.' Thus evaluations may be presupposed (if I am choosy, I may reject most boys and most clarets), but the acts themselves are only desired as pleasant – which confirms (though I shall argue in §5 that it is not required by) the claim that reason and desire tend to be at cross-purposes.

How do reason and desire operate? They were introduced as 'two kinds of thing that rule and lead, which we follow wherever they lead' (237d6–7). One may prevail over the other (e3), or one desire may prevail over reason and other desires (238a6–7, b8). Desire is a cause of movement which 'drags' one towards pleasures (a1). Reason itself moves in that it 'sets off' towards the right (b8); yet, if love has been strengthened enough by related desires, its 'pull' (*agôgê*) will carry the day (c1–3). In such language, conflicting motivations become quasi-physical forces, operating as it were spatially; there must be a mechanics of the mind, which might at the same time be a mechanics of parts of the body. But what is the relation of mind to body, and how does human agency straddle them? These are difficult questions within Plato's own theories; it is not surprising that they already arise within his presentation of popular psychology.

2

Of conclusions we expect consistency; reflection usually proceeds by way of incoherence. In the *Gorgias* we meet a Socrates who, even as he exposes the contradictions of others in his usual style, deserts any secure position of his own. (Readers impatient for coherence may proceed at once to §3.) Here, more than in any other dialogue, we meet the interface between Socrates and Plato, or early and middle Plato, and it is a geological fault.

What constitutes being just? In an early exchange, Socrates gets Polus to agree that it is having learnt, and now doing, what is just (460b6–8). Later, he tries out on Callicles a different conception: justice and temperance (which seem to be identified) consist of a certain structure and order within the soul (504b4–d3). Temperance is produced by tempering, which is restraining the soul from the things it desires (505b9–12). Socrates put to Polus that injustice is the greatest of evils, a malady of the soul (479b8, 480b1); but the point was not explained, nor Polus more than half persuaded (cf. his replies at 479d1–6). Clarification follows in opposition to Callicles, who identifies intemperance – construed as a policy of first maximizing, then satisfying, one's appetites – with freedom and happiness (491e5–492c8). Socrates argues that this policy is self-defeating, since unrestrained appetites are insatiable, like a leaking jar (493b1–3). The only route to fulfilment is self-control: one must succeed in ruling oneself, that is, one's pleasures and appetites (491d10–e1). Where does this leave the simpler thought that learning makes one just? Surely far behind: failure to rule oneself could lead to a divorce between knowledge, supplied by learning, and action, determined by strength of desire. If this more Platonic Socrates is right, the unjust man will learn through suffering that justice is best, but this will leave him short of *being* just, for which he will need to recover his ability – if it is not too late (525c1–2) – to exercise self-control.

There are other unclarities. We are told early on that all acts aim at the agent's good (468b1–8). What comes of this Socratic tenet once Callicles is permitted to define 'desires' such as hunger and thirst (by which he means appetites) as all being such as to be enjoyably satiated (494b7–c3)? Perhaps it is being supposed here that all acts aim at the agent's good even though all desires do not, since desires that do not aim at the good can only prevail if they are seconded by desires that do. As it happens, this fits how both Callicles and Socrates have just been speaking. Callicles' association of intemperance with freedom (492c4–5) demands that he should picture the intemperate man not as being carried away by his appetites, but as choosing to cultivate and gratify them (491e8–492a3). The only 'enslavement' (491e6) he envisages is of those who 'though at liberty to enjoy goods without hindrance', set up 'a master over themselves in the rules and speech and blame of the mass of men' (492b5–8). (Note how lucidly this anticipates Freud's conception of a superego created by the internalization of external prohibitions.) Socrates uses a vivid image to convey that attempting to satisfy unfettered appetite is foolish, but not that it is unfree: 'The uninitiated . . . carry water to this leaky jar with another leaky thing, a sieve' (493b5–7). Integral to Callicles' position is that he and other practitioners of intemperance take pleasure to be the good (cf. 495a2–6, b3–4, d3–4): their pursuing pleasure displays an evaluation and not a compulsion. Thus all acts may aim at the agent's good although not all desires do so. However, it is also possible that appetites too seek the good, but are fixated on a misidentification of it with the pleasure of the moment. Further uncertainty arises when Socrates asks Callicles an equivocal question: 'Do you agree with us too, that the good is the end of action' (descriptive), 'and that for the sake of it we should [*dein*] do all the other things?' (prescriptive, 499e7–9). This is confusing: saying that a thing *is* the case, and that it *should be* the case, are more easily alternatives. (Perhaps the good that we *do* pursue is intentional, that which we take to be the good, while the good that we *should* pursue is material, that which really is the good; but Plato can hardly have intended such a disambiguation.) Thus it may be that even all appetites aim at the good, or else that not even all choices do; Socrates seems happy to vacillate.

Socrates speaks not only of appetites, but of their locus in appetite: 'Once I heard from some wise man that we are dead now, our body is our tomb; and that of our soul with appetites in it is liable to be persuaded and to sway back and forth' (493a1–5). The juxtaposition strongly suggests that it is within the tomb of the body that the soul takes on an appetitive part (cf. 524d4–7). That this is still a part of the soul, with a rudimentary intelligence, fits the emphasis on its persuadability. Being persuadable (*pithanos*), it is likened to a jar (*pithos*): an intemperate appetite is like a leaky jar, which can never be filled (493a5–b3). Somewhat differently, the soul of an uninitiated fool is like a sieve with which he tries to carry water to this leaky jar (b5–c3); here appetite would appear to be relegated outside even a corrupt soul to the body (as at 517c7–d5). Earlier, Socrates even ascribed to the body the act of discriminating between cookery and medicine according to bodily gratification (465d2–3). Again, he seems happily indecisive, as is once explicit: 'I think it makes no difference' whether mixed pain and pleasure occur in soul or body (496e4–8). We might press him into this position: one part of the incarnate soul is appetite, while another – call it, again, judgement – may serve or rule appetite; a foolish judgement is unreliable and forgetful (493c3), and allows appetite to become insatiable. (What we actually read here is that a person may put his soul at the service of appetite; we shall find Plato putting a person as it were outside his constituents again.) Appetite is not always excessive, but not being 'closely sheathed' (b2) it is prone to excess. Callicles invited Socrates' attack when he recommended that appetites should not merely be filled but enlarged (491e8–492a3). It is true that Plato will later characterize appetite as insatiable by nature (*Rep* 4.442a6–7), on the metaphysical ground that even the unreal cannot be satisfied by the unreal (9.586b3–4).

Thus in the *Gorgias* we find Plato's thought in a state of transition.

Its inconsistencies suggest that he thought that coherence could wait until the transition was accomplished.

3

In the *Gorgias* Plato contrasts body and soul, appetite and judgement, without clearly connecting the contrasts (493a1–5); in the *Phaedo* he plainly associates body with appetite, and soul with judgement, in a manner that is subtly elaborated, but elusive to modern preconceptions. Since Descartes, there has been a dichotomy between body and mind of a recalcitrant kind: on the one hand, the physical, spatial, mechanical, unthinking, unconscious; on the other, the mental, non-spatial, at most quasi-mechanical, thinking, at least typically conscious. A lesson that is as easily learnt in the *Phaedo* as anywhere is that the modern mind–body problem arose not through a religious view of the soul, but through a scientific view of the body as a machine for living; on the older and Greek view, the body is a natural subject of life psychological as well as biological. It is true that a body without a soul is a dead corpse; in Greek, to be alive (*empsychos*) is to have a soul (*psychê*). But the life of an animated body was conceived to be mental as well as physical, and with no sense of strain; it is we, who have dissolved matter into the raw material of physics, who are at a loss how to find a place for consciousness. We cannot doubt that our problem has been a discovery and not an invention, but we need to think our way tentatively behind it if we are to take at their face value ways of speaking in the *Phaedo* that are alien to ours.

Once our eyes are open to it, we find recurrent evidence of a body that is conscious and non-Cartesian: we read of 'the pleasures that come by way of the body' (65a7), and 'the body and its desires' (66c7); the soul, bewitched by the 'passions and pleasures' of the body, may think nothing else real save what is corporeal (81b3–5); it may 'share opinions and pleasures with the body' and 'take for real whatever the body declares to be so' (83d6–7); it may comply with 'bodily feelings' such as hunger and thirst or oppose them (94b7–10); it converses 'with our appetites and passions and fears, as if with a distinct thing' (d5–6). It seems that it is the body that is the immediate subject of perceptions, which it then passes on to the soul. Ideally, the soul does not fully accept these (which would be to assume that appearance is reality), but either uses them for its own purposes (75e3–5, 79c2–5), or withdraws from them so far as possible

(65e6–66a6, 83a6–7). More precise than talk of the soul seeing or hearing (as when it is the single subject of perception, recollection, and pre-incarnate knowledge, 74d9ff.) is talk of its 'getting' or 'receiving' a perception (73c6–7, 76a1–2), and of its 'examining' (not perceiving) things 'as if through a prison' (82e1–4) or 'through the eyes' (83a4) or 'through other things', in contrast to its 'seeing' intelligible things 'itself' (b2–4). It fits this that Socrates equates relying on sight and hearing with taking the body as a partner (65a9–b2), and remarks that hearing, sight, pain, pleasure can bother the soul unless it dismisses the body (c6–8). Thus the living body (that is, body possessing a soul) is a subject both of sensations and of desires and beliefs, which must be noted by the soul, and may be accepted by it, voluntarily (cf. 84a4–5) or involuntarily (cf. 'is compelled' 83c5, d8). These mental states that start in the body and may or may not be accepted into the soul are also corporeal, which must be why the soul that is bewitched by them 'will have been interspersed with a corporeal element, ingrained in it by the body's company and intercourse' (81c4–6). 'This element is ponderous', heavy, earthy, and visible (c8–9), at the same time as it has desires of its own (e1). Plato implicitly holds a double-aspect view of such states, whether they remain in the body (troubling the soul as if from outside) or are admitted into the soul (becoming a fifth column within its citadel), without a metaphysics (divorcing extended body from conscious mind) to make it evidently problematic how the two aspects fit together.

Socrates repeatedly says of pleasure things only true of bodily pleasures (60b3–c7, 65c5–7, 68e8–69a1, 81b3–6, 83b5–7, d4–6, 84a4–5); also of desire things only true of bodily desires (66c2–4, 68c8–10, 81b2–4, 82e5–6, 83b5–7, c1–2). This is probably because 'desire' can restrictedly mean appetite, and 'pleasure' pleasant sensation. Less frequently, he adds a gloss: 'the pleasures that are through the body' (65a7), 'the desires in respect of the body' (82c3), 'the pleasures around the body' (114e1–2). Of course it is not his view that soul stands to body like Hume's unmotivating 'reason' to his 'passions': the Greeks never divorced cognition from desire in that way. It is no surprise that the soul is ascribed a desire for wisdom (66e2–3, cf. 65c9); it is wisdom-loving (*philosophos*, 68b3, c1, 11) and learning-loving (*philomathês*, 82c1, 83e5). We claim to be 'lovers' of wisdom (*erastai*, 66e2–3, cf. 68a2, 7), presumably with our souls (cf. 66b5–7); the man who 'has devoted himself to the pleasures of learning' can have 'confidence for his own soul' (114d8–e4). Yet the incarnate soul is at peril of sacrificing its original devotion to the divine objects that it resembles and contracting a corrupt attachment to the mortal objects that resemble the body (cf. 80a10–b5). This may be because it is flooded by the body's attitudes: the body 'fills us up' with loves or lusts (erôtes, 66c2–3, cf. 81a7); the soul may be 'compelled' to take on the pleasures and pains of the body together with the materialist metaphysics that accompanies them (83c5–8) and must constitute its 'folly' (67a7), thinking that only the corporeal is 'true' (81b4–5) and taking to be true 'whatever the body declares to be so' (83d6–7). It may also be because, with a second-order attitude (an attitude towards attitudes), the soul becomes enamoured of the body and its attitudes. The bad soul loves the body (81b3, cf. 83d6): 'always having intercourse with the body and tending it and loving it and being bewitched by it and by desires and pleasures' (81b2–4), it falls for it like a man for his mistress, so that, after death, it remains 'in a state of desire for the body' and still hovers around it (108a7–b1). Its wiser attitude is one not of a co-operator (82e6) but of an antagonist (like Odysseus reproving his heart, 94d6–e1): it is to 'find nothing of that sort pleasant', to 'take no part in those things', to 'care nothing for the pleasures that come by way of the body' (65a5–7). The *Republic* will elaborate two relevant thoughts: the 'most and greatest' so-called pleasures that make their way through the body to the soul are really just respites from pain (9.583c3–585a7, cf. *Pdo* 60b3–c7, *Phil* 42cff.), and the truer pleasures are those in truer things (585a8–586c6). The soul shares in such pleasures in the wrong way if it (a) permits unnecessary ones (64e1–65a2), and indeed (b) takes pleasure in them (a5); (a) depends upon (b) in that the motive for excess would be pleasure. For the soul to share in bodily pleasures is for it to welcome them, and even (if it is literally contaminated by the corporeal) to feel them itself.

'We ourselves are part body and part soul' (79b1–2), and yet it fits Plato's devaluation of the body that 'we' are often identified with our souls alone: Socrates can speak indifferently of the soul's withdrawing from the senses so as to think of reality by itself (83a6–b2), and of *our* being separated from our bodies so as to 'know through ourselves all that is unsullied' (67a7–b1); he can assure his friends that at death *he* will depart, leaving his body behind (115c4–e4). He can also (by a variation that we met in the *Gorgias*, and shall meet again in the *Republic*) speak of 'us', or the like, as if we stood outside both soul and body, opting between them (67e6–8, 78b9, 83a1–3, 107c6–8, 114d8–115a2). It is hard to take this as more than a way of speaking: at the level of analysis, soul and body are all that can constitute us.

About the nature of the soul, the *Phaedo* juxtaposes what look like three very different views, identifying the incarnate soul both (a) with a pure intellect that remains 'most likely' to be 'incomposite' (78c6–8), being invisible (79b12–15) and so 'constant' (a9), and retains an affinity to the 'pure', 'immortal', and 'unvarying' (d1–3), and a close similarity to the 'divine', 'immortal', 'single in form', 'unvarying' and 'constant' (80b1–3, cf. 81a4–5), (b) with a sullied intellect (67c3, 81b1–d4) that has come to 'partake of the visible' and 'be seen' (d4), and (c) with the cause of a body's being alive (105c9–11) and all its metabolic functions. We may surmise that it was partly to accommodate its biological role that Plato elsewhere allows the boundaries of the soul to expand at the moment of incarnation to encompass all the aspects of life: if appetite is both part of the soul itself (as was uncertainly asserted in the *Gorgias*, and will be asserted emphatically in the *Republic*), and intimately connected with the physical processes of digestion and growth, we can more easily conceive that soul animates body. What the *Phaedo* does try to elaborate is how the soul becomes the dupe and victim of the body, endorsing and sharing experiences and attitudes that only a body can engender. Here the notion of contamination is crucial, and not unproblematic: 'kneading together' (66b5) and 'interspersion' (81c4) are only easily interpretable as processes involving *two* physical stuffs, and yet physical talk about the soul (for example, as gathering itself together, 67c8, 83a7–8) sounds wholly metaphorical. However, if we dismiss contamination as mere imagery – perhaps encouraged by its use to explain the visibility of the ghosts that haunt tombs (81c11–d3), a phenomenon that *we* can hardly take seriously – we have no explanation of *how* a soul that is originally intellect can take on unintellectual states that are not easily shed at death. (In this way the *Phaedo* is an advance on the *Gorgias*, where Socrates supposes, in order to explain how souls after death are transparent to their judge, that a soul, 'whip-marked and full of scars', that has taken on the stain of its unjust actions is yet at death completely stripped of the body, 524d4–525a3.) After all, the concept of incarnation at birth is more familiar than that of intermixture after death, but not dissimilarly puzzling. The *Phaedo*'s soul is more like a corruptible intellectual than a safely delimited faculty of intellect. The intimacy of its liaison with the body resembles a relation between persons, even (I have suggested) between lovers. Plato can write as if aspects of incarnate life were multiple persons, or as if *we* were an extra element within ourselves – an ambivalence of expression that will recur even after he has enlarged his conception of the soul. Working in the *Phaedo* with a simple framework, he already applies it to reality in sensitive but equivocal ways.

4

Homer's Odysseus strikes his breast and chides his heart: 'Endure, my heart, for worse hast thou endured' (*Odyssey* 20.17–18). (Or as John Ruskin put it in a poem, perhaps less felicitously, 'Thou little bounder, rest.') Socrates cites this in the *Phaedo* to instance how the soul can guide and master 'the affections of the body', such as 'appetites and passions and fears' (94d5–e4), but in the *Republic* how reflection may rebuke rage, both elements within the soul (4.441b4–c2). Given that the body that has feelings is the body with a soul, there is no clear inconsistency, but the style of mapping has changed: we now find Plato opposing not soul and body, but 'parts' of the soul – a term, *meros*, that he first so uses at 442b11.[4] It might seem that we at once have a substantive issue: does the soul have parts? But that would be an illusion: until a criterion of partition is given to define the nature of a part and the principles of demarcation, the question lacks a sense; if a workable criterion is supplied, the question will become empirical. (There are not many initial restrictions on the kinds of thing that can have parts, and it is certainly not required that they be material: think of proofs, poems, and castles in the air. Nor should it be supposed that one criterion of partition, for one purpose, excludes others, for other purposes – a point to which I shall recur in Chapter 3 §3.) To discover what Plato means, we must identify his criterion; if it is well and appropriately defined, there can be no a priori objection to its application. The real problem is that he does not define it explicitly or coherently enough.

Plato starts from a thesis that we may call the Principle of Non-Contrariety: 'It is evident that the same thing will never do or suffer opposites simultaneously in the same respect and in relation to the same thing' (*Rep* 4.436b8–9). Thus any appearance of attaching contrary predicates to a single subject (that is, predicates that it cannot jointly satisfy) is to be dissolved by qualifying either subject or predicate. He at once gives two physical examples:

40

(a) If a man is standing still, but moving his hands and head, we should say not that he is simultaneously at rest and in motion, but that some of him is at rest, and some of him in motion (c9–d1).

(b) If a top is revolving round a central axis, we should say not that the whole of it is simultaneously at rest and in motion, but that it is at rest in respect of its axis, and in motion in respect of its circumference (d4–e4).

Clearly Plato could have reversed the redescriptions, qualifying predicate instead of subject, and subject instead of predicate: the man moves in respect of his hands and head, but not of his legs and torso; it is not the axis but the circumference of the top that moves. A later example invites the same variations:

(c) The arms of the archer do not simultaneously push the bow away and draw it near; rather, one arm pushes it away while the other pulls it to (439b8–11).

In Plato's statement of (c), it is the subject that gets qualified, as in (a), and not the predicate, as in (b); but it would be equally easy to say that the archer pushes with one arm and pulls with the other (or indeed that he pushes the bow-tree and pulls the bowstring). The options are open.

Plato then (437b1–3) generalizes with a series of opposites that hover between the physical and the mental: *prosagesthai* ('draw to') and *apôtheisthai* ('thrust away') are primarily physical; *ephiesthai* ('aim at') and *aparneisthai* ('refuse' or 'deny') are closer to the mental (though with the metaphorically physical prefixes *epi*, 'towards' and *apo*, 'away'); *epineuein* and *ananeuein* have two aspects, for they denote physical symbols (lowering or raising the chin) of mental acts (assent and dissent). Each pair expresses a binary contrast that is then applied to desires: desiring is associated with *ephiesthai*, *prosagesthai*, and *epineuein*, its contrary with their contraries (b7–c10). Now we find cases where thirst, i.e., a desire to drink, which drives the soul towards drinking like a beast, is opposed by something that draws the soul back (439a9–b5); when a man is thirsty and yet refuses to drink, there is something in his soul that tells him to drink, and something telling him not to that prevails (c2–7). But we excluded that the same thing 'by the same of itself' should act simultaneously in opposite ways in relation to the same thing (b5–6); so the soul must contain two forms (*eidê*, e2), whereby it desires oppositely.

Yet are Plato's various opposites really analogous to contrary desires? His argument invites the following objection. There is a clear distinction, also available in Greek, between desires and intentions. Plato's language has the effect of assimilating them, but they differ greatly in respect of contrariety: to have contrary desires, that is desires whose joint fulfilment is excluded, irrespective of their individual practicability, either by facts or by logic, is an inescapable aspect of the human condition, whereas to have contrary intentions is an empirical error or a logical fault. Indeed, neither desires nor intentions really fill Plato's bill: contrary desires are so easy that even their subject may be aware of their contrariety, and their ascription to a single subject requires no qualification to subject or predicate; contrary intentions are too problematic, in that they cannot survive the subject's awareness of their contrariety without modification. Thus I may consciously both desire immediately to drink, and desire immediately to eat, while realizing that I cannot simultaneously do both, without any appearance of self-contradiction; whereas an intention immediately to drink can only consciously co-exist with an intention immediately to eat if they are somehow insulated from any knowledge that I cannot do both. Plato tries to assimilate desiring to an act of drawing to, and desiring-that-not to an act of pushing away (437c8–10); but pushing and pulling are more opposed than contrary desires (which may belong unqualifiedly to a single subject who is aware that he has both but cannot fulfil both), and less opposed than contrary intentions (which cannot be reconciled with an awareness of their co-existence and contrariety by ascription to parts of a subject). Indeed, not only is consciously having contrary desires nothing like a contradiction, it may not even be a state of conflict: any adequately rich and varied life must be full of desires that are frequently overridden by others to which they are contrary, and yet it does not follow that it must be conflicted. Philosophers tend to call contrary desires, that is, desires whose fulfilment is jointly impossible, 'conflicting desires'; but for our purposes it is better to use 'conflicting' more restrictedly, so that desires only count as conflicting if they are veritably *in conflict*, for otherwise we risk obscuring the fact that having contrary desires is virtually a corollary of having many desires, and need not amount to the unhappy state of being conflicted. If I am free to do what I most desire to do, I may still feel some regrets – for example, I may wish I could do *more* of what I desire to do – but these may fall way short of mental conflict.

In defence of Plato, I suggest that what he really has in mind, without distinguishing it clearly in his thought, is not a relation that holds between any contrary desires, but one that only holds between them if they are both sufficiently tenacious and intense. What he says is plausible neither of mere desires nor of sheer intentions – two very different candidates that he appears to confuse. At least in English, there is an idiomatic difference between just *having a desire* to do something, and *wanting* to do it. Most desires are easily (and often) overridden, while if I really want to do something, I *feel set* on doing it.[5] Feeling set on something is closer, but still not identical, to intending to do it: forming an intention to do something goes with coming to believe that one will do it (though it is problematic to define just how prediction and intention relate), whereas I can feel set on something without having any idea whether it is practicable, perhaps even when I am fairly sure that it is impossible. Feeling set on something is a matter partly of the intensity of the desire (so that it is painful to frustrate it), and partly of its tenacity (so that it is difficult to displace it on to a different object). Plato's analogies of 'drawing to' versus 'thrusting away', and his language of 'aiming at' and 'refusing', more aptly apply not to states of merely having a desire for a thing, but to ones of actually wanting it. Thus Socrates says, 'The soul of the thirsty, in so far as it thirsts, wishes nothing else than to drink, and yearns for this and *its impulse is towards this*' (439a9–b1, of course my emphasis). Being conflicted comes of consciously feeling set on doing at least two things that are evidently (or just apparently) incompatible. One but not both of them may actually be intended. To mark the difference, we may speak of a 'weak contrariety' of desire when an agent merely has contrary desires, and of a 'strong contrariety' of desire, constituting mental conflict, when his desire is set in contrary directions. This need not restrict the applicability of Plato's theory: two weakly contrary desires that have a tendency to become conflicting may indicate two parts of the soul as well as two strongly contrary desires. Strong contrariety is always a state to evade or escape. The fact that it is part of the human condition calls for explanation: why is it that our desires tend to become set in contrary directions in ways that the pain of strong contrariety is unable to deter or correct? So construed, conflict of desire is at once a predicament and a problem.

An analogous difficulty arises later in the *Republic* when Plato explicitly extends his argument to beliefs:

> Often when this [sc., the part of the soul that calculates and measures] has measured and declares that certain things are

larger or smaller than others or equal to them, the opposite appears to be true simultaneously about the same things . . . . Did we not say that it is impossible for the same thing to hold opposite opinions simultaneously about the same things? . . . The part of the soul, therefore, that opines contrary to measurement could not be the same as that which opines in accordance with measurement.

(10.602e4–603a2, cf. also 603d1–2, 605c2)

Plato has in mind the illusions of appearance, as when a straight stick looks bent in water, and their exploitation by scene-painters (602c7–d4). He apparently supposes that these give rise to conflicting beliefs within the same mind. His conclusion is simple: the Principle of Non-Contrariety must apply equally to contrary beliefs as to desires, and both can be accommodated within a single mind by partition. This extension of his theory of parts to conflicting beliefs was already implicit in the general opposition of assent to dissent at 4.437b1, but it exposes him to a variant on my earlier objection about intentions: a subject cannot consciously hold contrary beliefs in the way that he can simultaneously be partly in motion and partly at rest. Partition only helps if it denies the subject awareness of either one or other of the beliefs, or of their incompatibility, but Plato is most interested in cases of conscious conflict. We have to suppose that his argument really applies not to pairs of beliefs but to pairs that contain at least one half-belief, whether this be a potential belief that is struggling to become a full belief, or a past belief that gets demoted through the emergence of actual or potential beliefs that conflict with it. There can be half-beliefs that come upon one without being fully accepted, and failures to form firm beliefs according to one's best judgement, but not two beliefs held simultaneously despite awareness of their inconsistency. In examples like that in Book 10, it is independently plausible that appearances present candidates for belief to the mind that register within it in a state of postulancy, perhaps generating impulsive and involuntary responses (as when one flinches from the train that approaches on the cinema screen) that fall short of actions. In other cases, one may act on a belief that, in a way, one knows to be false. Justin Gosling gives the example of a man who has fully tested the safety of a rope bridge, and yet distrusts it and stays put. Much in Plato's style, he diagnoses a 'division of judgement': 'By one route to a sort of judgment I am convinced it is safe; by another I am not' (1990: 15). Though one may well speak like that, it becomes paradoxical if taken literally. It seems better to say that the man is unable to be convinced either way, that is, fully to accept either belief. To the extent that he focuses rationally on his best evidence, he cannot seriously believe that the bridge is unsafe; to the extent that he focuses imaginatively on the action expected of him (which he cannot do without visions of falling), he cannot believe, in his heart of hearts, that the bridge is safe. He half-believes that the bridge is safe, and half-believes that it is not.[6] This counts as a relation not just of contrariety, but of strong contrariety, when neither belief is content to remain an idle half-belief, so that the subject feels torn between them. Again, this clarification, which Plato's text rather demands than invites, need not be taken to restrict the scope of his theory: two beliefs may count as tending to be in conflict (say if they are inconsistent, and survive through remaining at a distance within the mind) even if the effect of conflict must be to demote at least one of them into a half-belief.

Let us now return to Book 4, and contrariety between desires. Does strong contrariety supply Plato with the criterion to yield the partition he wants? One danger is that appetite, which he wishes to count as one part, may turn out to be liable to division within itself. Take the so-called 'oligarchic' man of Book 8 who puts down his drone-like appetites because he is aware that they compete with his overriding appetite for money (554b7–d3): his reason sides with his desire for money and against his other appetites (even making use of the former to inhibit the latter, c12–d1), and yet his appetite presumably remains a single part of his soul. Multiformity is characteristic of appetite (9.580d11) in a way that fits it to be likened to a many-headed monster (588c7–10), but the subject's awareness of the multiformity, and the dilemmas it poses, must not have the effect of partitioning appetite further. One restriction is to demand that the contrariety be non-contingent in that the object of one desire be, or entail, the negation of the object of the other; this is already exampled in Plato's opposition of a desire to drink (in the form of thirst) to a desire *not* to drink (in the form of a refusal to drink). It may be objected to this that if I have (a) a desire to eat and (b) a desire to drink, but know I can't do both, then (a) will generate (c) a desire not to drink, and (b) will generate (d) a desire not to eat, so that (a) and (b), which will not themselves count as problematically contrary, still generate the pairs (a) + (c) and (b) + (d), which will. Yet this is only damaging if we hoped to include all these desires within a single part of the soul, and it is not to be assumed that a desire and its negation will belong to the same part. It could be that such derivative desires do not fall within appetite: it is possible that (c) arises within reason if reason sees more point in satisfying (a) than (b) (cf. Penner 1971: 113–14). However, the objection *is* troublesome, for two reasons. Firstly, there are cases, if uncommon ones, of contradictory appetites: if I am suffering simultaneously from a dry throat and a full bladder, I may well both desire to drink and desire not to drink, and both desires may relate in the same heedless way to 'various repletions and pleasures' (4.439d8). This might force us to say that my throat wants (me) to drink while my bladder wants (me) to abstain, so that I am desiring differently in different parts of myself; this would be a fragmentation within appetite itself that Plato does not envisage. Secondly, he ascribes to a single part of the soul not only appetites, but also love of money as a means of satisfying them (9.580e5–581a1, cf. 4.436a1); and if thirst and a desire for the wherewithal belong together, so should thirst and an aversion to any impediment in the way of its satisfaction. Hence, if my appetite contains desires (a) and (b), and I know I cannot satisfy both, it will take on desires (c) and (d), which would segment appetite after all. Thus tightening the notion of contrariety of desire by requiring contradictory objects for partition still appears to yield more parts than Plato intends.

Plato is in difficulty, but I think that he has two ways of extricating himself. The first is to claim that, as a matter of fact, we find within appetite itself a tendency towards weak, but not strong, contrariety of desire. The fault-lines that underlie a tendency towards strong contrariety may fall outside. It may contingently be true that, while I may simultaneously be set appetitively upon now satisfying my thirst and rationally upon maintaining my health, though I know I cannot do both, yet I am never simultaneously set appetitively both upon satisfying my thirst and upon satisfying my hunger when I know I cannot do both. Pressing considerations of health can override my thirst although I still feel set on drinking (as is evidenced by feelings of conflict and frustration); an imperative hunger may always override my thirst by reducing my wanting to drink to my merely having a desire for drink (so that I still suffer from the sensation of thirst, and retain some desire to drink, but do not feel at odds with myself). Plato's second way out is to appeal to a secondary criterion. His example is not of a desire to drink and a desire not to drink colliding on the same level, but of this:

Are we to say, then, that some men though thirsty are not willing [*ouk ethelein*] to drink? ... Is it not that there is something in the soul that bids [*keleuon*] them drink and a something that forbids [*kôluon*], a different something that masters that which bids?

(4.439c2–7)

As is true interpersonally, the prohibition is a response to an impulse. While it is true that *keleuon* appears with *kôluon* as much for the jingle as for the sense, it is clear that *ethelein* signifies willingness rather than wishing: it connotes an attitude of endorsement towards a proposal already made (cf. *Gorg* 522e5–6). Irwin has argued that 'Plato needs to explain "rejection" as "rejection of the desire for the object"' (1977: 327); I think that he already has this in mind. He has the notion of a kind of desire that, taking a given desire as its object, adopts towards it an attitude that may be critical. If a desire to do something is of first order, a desire to have or lack that desire, or to act according or contrary to it, is of second order; so, in Plato, we may call the given desire 'lower-order', and the attitude towards it 'higher-order'. Yet a bare formal distinction between orders of desire does not suffice. Thirst is a desire for drink as the satiation of thirst, i.e., a desire for its own satisfaction; if I want to drink then I want my desire to drink to be satisfied, in an automatic and uninteresting way. Interesting are cases where the second-order desire is either critical, or not automatically accordant, cases where it is not a reflection of the first-order desire but a response to it. Rejection of a desire may take various forms: I may recoil from having it; I may recoil from ever fulfilling it; I may recoil from fulfilling it here and now. (It is not the case that the first of these entails the rest: one may recoil from having a desire in a way that leaves room, given that one has it all the same, for a willingness to pursue its satisfaction; contrariwise, as with Odysseus' curiosity to hear the seductive song of the sirens, one may wish to take on a desire so long as one runs no danger of acting on it.) Plato has in mind a rejection of a desire to drink that entails a desire not to drink. There will then be both a *contrariety* of desire, and a *confrontation* of desire: I not only want to act in a certain way and to act otherwise, but further have one desire that adversarily confronts another, a desire that looks another in the face and recoils from it. In addition to desires pointing away from one another, with one desire counteracting another simply as a corollary of pulling in a different direction, we have one desire

47

facing up to another, and attempting to countermand its effect upon action. The relations differ in their logical properties: contrariety is symmetrical (if *a* is contrary to *b*, *b* is contrary to *a*), while confrontation is asymmetrical (*a* can confront *b* without *b* confronting *a*). Within Plato's psychology, some parts may confront and be confronted, while others may only be confronted, since it is not in their nature to do any confronting. It is a plausible presumption that appetite lacks the capacity to be a subject of confrontation: confronting simply lies outside its repertory. Hence appetite cannot fall apart into further parts through confronting itself. Thus it is helpful to suppose that the relation of confrontation supplements that of strong contrariety in determining the soul's division into parts: distinct parts of the soul have an inherent tendency to contain desires that stand in relations both of strong contrariety and of confrontation. This yields a still richer sense in which desires can be not just weakly contrary, but conflicting.

5

We shall gain a fuller understanding of the principles of partition if we can identify the point of a long discussion of the precise objects of hunger and thirst (*Rep* 4.437d2–439b2). Here Plato insists that thirst is simply for drink, as hunger for food, and rejects a different view:

> Let no one disconcert us when off our guard with the objection that everybody desires not drink but good drink and not food but good food, on the ground that all men desire good things, and so, if thirst is a desire, it would be of good drink or of good whatever-it-may-be, and so similarly of other desires.
>
> (438a1–5)

How is this excluding an objection? The rejected view is itself ambiguous: it might be qualifying the object of thirst, as thirst conceives it, (a) as good drink, namely, only drink that is good of its kind, only a good kind of drink, or (b) as drink as a good, namely, drink only if it is good (here and now) to take, only if drinking (here and now) is a kind of good. Perhaps each would apply in a different case: reason might need to question the quality of the drink, or the utility of drinking. Plato reasons by a somewhat tedious induction from other cases that of a pair of correlates we must qualify both or neither: thus knowledge is of anything learned, while medical knowledge is of health and illness (c6–e8). He concedes that appetites can be qualified: though mere thirst is of mere drink, a hot thirst is for a cold drink, a cold thirst for a hot drink, great thirst for a large drink, small thirst for a little drink (437d11–e4). These cases look rather various themselves: while a little drink is better than nothing (though insufficient) for a large thirst, a hot drink may well be worse than nothing (because exacerbating) for a hot thirst. The use to which Plato puts the point is neither disambiguating nor cogent:

> The soul of the thirsty then, in so far as it thirsts, wishes nothing else than to drink, and yearns for this and its impulse is towards this . . . Therefore if anything draws it back when thirsty it must be something different in it from that which thirsts and drives it like a beast to drink.

> (439a9–b5)

If thirst is simply for drink, then an inhibiting thought of the form 'This is drink, but . . .' (it is only Coca-Cola, or I am suffering from dropsy) must draw its force not from thirst, but from some other motivation. The fallacy is that, though thirst exhausts the soul *qua* thirsty, it does not exhaust the soul *qua* appetitive, for thirst is not the only appetite. If the inhibiting thought was 'This is drink, but I want now to eat' (or, 'let me now eat'), its appeal would be to an imperative hunger, and not to anything outside appetite. If Plato has a better line of thought, it has to be rescued from his text.

One possibility is this: while Plato really knows that thirst is neither the only appetite, nor all appetite like mere thirst, he may be excluding the possibility that any appetite aims at goodness. His thinking may be that, if all desires aimed at the good, so that one only desired what one took to be good, then there could be false or vacillating beliefs about the good, but no conflict between desires. If this is right, one must reject Socrates' linkage between desire and the good if one is to retain more than an appearance of mental conflict (cf. Cornford 1912: 260–1 n. 2, Irwin 1977: 191–2). However, the reasoning is bad, and Plato knew it – or was only 3 minutes' thought from knowing it. This is evident from the later argument that I have quoted from Book 10 for a bipartition of the soul (602e4–603a2). This applies the Principle of Non-Contrariety equally to contrary beliefs and to desires, to the effect that both can be accommodated within a single mind by partition. I noted in §4 that the extension demands caution, but it is a different moral that I want now to draw from the passage. It is an important truism that all beliefs, in virtue of being beliefs, aim at truth: they have in common that truth is the primary criterion of their success (cf. 3.413a4–10). Thus the ignorance that is not mere lack of information but falsity of belief is an unintentional wandering of judgement that misses the mark it aims at (*Soph* 228c1–d2); in a limited application of Socrates' famous adage to error, the man who misjudges justice 'does not err willingly' (*Rep* 9.589c6). Yet this hardly seems an objection to a mental partition based on contrary beliefs; and if it is no objection to such a partition that all beliefs aim at truth, why should it tell against a partition based on contrary desires if all desires aim at the good? We could derive contrary desires from contrary beliefs about the good, with thirst saying 'It is good to drink' (or 'This is a good drink'), reason denying it, and neither believing the other. This would still leave intact a distinction between one desire's modifying another within a unitary soul, and one desire's confronting and then mastering another within a partite soul (cf. Bosanquet 1895: 154). Thus we do not have to ascribe to some desires another goal than the good in order to confirm the reality of mental conflict.[7]

In fact, once his denial that thirst is for good drink has played its role, Plato ceases to be careful to restrict appetite's conceptual repertory. Various passages ascribe to appetite beliefs that must be evaluative in some way: 4.442d3 hopes for consensus between reason and appetite that reason 'should' rule; 8.554d2 equates taming bad appetites by reason with 'persuading them that it is better not'; 9.574d5–e2 describe a conflict between respectable opinions about the fair and the base, and unspecified opinions associated with lawless desires. The evaluative concepts of which appetite is capable remain open: they certainly include 'pleasant' (4.436a11), and possibly 'truly pleasant' (9.586d8–e1); 442d3 and 554d2 strictly imply that they include 'good' and 'ought' – though it would be literal-minded to infer it confidently. An unqualified assertion that the good is 'that which every soul pursues and for its sake does all things' (6.505d11–e1) is itself ambiguous, but in its rhetorical context probably applies to all individual acts (and not just to all kinds of act); if so, then if appetite were indifferent to the good it would follow (more incredibly here than in the *Gorgias*) that it could never inspire action by itself. If Plato is uninsistent about restricting appetite's vocabulary, he is quite right to be so, for nothing of empirical substance hinges on it: it will fit the same phenomena to say that appetite aims only at pleasure and takes no interest in the good, or that it identifies the good with pleasure. Indeed, both may be true, according to different conceptions of the good: on a determinate conception, to pursue only pleasure may be to turn one's back on the good (cf. the man who is 'under compulsion to pursue the pleasant in preference to the good', *Phdr* 239c4–5); on an indeterminate one, to pursue anything is to take it as a goal and so as part of the good (cf. the medieval tag, 'Whatever is desired is desired under the aspect of the good'). What differentiates Socrates' position is that he aimed all desires not just at the good taken indefinitely, but at long-term happiness (*eudaimonia*) as conceived rationally (if often foolishly) by the agent. Again, belief and truth provide a helpful analogy: all beliefs aim at truth, indeterminately conceived (say as correspondence with reality); but some beliefs may irrationally identify reality with appearance, while others take reality to be captured not by looking but by measuring. What matters is not the terms that reason and unreason apply, but the principles by which they apply them.

In the light of the analogy between goodness and truth, it is charitable to understand Plato's bad argument (*Rep* 4.439a9–b5) as a hasty approximation to a better one for which he immediately provides the materials. What needs insistence is not that reason pursues the good and appetite not the good but the pleasant (a claim that we have just seen to be true in one way but false in another), but the following:

> Is it not a fact that that which inhibits such actions arises when it arises from the calculations of reason, but the impulses which draw and drag come through affections and diseases? . . . Not unreasonably shall we claim that they are two and different from one another, naming that in the soul whereby it reckons and reasons the rational [sc., part] and that with which it loves, hungers, thirsts, and feels the flutter and titillation of other desires, the irrational and appetitive [sc., part] – companion of various repletions and pleasures.
>
> (c9–d8)

It does not matter how reason expresses its conclusion, and Plato leaves this unspecified. (If he could have anticipated the argument of 9.583c3–586c6, Socrates could have represented reason as contradicting appetite's expectations of the 'pleasant', and thus using a term, though not an argument, readily intelligible to appetite.) What does matter is that reason reaches its decisions through a reckoning that carries no conviction with an appetite determined by 'various repletions and pleasures'. Reason and appetite constitute two alien points of view: appetite is a creature of physical needs and sensory appearance, while reason is the master of techniques for grasping theoretical and practical truth. This is why contrary desires can produce conflict: I may still feel set on drinking even when I know I must not and reject the thought of doing so, so long as my appetite and my reason are foreigners to one another. Strong contrariety and confrontation are relations of conflict between alien desires. Confrontation is an adversarial relation between two desires, one (or each) of which rejects the other from a point of view inimical to it. When a soul divides into parts we can distinguish points of view yielding lasting tendencies to desires in confrontation. Plato's surface emphases do inadequate justice to his deeper thoughts: he declares repetitiously that things are distinguished by contrarieties, and that thirst is only for drink; he describes illuminatingly how desires can stand in relations of strong contrariety and of confrontation, and how intelligent self-determination differs from brute causation.

I believe that the deeper reading is confirmed by the manner of Plato's introduction of 'spirit' as a third soul-part. To establish it accordingly, he needs both to find it tending towards relations of strong contrariety and confrontation with the two parts already identified, and to derive this tendency from a source that distances it from them; this is what he does. It must ease his task that, of all the parts of the soul, spirit is the most naturally stubborn and confrontational. First and foremost, it is that within us with which we feel anger (4.439e3); this was already implicit in its particular ascription, within a long tradition (cf. Newman 1887–1902: iii. 363–4, ad Aristotle *Pol* 4.7.1327b23), to Thracians, Scythians, and other northerners (435e6–7). To partition it off within the soul, Plato has to focus on cases in which anger is self-directed. He claims that this is common when a man is constrained to act contrary to his reasoning (440a8–b2). He cites the example of Leontius, torn between a desire to look at corpses, and a repugnance at doing so (439e7–10). This is not just a case of a weak contrariety of appetites, say curiosity versus squeamishness. When Leontius cries out, as it were to his eyes, 'There, you wretches, take your fill of the fine spectacle', he 'recoils' from looking even as he does look, and 'is angry' with himself for looking, thus confronting the desire (439e9–440a3). (It is evident from a fragment of Theopompus, if emended, that Leontius, whom we may call the first sexual pervert in history, was notoriously susceptible to pale complexions, whether as a cause or as a consequence of necrophilic tendencies, and it is doubtless these tendencies that he is really confronting in Plato's anecdote; cf. Adam 1902: i. 255.) To consolidate the separation of spirit from appetite, Socrates suggests, and Glaucon agrees, that spirit will never be found taking the side of appetite against reason (b4–7). This overstatement is rapidly qualified: it is the noble-minded man who refuses to resent ill-treatment that he concedes to be just (c1–6); it is only 'naturally', when uncorrupted by upbringing, that spirit is reason's auxiliary (441a2–3). Two considerations divorce spirit from reason, of which one is proposed by Glaucon and confirmed by Socrates, and the other proposed by Socrates and approved by Glaucon; together they indicate that, as a result of a radical difference in their sources, spirit and reason are liable to be related adversarily. They are that children are full of anger from birth, though reasoning comes later, and that their tendency to anger is shared with animals, who never reason (a7–b3, cf. 2.375a11–12). These two observations work together: it might have been that one and the same part of the soul displays itself in impulsive anger before it learns to exercise itself in reasoning, but the fact that such anger is common to children and animals indicates that its source is not inchoate reason but irrational instinct. Once reason has developed, we find it rebuking unreasoning anger as something other than itself (441b4–c2): as Odysseus strikes his breast (a physical act that proves parts of the body, cf. 436c9–d1), he chides his heart (a mental act that goes to prove parts of the soul). Thus we have a composite argument for a complex conclusion: spirit derives from a source of its own, which is common to men and to animals, a tendency to be at odds both with appetite and with reason.

What, then, is a part of the soul? It turns out to be the home of a family of desires and beliefs that have a tendency to stand in relations both of strong contrariety, and of confrontation, with members of any other family, but not of their own. The tendency is due to contrasting sources of desire and belief within the mind. (It is here that partition becomes explanatory and not just descriptive.) The confrontation may be one-way, or two-way if each part is capable of confronting the other. On this view, human desires form only a few clusters or clans – where the term 'clan' may add to the more general 'cluster' the connotations of relatedness and permanence. I have complained that Plato misclassifies the data to which his conception directly applies: these are more than mere desires (which are not themselves matter for strong contrariety), and less than full beliefs (which cannot survive awareness of mutual inconsistency intact). What his theory directly fits are states involving the presence of wanting, and of half-believing. However, I have suggested that this does not restrict its applicability: it applies to pairs of weakly contrary desires with a tendency to intensify and become conflicting wantings, and of contrary beliefs with a tendency (say if their contrariety becomes evident) to become conflicting half-beliefs. I have not said anything about confrontation between beliefs, but that is not hard to supply (so long as one of the beliefs is demoted into a half-belief): in Plato's own simplest example (10.602c10–11), reason not only insists that the stick remains straight when it is placed in water, but takes a dim view of the opposed tendency to take things to be as they look, to identify reality with appearance. My term 'home' is intentionally indefinite, but perhaps less misleading than any alternative. Plato never calls the parts a plurality of 'souls': rather, a part is what *we* do something *with*, in the sense not of an instrument by which we do it, but of an aspect of ourselves in respect of which we do it. Thus we learn with one part, feel anger with another, and desire sensual gratification with a third (4.436a8–b2); alternatively, it is the soul that does such things with them (439d5–8). When we read 'The soul of the thirsty, then, in so far as it thirsts, wishes nothing else than to drink' (a9–10), the qualification more likely attaches to the predicate than to the subject. It is true that, with typical verbal nonchalance, thirst may be predicated, within a few lines, of person, soul, and soul-part (a9–b5). As we saw, these variations are anticipated in the initial physical parallels: Plato writes that one arm of the archer pushes the bow away while the other pulls it to (b8–11), but the wording of the previous examples shows that he would be equally happy to say that the archer pushes with one arm and pulls with the other. Such indications imply that mental parts should not be taken to be subjects of mental activities, for a subject of an activity cannot also be the aspect of another subject in respect of which this subject performs it. If beliefs and desires are mental items, mental parts should rather be conceived on the analogy of physical spaces or fields that contain things. It fits that the parts are ascribed sizes, as mental subjects could not be: already at 431a8 the soul's better element is called smaller than 'the multitude of its worse'. This was doubtless suggested by the political analogy (likening its worse element to the mob, cf. b9–c3), but is confirmed later (442a5–6, 9.588d4–5). If the parts are not subjects, they are not agents either, though their contents are causes of action, constituting either forces (if we think of desires or of evaluative or normative beliefs) or conduits (if we think of dispassionate beliefs). It is a natural assumption that, in cases of conflict, action follows according to a play of forces and the relative strengths of opposing pulls (cf. 589a1–2).

A further indication is supplied in a striking passage which uses a hydraulic metaphor to describe a schooling of desire:

> When in a man the desires incline strongly to any one thing, they are weakened for other things. It is as if the stream had been diverted into another channel. . . . So when a man's desires have been taught to flow in the channel of learning and all that sort of thing, they will be concerned . . . with the pleasures of the soul in itself, and will be indifferent to those of which the body is the instrument.
>
> (6.485d1–12)

Presumably the force of a desire is more easily rechannelled within a part than between parts; we can picture each part as directly fuelled by a single source of energy, though the sources connect. Indeed, this may explain what I could earlier only write into a definition (of a psychic 'part') or posit as a convenient contingency (about the parts that Plato envisages): desires within a single part may not be liable to stand in relations of strong contrariety to one another for the reason that excess quantity of affect is readily displaceable from one to the other; hunger, say, may well compete with thirst (especially to the extent that they have distinct physiological origins), but their kinship is such that excess affect will quickly drain from one to the other, so that it is never the case that each is intense enough to be strongly contrary to the other. (This generalization will be qualified, in a manner faithful to its spirit, at the end of §6.) However, the point that is explicit here, and now relevant to us, is that displacement of affect is also possible between psychic parts; yet if these were subjects of desire like persons, strength of desire could not migrate between them. If we think of parts instead on the model of channels or fields, we can imagine a given quantity (or quantum) of affect retaining a kind of identity even after entering a new sphere of influence and fuelling a new kind of desire. Of course it may be difficult to take this literally: if we identify a quantum of affect by reference to the identity of some desire, we cannot allow one desire to steal the intensity of another. Yet Plato's willingness to apply such talk not only within but between parts confirms that they are rather fields than subjects.[8]

Such, I think, is the reading of Plato's language of parts that does central justice to the substance of his theory.[9] Yet this is complicated by a tendency to speak of the intrapersonal interpersonally, as if the soul consisted of various mini-persons or homunculi. He is given to speaking of the parts anthropomorphically: parts can give commands (4.439c6–7), or be obedient (441e6); they can raise faction (442d1, 444b1), or be meddlesome (443d2, 444b2). In his most vivid simile, he views each of us as containing a 'manifold and many-headed beast' like Cerberus, a lion, and a man (9.588c7–e1). He can also write as if each of us were not party to the factions of his soul, but stood outside them like a trainer or referee. Thus a man must not suffer the principles in his soul to do one another's work, but must harmonize them, linking and binding all three together (4.443d1–e1). Less happily, the psychic timarch, pulled between reason on the one side and spirit and appetite on the other, hands over the domination of reason to spirit (8.550a4–b7), while the oligarch thrusts spirit from his soul's throne, setting up the acquisitive aspect of appetite in its place (553b8–c6). (We may imagine, internalizing an earlier observation that all revolution originates from dissension within the ruling class, 545d5–7, that it is the man's own reason that hovers between the call of truth, and the demands of the rest of his soul; if so, it is his reason that is switching its allegiance. However, Plato is not at pains to describe things so.) Yet it is mysterious what is left over to motivate decision between one's soul-parts. These forms of expression, treating parts as persons or separating the man from his parts, are recurrent in Books 8 and 9, where they often occur together. We can take them to be a manner of speaking, a way of writing up internal conflict in the style of external drama. This fits the special style of these books, which, expounding parallels between political and psychic decline, naturally picture the soul in civic and interpersonal terms. More speculatively, we may surmise that such conceptions can faithfully capture an aspect of the way the mind pictures itself, a self-dramatizing mode in which it experiences, and transmutes, its own workings. Thus a man may draw upon the repertory of one part of his mind in addressing another part, whose repertory is different, as if it were another person; this may differentiate the repertories more sharply, and make the confrontation more personal. As I said in the Introduction, these approaches need not be taken as alternatives. The private world is both characterized and created in a public language, so that the personal apes the social, the intrapersonal the interpersonal. Plato's political models serve his own purposes in their specificity, but in their general role are apposite to self-images that mould the self. Dramatically is at once how Plato writes and how we live.[10]

To an extent, therefore, talk of homunculi, however problematic, fits the phenomenology of human mental life. However, it is likely that Plato is driven to it in part by his failure to realize that the data to which his theory directly applies are neither intentions (to which his language in Book 4 tends to assimilate desires), nor beliefs. When I am conflicted, Plato may well be supposing, *I* cannot be said to hold just one (or I would not be conflicted), or both (or I would be unintelligible), of a pair of evidently inconsistent intentions or beliefs. By whom then are they held? Presumably by different sub-persons within the person that I am, namely, homunculi. But this is both fantastic, and contrary to much else that he says (rehearsed above) to indicate that parts are fields and not subjects. So here we find the nub of an incoherence between two aspects of his theory, which connect with different ways of applying his Principle of Non-Contrariety to beliefs and desires. One aspect, explicit and schematic, is constituted by his application of the principle to consciously contrary desires as confused with intentions, and beliefs; these appear to demand ascription not to a single subject, but to soul-parts as subjects. The other aspect, implicit and concrete, is constituted by his recognition of relations of strong contrariety and confrontation that hold between consciously opposed states of wanting and of half-believing (or of intending and wanting, and of believing and half-believing); these can consistently be assigned to a single subject, though they relate to different parts of his mental make-up. Homunculi are in part a conceptual corollary of the first aspect, and in part both a presentational and a phenomenological complication of the second. I shall return to the topic of conflicting intentions and beliefs at the end of this book (Chapter 4 §5). For the time being, I set the issue of homunculi aside; there is much in Plato that we can understand and assess without reference to them.

6

In this section I shall examine Plato's three parts of the soul separately, facing up to some difficulties but sidestepping others; we can best consider after that what is most problematic in his division.

Reason (or 'the reasoning' part, *to logistikon*) has various operations and concerns, which Aristotle was later to separate out as theoretical or practical. On the one hand, it is both its task to discover the truth (*Rep* 9.580d10, 583a2), and also its passion (4.435e7, 9.580d10, 581b5–10, 586e4); on the other, it governs the entire soul, guarding against both internal and external dangers with knowledge of what is beneficial to each part of the soul and to the community of its parts (4.441e4–442c8). Less clear is how these roles connect. An indiscriminate love of truth (cf. 5.475b8–9) is private to reason, much as a love of money may be private to appetite (cf. 4.435e7–436a1), and there can be a tension between devotion to truth for its own sake, and the cultivation of those truths that bear on the activities of the other parts, and of the whole man as a social animal. Indeed, it is familiar that this tension becomes a feature of the lives of Plato's rational paradigms, the philosopher–rulers, forbidden to linger among their own contemplations (7.519c8–d6), and governing out of social necessity, not out of a dearth of goods of their own (520e2–521a6). Plato wishes rather to emphasize how distant they are from the self-seeking of ordinary rulers (e.g., 520e3) than to explain how their motivations connect. However, he has various reasons for holding that the best life of incarnate reason, the life in which it most nearly realizes its true nature within a world of change, is of a piece. One way in which theory points to practice is through its objects: to know the Forms is to love them, and to love the Forms is to wish to fashion oneself in imitation of them in a just and orderly life (6.500c2–d1) – the opposite assimilation to that which comes of taking pleasure in the ways of the wicked (*Laws* 2.656b1–6). Once reason itself possesses wisdom, it will desire that wisdom possess the soul of which it is part, which requires (*Rep* 4.442c5–8, cf. 444a1–2) that it rule wisely within the soul. This already offers the agent a prize of a kind: the man who is keen to become just and to practise virtue will be likened to a god so far as is possible for a man (10.613a7–b1, cf. 6.500d1, *Symp* 212a5–7, *Theaet* 176a8–b3, c1–3). There is further point in moulding not just oneself but one's community (cf. *Rep* 500d4–8): I love wisdom more if I wish it to characterize not only myself but my city, which requires (4.428e7–9) that this be ruled by the wise; in a striking expression, it is a 'service' to justice to extend its domain in governing a city (7.540e2–3). Selfishly, philosophers must wish to rule both in the city, and in their own souls (cf. 9.571e1–572a8), in order to protect themselves against interruptions to philosophizing. Here, interestingly, city and individual cannot be parallel, and internal demands are more stringent than external: it may be best for my philosophy that other philosophers rule; but, if I possess reason, I cannot hand over the rational governance of my other parts to the reason of others. (Here I differ from slaves who can only be ruled by reason if they submit to the rule of others, 590c8–d6.) Yet any selfish motivation must be secondary if philosophical rulers are to differ from most rulers in not being governed by 'a senseless and childish opinion about happiness' that conceives it as a private prerogative (5.466b4–c3). Plato disparages a narrow self-interest set on 'appropriating' (c1) or 'snatching' (7.521a6) goods for oneself. However, a generous self-interest that partly identifies one's own good with the good of others is very much a goal (3.412d4–7, 5.463e3–5). Reason loves its own operations, but these include not only the private grasp but the public propagation of truth (e.g., 2.380b6–c3) – except in a few cases where falsehood is medicinal (2.382c10, 3.389b2–9, 5.459d1–2). Thus its life is complex, and not without its hard choices; yet its motivations hang together, and do not threaten internal stasis.[11] It may, on occasion, hesitate between the thinking that is a holiday from acting, and the action that is an extension of thought, but the worst that it faces within itself is not conflict but weak contrariety, and that superable. Rational desires are not merely modified by reasoning (all the desires of the temperate man are that), but arise out of reasoning (4.439d1). As successful reasoning produces propositions that are mutually supporting and consistent, rational desires should tend towards reconciliation; contrariety should produce compromises, not stand-offs.[12]

Plato introduces appetite (or 'the desirous' part, *to epithymêtikon*) with the desires that, being most blatantly irrational, best give the lie to Socrates. He has no specific term at hand for the appetites, either in our idiomatic sense, or in the sense of whatever desires are to be assigned to this part, and he introduces them merely as 'a certain class consisting of desires' (*epithymiai*), of which the 'clearest' members are hunger and thirst (4.437d2–4). He later justifies calling this part the *epithymêtikon* (his coinage) on the ground of 'the intensity of desires for food and drink and sex and their accompaniments' (9.580e2–4). That indicates how similar *epithymia* is to our 'desire': both terms can be used widely to cover all appetencies, but tend, through connoting a certain phenomenology (cf. a 'state of desire'), to be used more narrowly of those kinds of desire of which the physical appetites, and notably hunger and thirst, are the paradigms. It is for clarity, and not faithfulness, that I use the term 'appetite' (which errs, however, on the other side, that of undue specificity). It is especially clear of appetites aiming at physical replenishment that they arise not from reasoning but from 'affections and diseases'

(4.439d2), that is, from physiological causes; they may be characterized as 'states of physical depletion' (9.585a8–b1, cf. *Tim* 70d7–8). To them Plato adds sexual desire (4.439d6), which, taken physiologically, belongs better in the case of the male with desires for evacuation. Along with hunger, thirst, and sexuality come other appetites akin (436a11–b1), or associated (9.580e4), or unspecified (4.439d7, cf. 437d2–3).

It is not evident how the dependence of appetites on bodily states of being full or empty fits with Plato's view that they are typically insatiable (9.581b3–4, 590b8). Does he merely mean that hunger and thirst keep coming back within cycles of depletion and replenishment? He more likely has in mind that they tend to fuel the sensuality (like that of the torrent-bird, *Gorg* 494b6) of hastening these cycles in order to get more of their pleasures. Such a policy of intemperance (about which Callicles and Socrates debated in the *Gorgias*) must be motivated by a new kind of desire for pleasure: the sensualist adds to our fluctuating appetites in need of satisfaction a lasting hedonism that maximizes appetites as a means towards maximal satisfaction. Where does such sensuality belong? Most likely there is no universal answer. It may be a product of reflection, at home within a corrupt reason; where it is rather a bad habit than a perverted policy, it may count as an appetite of a new kind.

Is there any way in which appetite might extend its repertory through the use of reasoning while remaining distinct from reason itself? We read that 'we called it . . . likewise the money-loving part, because money is the chief instrument for the gratification of such desires', that is, those aimed at food, drink, love, and their accompaniments (*Rep* 9.580e3–581a1, referring back to 4.436a1). This implies not merely that money helps one to satisfy one's appetites, but that appetite acquires a standing desire for money on that ground. Does it make the connection itself, or does it depend on reason to point it out? A degree of dependence on reason is implied in a passage describing a dominant appetite that allows reason 'to calculate and consider nothing but the ways of making more money from a little' (8.553d3–4); clearly appetite can do with reason's help. However, if it has a primitive power to reason from ends to means, it may desire money as a means without being skilled at the art of money-making.[13] If it is capable of accepting that one thing is a means to another, it must possess the concept of a means; and how can it do this if it is incapable of performing even the most rudimentary means-end reasoning itself? In fact, it is tempting to ascribe some grasp of ends and means to human appetite even before we bring in money: plausibly it not merely thinks of drink with pleasure (as any animal may do), but desires it as a means to the pleasure of satisfying thirst (cf. 4.436a11 on our desiring with our appetite 'the pleasures associated with nutrition and generation').[14] Given that we are self-conscious language-users, we may suppose that our appetites are distinctively human (even if 'beastlike' by comparison with our other desires, 439b4) and, as it were, saturated by the notion of doing one thing for the sake of another. In the instance of consciously desiring drink in order to experience the pleasure of satisfying thirst, appetite's reasoning achieves an adaptation of instinct; in that of purposefully desiring money for buying drink, it dictates a new habit. It remains restricted, and restrictedly self-determining: it moves from ends to means by only the most familiar of paths, and it cannot sort out which of a pair of ends (say, satisfying hunger or satisfying thirst) should be preferred. It can repeat a past success, but not calculate a fresh expedient; it is incapable of deliberation or choice. Distinctive of appetite from reason is not a total incapacity to think, but a mode of thinking that is mechanical.

More needs to be said to justify the ascription to appetite of new desires arising out of old appetites through habit. A plausible thought is that it can only contain desires that share the phenomenology of physiologically generated appetites, and so fit F.H. Bradley's characterization of desire: 'For desire we must have three elements – an idea conflicting with reality, that idea felt to be pleasant, and the reality felt to be painful; and these elements felt as one whole state make up desire' (1935: i. 263). We must hesitate to infer appetites for things that it is difficult to think of as pleasures and with pleasure (two features logically distinct but connected within our psychology); equally, we must have doubts about appetitive aversions from things not easily thought of as painful and with pain. In an example of Terry Penner's (1971: 113–14), I may have an appetite for a drink that I know I can only get by exchanging my warm bed for a cold room, and yet strictly lack any desire, let alone appetite, to get up: even if I recognize that I have a reason to get up (one that may be overridden by other reasons), I will not *desire* to get up if what suffuses the idea of getting up is the discomfort of shivering and not the consolation of the drink. In such a case, where thoughts of the end fail to colour thoughts of the means (in the way they so easily succeed in doing when one comes to love money), there is ground to deny that an awareness of ends and means suffices to generate a new appetite. Idiomatically, this seems right, but what if I do get out of bed in order to get the drink, though reason and spirit tell me not to and only appetite motivates me? Plato had better deny that this ever actually occurs: appetite operating alone cannot motivate unappetizing actions, and what look like exceptions must in fact involve the transient suborning of reason to act as appetite's auxiliary. This claim may be falsifiable, and yet not false.

If we stress the phenomenology of appetite, we may be able to resolve a related uncertainty: does it love money only as a means, or also as an end? Valuing money for its own sake is suggested by a description of appetite as not only 'money-loving' but 'gain-loving' (9.581a6–7). The suggestion is confirmed by the ranking of 'gain-loving' alongside 'wisdom-loving' and 'victory-loving' (c3), given that reason loves wisdom for its own sake and (as we shall see) spirit victory for its own sake. There follow mentions of the 'money-maker', who doesn't sound like a sensualist (c10–d3, cf. 'the thrifty and money-making man', 8.555a9), and 'the pleasure that comes from money' (581d5–6), which must be intrinsic if it is to be single. Plato sometimes connects the insatiability of appetite to its attachment to money (4.442a6–7, cf. *Pdo* 66c7–d2). (Not that he is consistent: he can also oppose 'the acquisitive appetites' to 'the unnecessary ones whose object is entertainment and display', 9.572c2–4, as if all acquisition was out of necessity, and it was impossible, despite Volpone, to enjoy one's wealth without spending it.) This already makes some sense if there is no definite limit to possible future expenditure, but it makes fuller sense once money is also desired for its own sake, and so unlimitedly: as goals arising from the conversion of means into ends offer no real satisfaction, the desire for them can be exhausted but never sated. A tendency for appetite to slide between instrumental and intrinsic valuings of money fits its phenomenology: only seductive thoughts speak to it, and they seduce it into desiring to translate them into actuality for its own sake. Appetite's primitive thinking, which encompasses only simple and familiar links between ends and means, and can only pursue means if they share the attraction of ends, tends to subvert its respect for the distinction.

An unexpected appetite that Plato does countenance is one for philosophizing. The democratic man, though a creature of appetite, is 'manifold and full of very many dispositions' (8.561e3–4), alternating unpredictably between wine and water, sloth and exercise, war and business, politics and philosophy (c7–d5). Under the sway of 'the appetite of the moment' (c7), he acts as he feels (d3) in a life that he calls pleasant, free, and happy (d6–7). Variable in the objects of his activities, he is constant in his manner of pursuing them. In the terminology of Stephen Schiffer, he treats all his desires as 'reason-providing' and not 'reason-following' (1976: §4); for he knows no better reason for an activity than that it happens to attract him, and no reasons for desiring one thing rather than another. Pleasure is his only value, and it is a shifting target that does nothing to set his appetites in one direction. We have still to ask where his non-physiological appetites, including his taste for philosophy, come from. It may well be that they are borrowed from other parts of the soul, and then transformed by the nature of appetite. If this is so, appetite can be eclectic in its objects so long as it pursues them appetitively. A love of philosophy will count as an appetite if it is pursued just for fun, and not (which is harder work) out of a passion for truth. This seems a complication to be welcomed.

I have already discussed appetite's evaluative repertory, in fact to nugatory effect: it may entertain thoughts about the 'good' so long as they reduce to thoughts about its goals. Its first abstract goal appears to be pleasure: it pursues not just food and drink but 'the pleasures associated with nutrition and generation' (4.436a11); it later pursues not just money but 'the pleasure that comes from money' (9.581d5–6). 'Good' may then be admitted into its vocabulary alongside 'pleasant' so long as it is 'pleasant' (in a phrase of J.L. Austin) that wears the trousers, so long (to change the metaphor) as 'good' is a passenger. Does appetite possess the concept 'must'? It does, if we take Plato at his word: temperance needs agreement that reason 'must' or 'ought to' rule (*dein*, 4.432a6–9, 442d1). Further, I have said that appetite can desire one thing as a means to another. Can it desire it as a sufficient means? Can it desire it as a necessary means? Presumably we must answer yes to the first question (how else could it have a concept of means at all?); so we may also answer yes to the second. And to desire one thing as necessary for another is to judge that, for the first, one *must* have the second. So appetite should be allowed the use of 'good' and 'must'; what distinguishes it is how it applies them. This leads into a more substantive question: on what ground can appetite appreciate that reason must rule (or 'ought to' rule, *dei*)? Plato wants a contrast between the temperance which persuades appetite that it 'had better not' and tames it by giving it a reason (*logos*), and the seeming justice of the internal oligarch which 'by some better element in himself forcibly keeps down other evil desires dwelling within . . . by compulsion and fear' (8.554c12–d3). This connects with a subsidiary question: if appetite is capable of agreement, need the producers within Plato's utopia possess anything but appetite? If they need reason, while appetite does not, the nature of the agreement, and so temperance itself, would seem not to be the same within the soul and within the city (*pace* 4.435e1–3, 442d2–3). It appears that, while friendship is a goal within both (cf. 1.351d5–6, 4.443d5, 9.590d6), and that to this extent internal and external temperance are the same, producers are capable of a richer friendship with their rulers than appetite is with reason: while appetite remains self-centred, producers can identify with their fellow citizens of any class (cf. 5.462c7–8, 464a4–6). (Although these passages say nothing about producers in particular, what is true of all citizens must be true of producers, and Plato thinks best of that city in which 'the greatest number' identify with one another, 462c7; cf. Price 1989: 186.) Plausibly, it is in virtue of their reason, simple though it is, that producers can be altruists. This might suggest a temperate appetite incapable of altruism but not of an enlightened self-interest that recognizes that it will best avoid appetitive frustration, and most achieve appetitive fulfilment, if it accepts the guidance that reason offers on behalf of the whole soul (4.441e4–5) and with knowledge of what will benefit each part (442c6–7). In practice, this would mean at least giving priority to necessary appetites (those we cannot divert, or whose satisfaction benefits us, 8.558d11–e2). In theory, there is a problem: how can appetite (capable, even on my fairly generous view, only of the simplest means–ends reasoning) form views even about its own best advantage? In its lack of a reflective intelligence, it must be incapable of considering all its pleasures impartially, that is, from a point of view that corrects the errors of perspective that featured in the *Protagoras*. If so, how can it even understand judgements about what it will enjoy most in the long term? There is a further problem: if appetite were capable of taking a view about its best advantage, what would preclude that this might conflict with, and perhaps be overridden by, a recalcitrant hunger or thirst?[15] It may be wiser to attempt to interpret the ideal of appetite's being 'persuaded' by 'reason' (554d2), and 'agreeing' that reason 'must' rule (4.442d1), in a way that pays little attention to the literal meaning of the words. The thought may be that reason's task is to give appetite longer views by drawing to its attention long-term pains surpassing short-term pleasures, and hence sparing it the turmoil and ruefulness that fill the tyrannized soul (9.577e1–3); we may suppose that appetite is capable of responding to deterrent thoughts that it lacks the foresight to summon up itself. If this is right, reason 'persuades' appetite, and appetite 'agrees' with reason, not in that appetite adopts an explicitly obedient attitude towards reason, but in that it develops under reason's influence (it is 'led' by it, 4.431b6) in such a way that it come to discard those desires that would defeat the ends of appetite as of the soul as a whole. What 'persuasion' and 'agreement' come to is a function of intelligence, and the temperance of spirit, and of reason itself, is more complex (and more literally 'agreement') than that of appetite. Thus educating *men* with 'persuasion' rather than with 'force' demands 'the true Muse, the companion of philosophical speech' (8.548b7–c1), which is reminiscent of the 'fair speech and instruction' that stretch and nourish reason (4.441e9–442a1) but can hardly be what 'persuades' *appetite* rather than repressing it with 'force' (8.554d1–2). Reason's goal must be a programme of training appetite that works so well that it can approve the satisfaction of all the appetites that remain. About our chances of achieving temperance so understood Plato vacillates (8.559b8–10 and 9.586d4–587a1 seem more hopeful than 9.571b4–c1 and 572b3–7). It seems a demanding but intelligible ideal.

Plato emphasizes that appetite is multiform (9.580d11) and many-headed (588c7–8), but it is 'the spirited' part (*to thymoeides*) that has seemed to many unduly protean. In its primitive form, it is displayed even by newborn children (4.441a7–b1) and animals (b2–3, cf. 2.375a11–12). It shares with appetite an aspect of physio-logical disturbance: it 'seethes' or 'boils' (*zei*, 440c7, cf. *Tim* 70c1–4); in the *Cratylus*, *thymos* ('passion' or 'anger') even receives the etymology 'the *thysis* and *zesis* of the soul' ('rushing and boiling', 419e1–2). At its more civilized, spirit takes on the evalu-ative activities of admiring, honouring, and taking pride in (*Rep* 8.553d4–6). It thus occupies a midpoint between the other two parts (*meson*, 550b4, 6). Yet there is a connecting thread to be traced. From its physiology spirit takes a native belligerence; as the seat of anger (4.439e3), it is prone to savagery (3.410d6–7). If we may use Aristotelian jargon to capture an anticipation of Aristotle, there is a correspondence between its material aspect (the boiling) and its formal (aggressiveness). This initially gives it not so much any distinctive conception of the good (like appetite's equation of the good with pleasure) as a type of orientation, aggressive and self-conscious, towards the good. With a special intensity in noble souls (4.440c2, d1), it is inhibited by the thought of being in the wrong (c1–5) and exercised by that of being wronged (c7–8). When its anger is directed at oneself (e.g., b1–2), this gives rise to shame (8.560a6–7). It is sooner provoked by wrongs to be resisted than stimulated by goods to be achieved; thus it speaks rather in terms of 'right' and 'wrong', 'ought' and 'ought not', than of 'good' and 'bad'. (We shall find Aristotle making the same point, *NE* 7.6.1149a32–4.) This helps explain why it is by nature reason's auxiliary (4.441a2–3): it is receptive of another's values, translating them into its own terms (cf. 442c1–3). However, its temperament also inclines it towards values of its own: we later, in Books 8 and 9, read repeatedly that it is set on honour (for the pugnacious love honour, 9.583a8); its love of that goes with a love of victory (8.545a2–3, 548c6–7, 550b6–7, 9.581b2–3, 582e4–5, 586c9). Indeed, its very self-righteousness risks becoming its own end, as is well stated by Christopher Gill:

> It is possible to see how the natural impulse of the *thymoeides* to be 'in the right' could, if unrestrained, become an ideal in itself, so that moral indignation would be converted into *amour-propre*; and this seems to be what Plato describes as the 'ambitious' type of man in Book 8.
>
> (1985: 8)

Its concern to keep up evaluative appearances makes it prone to a more unnatural corruption: flattery may make smooth a descent into subservience to appetite, so that it becomes habituated to the contumely that it ought most to resent (590b6–8); in its loss of freedom, it then comes to resemble less a lion (who is 'free' in character, cf. Aristotle *Hist an* 1.1.488b16–17) than an ape (590b9), and Thersites rather than Ajax (cf. 10.620b1–c3).[16]

Thus there is a unity to Plato's spirit: its different forms and manifestations connect. Yet is it securely a single part according to his criteria? It was partly in order to avoid further partition of appetite that I drew attention not just to contrariety, to which appetite is prone in its weak form (though perhaps not, I suggested, in its strong one), but to confrontation, of which it is plausible to hold it incapable. But what then of spirit, not only capable of confrontation but confrontational by nature, and often resistant to rational discipline? Why, for example, should shame not come apart from one-upmanship? The good horse of the *Phaedrus* is 'a lover of honour when joined with restraint and a sense of shame' (253d6); but why should there not be a conflict involving confrontation between the vanity that would boast of a successful seduction (cf. 232a1–6), and the shame that holds any but a Don Juan back? Indeed, Plato there has the horse of appetite revile the charioteer who would restrain it for cowardice and unmanliness (254c7–8); this should surprise us after the *Republic*, and implicitly concedes that a false courage (with which contrast 'true glory', 253d7) can decry a sense of shame, and so align itself with a separate part.[17] There is even an indication in the *Republic* itself. The 'false and deceptive words and opinions' that pervert the values of the democratic soul exist before they take over its reason (8.560c2–3); they must be ascribed to spirit rather than to appetite (unless we risk subdividing appetite by making *it* confrontational). Among the values they 'thrust forth as a dishonoured fugitive' is that of shame, which they miscall 'simplicity' (d2–3), and yet it will be emphatic in the *Phaedrus* that shame falls within spirit's own repertory (253d6, 254a2, c4). (Cf. *Rep* 9.571c9 and *Phdr* 256a6, where it is implicit that shame belongs to spirit, and wisdom or reasoning to reason.) Thus spirit is liable to become divided against itself in a way that threatens its singleness as a part. However, an answer to this complaint is implicit in a more careful reading of my characterization of a 'part'.[18] I wrote above (in §5) that a part of the soul is 'the home of a family of desires and beliefs that have a tendency to stand in relations both of strong contrariety, and of confrontation, with members of any other family, but not of their own'. We have now seen that the contents of spirit may confront each other, but what is the cause of this? It appears to be not any inherent tendency within spirit towards self-confrontation or self-contrariety (of the strong kind), but rather the danger that, when a rational desire conflicts with an appetite, spirit may side with *both* of them. Thus, in the instance touched upon in the *Phaedrus*, it may supply both a vanity that seconds sexual appetite, and a sense of shame that seconds rational restraint. Confrontation within spirit may always be parasitic upon confrontation elsewhere. The same may be true of strong contrariety: it may only be if both vanity and shame, say, are strengthened and stiffened from outside that each can retain enough affect to be strongly contrary to the other. What threatens to divide spirit against itself is not any intrinsic fissiparity, and hence it would be a mistake to try to divide its contents between different parts. Despite its liability to come apart within an already divided soul, it can still strictly count as a single part.

Thus supplementing strong contrariety by confrontation as criteria of partition is useful, if not indispensable, for excluding indefinite further division within appetite (since appetite cannot confront appetite), but is superfluous in relation to reason (since there reflection should resolve contrariety). It also does nothing in relation to spirit: spirit is confrontational and not reflective, and is saved from sub-partition only by the fact that it contains no *inherent* tendency either towards internal confrontation or towards strong self-contrariety. The fact that the supplementation does not achieve more may explain why, within Plato's presentation, confrontation remains second string to contrariety. Even with these two criteria to help him, he still faces problems.

In *Republic* Book 10 Plato recalls the Principle of Non-Contrariety, and applies it to opposite opinions that indicate a divided mind (602e8–603a2, d1–2). A decent man who loses his son will feel pain, but be moderate in his grief (e3–8). Yet even he will feel pulled two ways:

> Now is it not reason and law that exhorts him to resist, while that which urges him to give way to his grief is the bare feeling itself? . . . And where there are two opposite impulses in a man at the same time about the same thing we say that there must needs be two things in him.
>
> (604a10–b4)

So we must distinguish the best in us, which conforms to deliberation, from an irrational and idle element which drags us insatiably into lamentation (d5–10). For his purpose here, which is to identify 'that element of the mind to which mimetic poetry appeals' (603b10–c1), Plato need not advance beyond a bipartition (though 'the fretful and complicated character' of this element, 605a5, may deny it the unity of a part proper), but how well does his new example fit his fuller theory? Not easily. Appetite was set on sensual pleasure, and spirit on social aggression; grief is alien to both. It is true that a connection can be made: the wider part where grief is at home is called 'a friend of cowardice' (604d10), and a spirit relaxed by luxury and effeminacy becomes cowardly (9.590b3–4). Yet even if a despirited soul would be more prone to grief, grief is not merely a lack of exhilaration, and cannot have its roots in spirit as anger does. And the difficulty can be generalized. While spirit and appetite were originally separated by a case of conflict (that of Leontius), their tendency to conflict with one another, and with reason, was grounded on positive characterizations of their temperament and physiology. Emotions are accompanied, even perhaps constituted, by patterns of belief and desire, and so are liable to be party to contrariety and confrontation; but many of them are foreign to those few families of beliefs and desires that constitute Plato's tripartition. (Plato betrays this when he writes, at 10.606d1–2, of 'the sexual feelings and anger and all the appetitive and painful and pleasant feelings in the soul' – a listing that plainly does not fall into two groups.) Too much of the *Republic* – in fact, all of it outside the treatments of music and poetry in Books 3 and 10 – focuses on too few of the phenomena.[19]

What might explain the restrictions of Plato's focus? Four lines of thought make them less surprising. Firstly, we have seen that spirit is liable to self-confrontation, but can still count as a single part since the liability is not inherent, but parasitic upon conflict elsewhere. However, incorporation within spirit of a wide range of emotions would have raised the danger of an inherent tendency towards conflict (evidenced, say, when I am angry with myself for losing face by bursting into tears), and forced a reconsideration foreign to the primary purposes of the *Republic* (which are rather political and metaphysical than psychological). It is possible that Plato was aware of this: he alludes to other parts that may exist 'between' the three (4.443d7), and emphasizes that another and longer approach would be needed to give an accurate articulation of the soul (435c9–d8, 6.504b1–c4). Secondly, there is the analogy with the state: while Socrates claims to be equally sensitive to the demands of a political utopia and the data of empirical psychology (4.434d6–435a3), it is an inevitable suspicion that spirit is being assigned the qualities specially relevant to the tasks of the auxiliaries. These are military above all, so that courage becomes its salient virtue (cf. 429b1–3); yet other emotions demand other virtues (as Aristotle was fully to explore). Thirdly, Plato was all too receptive of an old moralistic commonplace contrasting just three ways of life, set on either wisdom, or honour, or wealth (*Apol* 29d7–e3, *Pdo* 68b8–c3, 82c2–8, *Rep* 1.347b1–6, 9.581c3–4).[20] A similar schematism is imposed on the loves of the *Symposium*: Diotima makes no division within the soul, but she allows lovers to rescue their lives from mortality in just three ways, through the procreation of physical descendants (208e1–5), the preservation of glory in myth or poetry (c2–e1, 209d1–d4), or the propagation of wisdom and virtue in others (209e5–210c7, d4–e4).

Thus a familiar categorization of life-options distracts Plato from properly acknowledging the richness of our psychological repertory. Finally, and more speculatively, his conception of spirit captures in its specificity that perennial aspect of psychic reality identified by Freud as the superego (cf. Price 1990: 262–4). Plato's neglect of most of the emotions was over-determined.

This neglect remains a fault, for emotions, as patterns of belief and desire, lend themselves as well as anything to the relations of contrariety and confrontation that divide Plato's psychic parts. This reason would not need to be given if Charles Kahn were correct in contrasting Plato's division from anything in Aristotle as follows:

> The tripartition of the *Republic* is not the division of a faculty of desire but a division of the psyche itself . . . . When Aristotle divides desires into three parts, he distinguishes all three from reason, sense-perception, and the like. When Plato divides the psyche into three parts, he divides it without remainder.
>
> (1987/8: 80)

If Kahn is right, emotions must be assigned to parts just because *all* mental phenomena must be. What makes his assumption plausible is simply the absence of any explicit warning to the contrary: Plato repeatedly writes of parts of the soul (*merê*), or kinds of soul (*genê*), with no acknowledgement that many elements of the soul may be left over. And yet, on reflection, there is implicit indication enough (cf. Cornford 1912: 262). The *Republic*'s criteria do not directly apply to sense-perception: it is a judgement that things are as they appear that cannot be assigned to the same subject as a judgement that they are not (10.603a1–2, cf. d1–2). Plato's assessment of the senses varies with the judgements he associates with them. In the *Phaedo*, he concedes that sight and hearing are the best of the senses, and yet denies that they provide any 'truth' (65b1–6); he lumps them together with the other senses as a physical medium through which the soul may be distracted and deceived (65c5–9, 79c2–8, 83a4–5), 'taking for real whatever the body declares to be so' (83d6). It is the body's assumption that appearance is reality, its metaphysics of a Mephistopheles, that makes the data of the senses so dangerous; sensibilia in themselves, abstracted from the intense pleasures and pains that fuel the metaphysics (c5–8), would be insignificant. In the *Phaedrus*, sight is granted a vision of Beauty itself (250d3–e1) in the form of a beautiful face or body (251a2–3), a paradoxical experience that eludes the lover's understanding (and may defeat ours), generating an intense fear (a3–4) and a confused idolatry: he would sacrifice to the boy 'as to a statue and a god' (a6–7, cf. 252d6–7), though the boy is neither and nothing could be both. This bifarious seeing (in which eye becomes mind's eye) is ascribed to the charioteer of the soul, namely reason (253e5, 254b5). Baffling in itself, it is rational in cause and effect: only one who recently 'beheld' much of the Forms (a seeing that was purely intellectual, 251a1–2) can catch sight of Beauty now, and his dazzling vision is the precursor of a clarifying recollection that detaches Form from face (254b4–8). We cannot infer that sight in general, let alone the other senses, belongs to any one part of the soul. In the *Timaeus*, the organs of sight and hearing are singled out as special servants to reason, all being located in the head (45a6–b1, cf. *Laws* 12.961d8–10). Yet each perception affects the soul as a whole: thus sound causes a motion that starts in the head and ends in the liver (*Tim* 67b2–5). We must conclude, I think, that Plato's tripartition is not of all the soul's operations, but only of those that lend themselves to the application of his criteria.

Unfortunately, there are further problems in using the criteria to yield a tripartition even of the mental states of belief and desire (or of half-believing and wanting) that do invite their application. I have spoken of families of desires and beliefs that have a tendency to stand in relations of strong contrariety and confrontation with members of any other family. How, firstly, does this apply to beliefs? It is striking that Plato only applies his own explicit Principle of Non-Contrariety to beliefs in the context of a bipartition: beliefs that come of calculation and measurement tend to contradict others that come of domination by appearance (*Rep* 10.602d6–603a2). (I added in §5 that reason takes a dim view of these beliefs, which is a form of confrontation.) There is an unemphatic contrast between 'the best part of the soul', which is single, and 'the inferior elements in us', which are plural (a4–8), but Plato makes no attempt to make out either that spirit and appetite are the dupes of appearance, or that all delusion is either spirited or appetitive. The only irrational beliefs that seem as accommodable as desires are evaluations that are their propositional correlates: clear examples consist of, or derive from, commendations of victory and honour (for spirit) or of sensual pleasure (for appetite). Also accommodable are ungrounded judgements, of circumstances rather than of ends or means, that collaborate with desires and are motivated by them; these may be factual ('He says things behind my back') or evaluative ('She is beautiful'). In relation to irrational beliefs that are not parasitic upon desire (such as those in Book 10 that come of visual illusion), Plato appears not to take his own tripartition seriously. What, next, of desires themselves? They are to be assigned to parts in ways that correlate with, and are explained by, their sources within our psychology. But what if what looks like a single desire has several sources? Alcibiades may have wanted to win his Olympic chariot victory both out of a sense of what he owed his city, and out of one-upmanship, and in hopes of free food in the Prytaneum ever afterwards. We might say that, if so, he had *three* desires to win, identical in their object but distinct in their natures. However, Plato needs to concede that modifications may be dictated to desires belonging to one part of the soul by motivations within another. He provides implicit examples in which different kinds of motivation enter into collaboration. In the *Sophist*, the sophist is located by the method of division as 'the money-making species of the eristic, disputatious, controversial, pugnacious, combative, acquisitive family' (226a1–4), so that he turns out 'a many-sided animal, and not to be caught with one hand, as they say' (a6–7). In partite terms, he has found a way of exploiting spirit for the sake of appetite, but one that demands compromises: his pugnacity must be bated, for he can also be described as 'that sort of hireling whose conversation is pleasing and who baits his hook only with pleasure and exacts nothing but his maintenance in return' (222e5–7). A different mode of combining spirit and appetite is described in the *Republic* itself: the oligarchic man, who is misled by appetite into taking pride only in riches (8.553d4–7), will henceforth be motivated by spirit as well as appetite in his money-making, so that his avarice will surely be enlivened by flamboyance (*pace* 555a1–2). (He may well find himself torn between economy and conspicuous consumption.) We can further suppose that, although he only allows his reason to calculate how to make money (553d3–4), he may find some satisfaction in getting things right, or grasping the truth, for its own sake. Plato needs to allow that many desires are multiply motivated, and represent compromise formations between elements belonging to different parts of the soul.[21]

What I have just discussed is perhaps rather a complication for his tripartition than an objection to it. More serious, as we saw before, is that it seems able to accommodate neither irrational beliefs that do not come of spirit or appetite, nor desires and beliefs that belong with emotions that are not spirited. In its insights and pretensions the theory is splendid, but it splendidly overreaches itself.

8

The *Phaedo* mapped the divided mind over soul and body, while the *Republic* maps out the soul. As the body that is party to mental conflict is the body with a soul, the contrast may be notional. Tripartition is a novelty, but perhaps not a radical innovation. More radical would be any discarding of the *Phaedo*'s doctrine that the soul is in origin simple and purely rational, and takes on complexity and conflict only as it assumes a body. When Plato advances in *Republic* Book 10 away from describing the soul as we find it within the body to identifying its 'ancient' and 'true' nature (a deeply Platonic equivalence, 611d2, 612a3–4), he rather multiplies options than excludes any; he hardly even seems concerned to indicate unambiguously just what the options are.

Much of what he proposes permits, and even suggests, the *Phaedo* picture of an originally simple soul ('single in form', *monoeidês*, 612a4, cf. *Pdo* 80b2) taking on mental accretions like the sea-god Glaucus encrusted with shells and seaweed (611c7–d7), so that the immortal is contaminated by the mortal, the purely mental by the partly physical. However, he also moots an alternative picture of an immortal soul always manifold ('many in form', 612a4), but consisting of elements put together in the finest manner (cf. 611b6). This alternative in turn might be explicated in two ways. The soul that is *not* put together in the finest manner and will 'not easily' be immortal (most likely an understatement, b5–7) may be the corrupt soul of Books 8 and 9, marred by 'other evils' on top of 'communion with the body' (611b10–c2); the description in Book 4 (443d3–e2) of the unity which can be achieved through temperance within the tripartite soul may have implied that there is no inherent deficiency in the interrelations of its parts (which need not imply that these are all ideal). Or else, the imperfectly related soul may be the tripartite soul of Book 4, 'marred by communion with the body' (10.611b10–c2) and so at least always liable to corruption, in contrast to a finer but also composite soul that exists before incarnation and outside the cycle of rebirth; even if it happens to be triple in composition, this soul will not be tripartite in the sense of 'part' that implies at least a tendency to conflict. An inherent complexity of a kind is confirmed by the signal fact that the proof of the immortality of the soul in Book 10 (608d3–611a3) rests on its indestructibility by its proper vices, injustice, self-indulgence, cowardice, and ignorance; for their nature was defined in Book 4 in terms of the tripartite soul

(444a10–b8). Yet Socrates may be indicating that the soul free of the body enjoys complexity without partition when he remarks that, viewed in its purity, it will permit a far clearer sight of the varieties of justice and injustice (611c4–5).[22] It tells with some force on the other side, that of identifying the true soul with a simple rational substance as in the *Phaedo*, that it is called 'akin to the divine and the immortal and to eternal being' (e2–3, cf. *Pdo* 80b1–3). However, so long as it is harmonious and fully follows reason (cf. 9.586e4–5), it may be counted indirectly as 'all following' reality (10.611e4) even if it extends beyond reason; and, if it is triple but not tripartite, it may resemble the soul of the world in the *Timaeus* which, though compounded of the Same, the Different, and Existence, is described as 'invisible and endowed with reason and harmony, being the best creation of the best of intelligible and eternal things' (36e6–37a2). Plato concludes here by leaving the options open (612a3–5). We shall find two of them developed later: in the *Timaeus* the human soul is described as originally complex but not partite, while in the *Phaedrus* it is presented (we have to consider how seriously) as originally tripartite.

Early in his second speech in the *Phaedrus*, Socrates offers a proof of the immortality of 'all soul' (245c5), by which he evidently means soul both human and divine (cf. c3). He proceeds to symbolize the form of the soul as follows:

> Let it then resemble the combined power of a winged team of horses and charioteer. Now in the case of gods, horses and charioteers are all both good and of good stock; whereas in the case of the rest there is a mixture. In the first place our driver has charge of a pair; secondly one of them is noble and good, while the other is opposite and of opposite stock.
>
> (246a6–b3)

Perhaps consideration of these divine souls might clarify how a soul can be complex and yet perfect. The charioteer is the emblem of reason, both in its grasp of reality outside the soul ('the plain of truth' offers 'the pasturage which is fitting for the best part of the soul', 248b6–7), and in its imposition of order within the soul (as will be spelt out in relation to incarnate souls). If gods are wholly rational, why are they assigned horses at all? One explanation is solely at the level of imagery: even winged chariots need horses. But that cannot be all, for Plato makes the most of the necessity: Socrates adds that they have their own nourishment, not the pasturage of the plain of truth, but ambrosia and nectar in their own manger (247e4–6). Emil Groag inferred that even divine souls have a sensuous side demanding sensuous satisfaction; he ascribed to them a unity of will, not of soul (1915: 208). This takes the text seriously, and is not inexplicable: Plato could be presenting here a strange view of gods in order to convey an ideal, that of the perfect responsiveness of appetite to reason, that would be human if it were not humanly impracticable – only a divine appetite, if there were such a thing, could be wholly at one with reason. However, Groag overlooks a further detail: it is the charioteer, after his own feasting, who supplies the ambrosia and nectar. Though only intellect (*dianoia*) can ingest insight and knowledge, these then nourish the mind of every soul 'that is concerned to receive what is appropriate to it' (d1–3); the horses cannot be fed independently of the charioteer. Only suggestions are possible, but it seems better to propose that the chariot with its horses nourished by the charioteer symbolizes that the gods' life is practical as well as theoretical, but with practice wholly informed by theory and owing to it its divine nature (just as the Homeric gods owe their immortality to ambrosia and nectar). 'All soul has the care of all that is soulless, and ranges about the whole universe' (246b6–7): divine life is unified but not uniform, and complex without conflict. How many aspects are there to a divine soul? Unlike the question about the number of soul-parts (given a good criterion of partition) this one has no answer, as Socrates may be acknowledging when he leaves open how many horses there are to a divine team.

However, *if* this is right (and no more speculative than it has to be), it obscures the issue raised in *Republic* Book 10 as to whether the true nature of the soul is multiform or single in form (612a3–4). It is no news to the *Phaedo* that the soul has at least a dual role, grasping truth (65b9) but also exercising rule (94b4–5). If we now distinguish practical from theoretical intellect (while still insisting, with Plato as against Aristotle, that practical thinking is nothing but an application of theoretical), we recognize the complexities of reason without extending the soul outside reason. If rational activity has two forms, is reason itself multiform? We might answer yes, bearing in mind Plato's discrimination between powers or capacities (*dynameis*) in *Republic* Book 5 on the basis of differences between objects and operations (477c9–d5); or we might answer no, on the ground that its operations are not independent of each other. Divine souls exemplify a complexity of rational functioning that may yet be accommodable within the simplicity ascribed to the soul (at least before incarnation and contamination) in the *Phaedo*. Where the soul is wholly rational, and its rationality has different operations but a single source, any new talk of multiformity, if that means that reason has many roles, expresses rather a shift in emphasis than a change of mind from the old talk of singleness in form, if that meant that those roles are all rational. Only in the *Timaeus* (as we shall see in §9) will the obscurity be dispelled.

We might expect to find light cast on the possibility of psychic complexes without parts once the Socrates of the *Phaedrus* turns to souls in heaven that are not gods. Instead, he ascribes to them a complexity that is also a partition. It is true that the term 'part' does not appear, but it never did much work, and there is evidence enough of conflict even here: one of the horses is opposite (or opposed, *enantios*) to the other (246b3), and, unless it has been well trained, the bad horse will weigh the driver down (no doubt against his will, 247b3–5). The nature of the horses before incarnation is somewhat mysterious, as the sketchiness of Socrates' description, and the bareness of his labels ('good' and 'bad' horse), may concede; it is particularly difficult to envisage an unembodied appetite. Talk of weight may remind us of how, in the *Phaedo*, a bodily element can remain attached to the soul to weigh it down even after death (81c8–10), and this may suggest that the divided soul of the *Phaedrus* is always liable to incarnation for the reason that it already carries with it the residuum of a previous body (cf. *Pdo* 81c9–d2). Yet the *Phaedrus* twice describes a first incarnation (248d1–2, 249a5), which can hardly, with no indication, mean the next one; and it says that the soul 'lays hold of something solid' and takes on 'an earthly body' *after* it has shed its feathers (246c2–4). It remains true that the identity of the horses seems parasitic upon the possibility of incarnation: the bad horse can only, before it fully possesses appetites, have the desire to become appetite (and so too for the good horse in relation to spirit). By carrying back the soul's tripartition into its prehistory, Plato can hope to use the tasks and trials of the soul in heaven to highlight those of the lover on earth: a fall from heaven is the converse, almost as if a film were being run backwards, of the ascent from earth. If this is all there is to it (which we cannot tell), we may interpret the prehistory as myth. Plato is cultivating ambiguity: that the human soul was originally tripartite may or may not have been mooted as possible in *Republic* Book 10, and may or may not be meant as actual in the *Phaedrus*; I incline to think that it is never a serious option.

Only Forms are what they are in themselves, and paying attention to them is the external, though dependable, cause even of the gods' divinity (*Phdr* 249c6). Other souls are always liable to incarnation, though some may escape it always (248c4–5). The cause of incarnation is cognitive failure: if, during the celestial progress, the driver's head (that is, his contemplative reason) fails to rise high enough and catches *no* glimpse of the Forms, the soul will shed its plumage and fall to earth (a1–c8); only a soul that has at some time seen the truth will become a man (249b5–6, 249e4–250a1), and the soul that has seen *most* will become a lover and philosopher (248a1–d3). (Consistency is, at best, barely achieved; but it may matter less in a myth.) The cause of cognitive failure is the driver's incompetence (b2) at managing a team that can only be guided with difficulty (247b3), a practical deficiency that prevents theoretical success – though no clue is given to the cause of the deficiency. Significantly, it is *both* horses that impede his progress (248a4–6); to vary the simile, we may imagine the good horse as a faithful hound that never resists its master, but often tries its patience. It is the driver who is described as the victim of confusion and force, but it must be the good horse who is opposed by the driver, not the driver by the good horse. Their confrontation, at least, is one-way.

It is only after incarnation that the good and bad horse become fully characteristic, and easily identifiable with spirit and appetite as described in the *Republic*; yet there is some modification of view, or (I rather think) simplification of presentation. The good horse has a thirst for honour and renown (temperance and a sense of shame permitting), and is governed by the word of command alone (253d6–e1). So, in the *Republic*, love of honour manifests domination by spirit (8.548c6–7); a claim there that spirit never takes sides with appetite against reason (4.440b4–6) was soon qualified (441a2–c2), but holds good here. The bad horse is prone to outrage or excess (*hybris*), and hardly even yields to whip and goad (*Phdr* 253e3–5). Simple dramatic contrast is eclipsing fact and theory: Plato really understood well that, within erotic relations, respect for the other may be undermined not just by appetite's sexuality, but by spirit's one-upmanship (cf. 232a1–6) or resentment (cf. 252c4–7). The bad horse is further blackened by the ascription of vices proper to spirit. It is called a 'companion of imposture' or 'false pretensions' (*alazoneia*, 253e3), which would seem to go best with spirit's concern to keep face; a complaint that temperance is unmanly, here made by the bad horse (254c8), occurs in the *Republic* (at 8.560d3) within 'impostorous speeches' (*alazones logoi*), dismissing reason's values and advertising shamelessness as manly, that (I argued earlier) are best ascribed to spirit (560c2–561a1). Further, while the *Republic* located irrational anger within spirit (4.441c2), Socrates here in the *Phaedrus* ascribes anti-rational anger that confronts reason to the bad horse (254c7). We must suppose that, tailoring his content as well as his style to the purpose of persuading the barely philosophical Phaedrus (cf. 271b1–5), he is sacrificing some finer points of his psychology.

The narrative of the breaking in of the bad horse (253e5–255a1) achieves some subtlety within those limits. It is the charioteer who 'catches sight of the light of his beloved', which fills him 'with tickling and pricks of longing' (253e5–254a1). Here a cognitive experience is itself intensely *felt*; indeed, the feeling is integral to the cognition, guaranteeing that (as the charioteer has yet explicitly to comprehend) to look at the boy's face is to recollect the Form of Beauty (cf. 250c8–251a7). Rather as the divine charioteer wins food for his horses through his vision of the Forms (247d1–e6), the effect of the idealizing perception of the boy is to warm the whole soul (253e5–6). The good horse is then pulled between two forces: that of shame within, which holds it back, and that of sexual arousal without, which forces it and the charioteer to approach the boy and – in a compromise formation that harnesses reason's persuasiveness to appetite's ends – plead the pleasures of making love (254a1–7). At first they recoil as from 'shocking and forbidden things' (just as they did from the perverted temptations of Leontius, *Rep* 4.439e7–440b4), but in time they agree to comply, knowing no better respite from importunity (254a7–b3). There follows the crucial reversal, often to be repeated, whereby appetite defeats its own purposes. Compelled to come really close to the boy, driver and horses see his face 'flashing like lightning'; the effect on the driver is to carry his mind back to the Forms, so that an implicit perception of Beauty itself inspires an explicit memory not only of Beauty but of companion Forms, most urgently that of Temperance (b3–7). The upshot is dramatic, and partly unexpected: the driver falls on his back, compelled by a necessity of his own to force *both* horses down on to their haunches (b7–c2). The good horse was obedient before (a1), and offers no resistance now (c2); why should it be treated so? It shared reason's notion of the shocking and forbidden, but that, going with a deference to 'the accepted standards of propriety and good taste' (252a4–5), was overridable once the driver and the good horse lapsed into listening to the solicitations of appetite. Reason's new apprehension of Temperance itself replaces a negotiable distaste for conventional impropriety by an unanswerable dictate of authentic moral experience. The driver is issuing commands that the good horse can obey in a language that it cannot understand. It feels now not just a sense of shame (*aidôs*, 254a2) but ashamed (*aischynê*, c4), since it is recoiling not just from a possible but from an actual willingness on its part to succumb. It cannot share the driver's transformation of consciousness, though we may suppose that, as it is broken in, it acquires convictions in place of conventions. The horses withdraw again, but the bad horse's rout renews the battle: at a distance from the boy, it recovers its spirits while the driver's memory of the Forms becomes the memory of a memory (being an intuition unsecured by any philosophical tether, cf. *Meno* 98a7–8). So appetite forces the lover to return close to the boy, and the reversal has to recur: the driver has the same experience, only more intensely, and punishes the bad horse – and presumably, though we hear no more, the good one too – still more cruelly (254e1–5). After many more recurrences, the bad horse 'nearly dies with fright' at the sight of the boy (no doubt by Pavlovian association between that and rough treatment), and the lover's soul is safely given over to a sense of shame (presumably in the good horse) and feelings of fear (especially in the bad, 254e5–255a1).

The lover's last temptation has a new twist: by a reflux of erotic desire, the boy falls in love with the lover, and is now tempted in his turn to see, touch, kiss, and lie down beside him – which, indeed, he does (255b7–e4).[23] Their bad horses become unholy allies: the lover's, who knows well what it wants, demands a little pleasure after so much pain (as if it were capable of the language of desert); the boy's, sexually aroused in a context that escapes his comprehension and control, is keen to comply (255e4–256a5). The lover's good horse resists with shame and his driver with reasoning, for they are now protected by moral convictions and ideal intuitions, respectively. If their better thoughts prevail, the lovers will enjoy a blessed life of philosophy and mental harmony, of internal order and mastery, enslaving the origin of psychic vice and liberating that of psychic virtue (a5–b3). Talk of harmony is consistent with that of slavery: though slavery may be resented, the *Republic* envisaged producers who are willing 'slaves' (cf. 9.590c9, d2). Yet the language of temperance, of persuasion and consensus (cf. 4.442d3, 8.554d2), is not used of the bad horse: we are not told here that it is brought home to appetite that even its own goals would be frustrated by sexual indulgence. We need not suppose that Plato has changed his mind: no doubt he would still claim that such indulgence brings no real satisfaction. Yet it is left partly elusive just how the horses' training is to be understood: outside metaphor, what are the driver's sanctions, and the horses' fears? Spirit carries its penalty, shame, in its own repertory, but where is the Achilles' heel of appetite?

Less happy as yet, but still with hopes of ultimate felicity, is the state of more vulgar lovers who, spirited and unphilosophic, pursue honour rather than wisdom (256b7–c1). Governed not by moral understanding but by 'the accepted standards of propriety and good taste' (252a4–5), they are neither complacently indulgent nor reliably abstinent. Through a failure of attention that lets them be taken off their guard, they may find themselves actually making love; and this may continue, though only now and then, since their minds are divided (256c1–7). If their friendship is cemented through a lifetime, they will have begun to regrow their feathers, and will lead a glittering life together in the heavens until eventually, because of their love, they acquire matching plumage (c7–e2). We should be puzzled quite how to take this. It allows a series of erotic gradations that correspond to the parts of the soul: philosophic lovers are enthusiastically chaste (a7–b7), and spirited lovers occasionally and unenthusiastically unchaste (c5–7), while sensual non-lovers display a sinful good sense whose wages is death (256e4–257a2). Yet the lenience towards the second-best lovers surprises: Socrates is presenting what may seem humanity to us but must have seemed sentimentality to Plato, whose usual view is that philosophy demands companionship (cf. *7th Letter* 341c6–d1), but not that lesser activities take on value through being pursued in company. Here more than anywhere, perhaps, we have to remember the ageing but callow Phaedrus, stretched out on the grass by Socrates' side: Socrates is offering a second-rate idyll to a second-rate mind.

However, even if we play down Socrates' permissive attitude towards an unideal friendship, we have yet to consider a possible claim that, still more remarkably, he is paying a new respect to the lower parts of the soul by revaluing passion and sexuality in his linkage of philosophical salvation, passionate pederasty, and sexual desire (*pro*: Nussbaum 1986: ch. 7; *contra*: Rowe 1990). I doubt this claim, and have anticipated or answered aspects of it already. If we are to escape the heritage both of Hume (who opposed 'reason' and 'passion') and of Freud (who connected passion and sexuality), we need to separate a reappraisal of passion from a reappraisal of the lower parts. The lover and philosopher is the person who saw most before incarnation (248d2–4), of which he retains a memory sensitive to visible likenesses (250a5ff.). The madness that these can inspire in him affects his reason, and the rest of his soul *only through this* (cf. 253e5–6). To the extent that it is an emotive mode of apprehending the Forms, it attacks his highest part, which is here never called 'the reasoning' part (*to logistikon*), but, colourlessly, 'mind' (*nous*, 247c8) or 'thought' (*dianoia*, d1). Plato is implicitly distinguishing two senses of 'reason': (a) that which desires and grasps truth (cf. *Rep* 9.581b5–6); (b) a way of grasping truth, namely, rationally (cf. the term *logistikos*, first at 4.439d5). New in the *Phaedrus* is an acknowledgement that reason can capture reality irrationally; reason and passion have kissed each other. The revaluation of erotic 'madness' is striking and substantial (contrast *Rep* 3.402e3–403b2), but not to be confused with the formal question where this madness should primarily be located. It is true that some of the imagery may be troublesome. (It is no help at all that the same Greek word, *pteron*, may mean 'wing' or 'feathers': all that we can be certain of is that it is wings that are broken, 248b3, and feathers that are shed, c8, and regrown, 251b6; but translation has to disambiguate, and may do so wrongly.) When the driver sees the boy and warms the soul (253e5–6), the effect is to set the feathers regrowing 'under the whole form of the soul, for formerly the whole of it was feathered' (251b6–7). How are feathers and wings related? Plato is unspecific, but some might picture the soul as bearing three pairs of wings, one for each part of the soul; if so, even appetite plays a saving role. (Possibly it belongs insecurely between heaven and earth, dragging us down from heaven, 247b3–5, and yet raising us up from earth.) I would not argue against this that appetite regains its feathers not through sexual awakening but through its subjugation by reason and spirit (cf. 254e5–255a1): regrowing one's feathers is experienced as liberating, while the taming of appetite is terrorizing. I would rather suppose that the soul has only a single pair of wings, attached to it as a whole (cf. 246a6–7, e5). Yet the whole soul was feathered, as birds are, and the regrowth of its feathers, necessary for its wings to function again, affects all its parts. This symbolizes that the saving madness of love seizes all the soul, but the lower parts respond in ways that threaten its salvation. The taming of appetite produces a better balanced soul, like a biplane no longer liable to plunges, responsive to its pilot and poised for ascent. Sexual arousal is a corollary of erotic inspiration that is not easily set at rest; Plato presents it as an aspect of the human condition, and not as a remedy for it.

9

The *Timaeus* elaborates two aspects of the *Phaedrus'* inheritance from the *Republic*, complexity within reason and tripartition within the soul. There is the contrast that tripartition now clearly arises out of incarnation. Socrates' second speech in the *Phaedrus* was partly myth, and its contrary view may only have been part of a dramatic re-enactment in heaven of reality on earth.

Timaeus describes the Creator as compounding in his mixing bowl a blend of Existence, the Same, and the Different. From this he forms the world-soul to serve a created corporeal world as 'a divine beginning of ceaseless and intelligent life for all time' (36e2–5), giving it the proportions that it needs in order to function as the subject both of knowledge and of true opinion: reasoning about the sensible world is imparted to the whole soul by the circle of the Different, and so gives rise to 'judgements and beliefs that are sure and true'; reasoning about the intelligible world is reported by the circle of the Same, and so gives rise to comprehension and knowledge (37b3–c3). That within which these things take place is soul (c3–5): Plato is envisaging a variety of cognitive states, rooted in a variety of constituents but only a single subject, and that wholly rational. He is thus faithful to the intellectualism of the *Phaedo*, while at last giving content to the *Republic*'s distinction between the 'multiform' and the 'single in form' (10.612a4) by supplementing the old recognition that even wholly rational souls function variously by grounding that variety on a complexity of composition.

Next are created, out of the same elements progressively diluted, two classes of souls with many members. Divine souls are embodied in stars, 'made for the most part of fire', either moving together as if set in a solid sphere, or pursuing their own orbits (40a2–b8). The Creator tells them that, together with all his direct creation, they are not indissoluble, and yet, by his will, shall never suffer dissolution (41a8–b6): not essentially immortal, and yet fit for immortality, they have been well put together in a good state, unlike the imperfectly compounded and perishing souls of *Republic* Book 10 (611b5–6). Human souls are first assigned each to a star, in which they are placed as if in a chariot, passengers rather than drivers in a temporary vehicle in which they can be shown the laws of destiny before they receive an incarnation, imposed and not merited, in an 'instrument of time', that is, a human body (41d8–42a1). Incarnation makes them innately prone to 'sensation arising from forced affections', 'love mixed with pleasure and pain' (in contrast to the loves of reason), and 'fear and anger and all the feelings that accompany these and all that are of a contrary nature' (42a3–b1). Mastery *of* these produces justice, mastery *by* them injustice (b2). The 'irrational turbulence' is an 'accretion' to the soul from the four elements (as was emblematized by Glaucus at *Republic* 10.611c7–d6). Mastering this by reason, so that it falls in behind the orbit of the Same, restores the soul to 'the form of its first and best condition' (42c4–d2). How reason can act so upon the corporeal is not yet explained. Those who live well will return to the 'habitation' of their consort star, while others will be reincarnated as women (b2–c1); thus each enters into co-operation with his own fate (cf. e3–4). It is no accident that the Creator embodies gods *as* stars but merely deposits human souls *in* them: otherwise the latter's leaving them would be excluded as the undoing of his creation. It is created gods who make human souls properly incarnate, and this is why human bodies are mortal (41b7–d3).

How does the deputed task of moulding mortal bodies go with that of composing a mortal soul (cf. 42d5–e1)? The 'circuits of the immortal soul' (43a4–5), which are solely rotating or orbital, are placed appropriately in the spherical part of the body, the head. This is then supplied with the rest of the body 'as a vehicle for ease of travel', possessing all the other forms of motion (up and down, left and right, backwards and forwards, 44d3–45a3). However, these remarks do nothing to differentiate inhabiting a body (which is incarnation) from inhabiting a star (which is not); indeed, the terms 'vehicle' and 'habitation' are used for both (41e2, 44e2, 69c7; 42b4, 45a1). A crucial difference must be that, while the star-chariot was directed by the Creator (44e1–2), a body-chariot, being alive, directs its own motions (e2–e5). If the soul is to animate and move the body, it has to be transformed, taking on a mortal part which serves as conduit between the rational and the material. The disorderly motions of young children arise from a confusion of activity and passivity, as the soul's natural circuits are distorted by incoming sensations (43a6–44a7). Regrettably, no mechanism of motion is set out; we shall later find that the omission evades a problem.

The mortal form of soul that comes with the body below the head is assigned a lurid repertory of mental states, 'dread and necessary affections: first pleasure, the strongest lure of evil; next, pains that take flight from good; confidence moreover and fear, a pair of unwise counsellors; anger hard to entreat, and hope too easily led astray'; with these are combined 'irrational sense and desire that shrinks from no venture' (69c8–d5). It is not made clear how all these fall within the old partition into spirit and appetite that follows. The role of spirit is familiar, and suited by its location:

> That within the soul which is of a manly spirit and ambitious of victory they housed nearer to the head, between the midriff and the neck, so that it might be within hearing of the discourse of reason and join with it in restraining by force the appetites, whenever these should not willingly consent to obey the word of command from the citadel.[24]
>
> (70a2–7)

Reason is now not just a metaphorical citadel of the soul (*Rep* 8.560b8), but the occupant of a citadel within the body that is the head. It is divided from the rest of the body by the neck 'as an isthmus and boundary' (*Tim* 69e1), but messages can get across. When spirit hears from reason that some act of wrong is being committed, either by another person or by the appetites themselves, it boils with anger, and the heart communicates its reaction throughout the whole body, which perceives the (rational) commands and (spirited) threats and falls into obedience (70a7–b8). Appetite too is described in familiar terms, and given a location that fits its function and diminishes its dangers:

> That within the soul whose desire is set on meat and drink and all that it has need of for the sake of the body's nature, they housed between the midriff and the boundary towards the navel, constructing in all this region as it were a manger for the body's nourishment . . . . Accordingly, they stationed it here with the intent that, always feeding at its stall and dwelling as far as possible from the seat of counsel, it might cause the least possible tumult and clamour and allow the highest part to take thought in peace for the common profit of all and each.
>
> (70d7–71a3)

Plato is at last providing an apologia for the body, ultimately on the ground of a principle of plenitude (41b7–c2), as the field of a special kind of interaction between mind and matter. Hence he stresses those appetites classified as 'necessary' in the *Republic* (8.558d11–e2), even as he recognizes that they too are liable to distract reason from reflections there also said to serve the whole soul (4.441e4–5, 442c5–8). Yet he remains faithful to the *Republic*'s complaint that appetite is characteristically insatiable (9.586b3–4) by supposing that those who framed us could predict our 'intemperance' over food and drink (presumably as inescapable, 72e3–5). By setting appetite at such a distance from reason (so as to distract it less, 70e6–7), and providing a lower belly to hold excess intake (so as to spare us fatal disease, 72e6–73a3), they did what they could to reduce the mental and physical effects. Strictly, the intemperance is of the soul and not of the body: the intricacy of our intestines denies us the physiological excuse for physical insatiability (a3–6) of the torrent-bird (cf. *Gorg* 494b6).

How does reason communicate with the other parts of the soul and win their co-operation? Spirit, it seems, is close enough to reason within the body to overhear its internal speech (70a2–5) even before receiving its announcements (as it does at b3–5). Naturally obedient, it is keen to listen and does not have to be addressed. The swelling of anger supervenes on the action of fire. For any physiological risk of excess here Plato furnishes a physiological remedy, the cooling of the heart through the lungs, which enables the heart to serve reason spiritedly (c1–d6). How a physical mean between heat and cold makes spirit responsive and even 'obedient' (a5) is not explained; somehow it must make spirit perfectly balanced, like a rock resting on a single point, so that a small impulse, starting from the head, is sufficient to direct it. Plato is more informative about the operations of reason and spirit upon appetite. Here he retains the metaphor of obedience (b8), but imagines two mechanisms, each of matter on behalf of mind. The first connects spirit and appetite: the heart is the fountain of blood that 'moves impetuously round throughout all the members', and thus communicates to 'every sentient part of the body' reason's decision and spirit's resolve (a7–c1). The second connects reason and appetite, and evidences a greater sensitivity at once to the general problem of how mind can interact with matter, and to the local one of how reason can communicate to appetite. Appetite could not understand argument and would not obey it, for it has 'no part in belief arising from reasoning and mind, but only in feelings of pleasure and pain together with desires' (77b5–6), and so is best guided by images and appearances (71a3–7). Reason's thoughts have the power to convey to the liver impressions that, received as if by a mirror, are reflected as images (b3–5). The liver possesses sweetness and bitterness, and both serve: when reason is harsh and threatening, it plays a role 'akin' to the liver's bitterness by colouring it biliously and wrinkling, shrinking, and painfully obstructing it; when reason is gentle, it exploits the liver's sweetness, straightening, smoothing, and freeing it (b5–d1). Here Plato enriches his account of appetite in the *Republic*, at last doing justice to its phenomenology by recognizing its dependence on the sensory imagination, its responsiveness less to thoughts than to images (cf. *Phil* 40a9–13). Yet he also revalues appetite by making it the subject of that 'true and inspired divination' which comes of 'divine possession' (71d3–e6). This is remarkable, and yet it rather confirms than contradicts the *Phaedrus*, which discussed divination before partition, but ranked the prophet four ranks below the lover and philosopher (248d2–7). I argued that it is the lover's reason that is inspired; it fits the lower valuing of the prophet if, as is now explicit in the *Timaeus*, the vehicle of his inspiration is the liver as the organ of appetite. Whereas the lover's ideal perceptions have only to be completed and corrected through a deliberate method of collection (*Phdr* 265d3–5), the dreamer's inspired images have to be translated into a different language, transposed from one part of the soul into another (*Tim* 71e6–72a6). Indeed, while the lover's experience is uncommunicable (which is why each of us must fall in love for himself), it is typically one man who enjoys the prophetic vision, and another who supplies the interpretation: diviners provide the raw material of expositors (72a6–b5).

Thus the body is designed to embody reason in ways that enable it to be active and mobile in the sensible world. The lower soul that it brings in its train is made generally subservient to reason through bodily mechanisms. Faults in the soul are not all to be laid at the body's door, for we are intemperate despite our intestines (72e3–73a6). Psychic ills that do arise from the body are caused rather by its disorders than by its deficiencies. Folly (*anoia*) is a disease of the soul, and of folly there are two kinds, madness (*mania*) and ignorance (*amathia*, 86b2–4). These seem to be two aspects of folly rather than two species: impatience and frenzy produce an inability to perceive or to reflect (b7–c3), for hyperactivity in one area causes inactivity elsewhere. An excess of pleasure, with associated pains, may come of a marrow full of overflowing seed; this is the cause of sexual intemperance (c3–d5). An excess of pain may come of vapours from phlegm or bile roaming through the body and confusing the motion of the soul; they generate within its three regions (*topoi*) peevishness and despondency (presumably within appetite), or rashness and timidity (within spirit), or forgetfulness and slowness in learning (within reason, 86e3–87a7). The best way into understanding this may be by way of the last pair. A mind slow to take things in contrasts with one quick to lose them just as a tablet too hard to receive imprints contrasts with one too soft to retain them (cf. *Theaet* 191c8–e1); the analogy brings out that being slow and being forgetful are extremes on a single continuum. Slowness in learning is a form of inactivity, forgetfulness of activity; they are here rooted in a physiological contrast between phlegm that is cold and slow and bile that is hot and quick (cf. 85e2–4, *Rep* 8.564b4–10; Tracy 1969: 129–33). The same contrast is drawn within spirit and appetite, in ways that slightly confuse the boundary between them. Peevishness (*dyskolia*) was associated in the *Republic* with spirit (3.411c2, 9.586c9, 590a9); indulging appetite may exacerbate it, but it comes with irascibility (*Laws* 7.791d5–7), which is certainly a defect of spirit (cf. *Rep* 3.411c1). Despondency (*dysthymia*) contrasts well with peevishness, being connected with dryness and coldness (cf. *Laws* 2.666b7–c2), but is also unexpected as a vice of appetite: its etymology evidently links it to a sluggishness not of appetite, but of spirit or anger (*thymos*, cf. *athymos*, *Rep* 3.411b7, 5.456a5). As in the case of anti-rational anger (*Phdr* 254c7), Plato is ascribing to appetite attitudes that are proper not to it but to a spirit that shares its sufferings. More felicitous is the extension of spirit to take in not only rashness but timidity, and thus to become not a single tendency but a field of opposites (within which, just as in Aristotle, courage would be a mean). This is not wholly new: early in the *Republic* Plato sensitively distinguished the effects of softening a man's spirited side, which may be faint-heartedness (if it was spiritless to begin with), or peevishness (if it was high-spirited and now becomes unstable, 3.411a5–c2). Yet he later wrote of spirit in relation to the other parts of the soul as if its attitudes were always high-spirited, and it was corruptible only by resisting reason or subserving appetite. He never, for example, envisaged a man who, irrespective of the calls either of truth or of pleasure, subordinates everything not to the rash courting of danger but to the cowardly evading of it. Now, in the *Timaeus*, spirit's repertory is extended to include attitudes contrasting with anger in the context of a physiological underpinning (the temperature of the heart) common to them all.

In several ways, this novelty within Plato's conception of spirit may help him out of old difficulties. One arose out of spirit's confrontational nature (as I noted in §7): if we enlarge its emotional repertory, we run the danger of finding within it an inherent tendency to conflict. Its new, or at least newly explicit, localization within the breast offers a way of limiting the damage. It can now be reconceived as a psychic domain grounded in one area of the body, whose physiology can only be understood (as at 70a7–b8) as enabling a united spirit to perform its proper functions. Though strictly not a single part if it contains obstacles to unity within itself, it will still be co-ordinate with reason and appetite, which are strictly parts, since these permit, though they do not demand, the same reconception. Further, the problem about the location of emotions that belong neither with the appetites, nor with self-assertive passions such as anger and emulation, is now eased by the well-motivated admission within spirit of emotions that belong within the same range as its more characteristic manifestations by being rooted in opposite states of the human metabolism: thus timidity may be admitted alongside rashness, cowardice alongside courage, modesty alongside boastfulness, and so on. So far, the problem is only eased, not solved: many other emotions are still unaccommodated, including grief (a prime topic of *Republic* Book 10). However, a richer account of the mental states supervenient upon the various conditions of the heart might take in these as well. Again, spirit will turn out to contain a miscellany of attitudes located together within an area of the body whose function, sabotaged by disunity, is to serve a single teleology.

Yet another objection may be disarmed as well. In §4, I saw it as a difficulty for Plato's official criterion of partition in the *Republic* that neither desires nor intentions, as we ordinarily understand them, really fit his application of the Principle of Non-Contrariety: consciously contrary desires are too little of a problem to demand different parts, while consciously contrary intentions are too much of a problem for them to accommodate. I suggested that what Plato had in mind was not simply having contrary desires, but consciously *wanting* contraries. That refinement is unnecessary if we suppose that desires are not merely analogous (as in *Republic* Book 4), but identical, to pushings and pullings of a kind. Then the logic of the facts, unlike that of the concept of desire, will be the same as that of rest and motion: desiring can be identified not just with attraction but with a kind of pulling, desiring-that-not not just with repulsion but with a kind of pushing, and not desiring with being at rest. While Plato's metaphysics of mind and body are murky, such identifications may be implicit in the localization of parts of the soul within different parts of the body, to the effect that the play of desires becomes a play of local and physical forces. There were intimations of localization in the *Republic*: if appetite is a 'companion' of repletions (4.439d8) which have a location (say in the belly), then perhaps appetite has a location also; reason metaphorically occupies the 'citadel of the soul' (*tês psychês akropolis*) in the *Republic* (8.560b7–8), rather as it literally occupies 'the top of the body' (*akron to sôma*) in the *Timaeus* (90a5); and, within what is admitted to be only an 'image' (*eikôn*), man, lion, and Cerberus must occupy different areas within the 'wrapping' that is the human frame (*Rep* 9.588c7–e1). But only now has localization become both literal and explicit. If we connect parts to locations, we need to reflect how they are to be counted: we must hesitate to find a different psychic part whenever there is a possibility of identifying desires with physical movements in different parts of the body – especially if the movements are co-operative rather than conflicting, so that we could instead identify the totality of them with some consistent set of desires. Still, there emerges hope of a theory, yet to be elaborated, that could justify talk of desires in terms of movements.

However, such speculations bring us close to a deep difficulty. Though the *Timaeus* is informative (in pages I have neglected) about the means of perception, it is silent about the mechanics of motion. How, within Plato's account, is the sum of desire to effect movement? As parts of the soul occupy different parts of the body, and any part of the soul may be overridden in action, no part of the body can be singled out as containing *the* place where motion starts. To tell an intelligible story, Plato would need to identify some central organ of desire which would register relevant considerations, resolve any divergences – ideally by rational thinking, otherwise through a play of forces (cf. 43a6–b2) – and then act upon other parts of the body. But then that organ would plausibly be the seat of desire, so that the parts of the soul would share a single focal location. Given Plato's silence, we cannot tell whether this objection is fatal; but neither can we tell whether his psycho-physical fictions capture even a possibility.

10

Republic Book 10 pointed us in contrary directions. Its mapping of the incarnate soul left open how we were to trace this to its origins, whether through thinking away its complexity, or only its contrariety: is the *Ur*-soul simple or complex, and, if it is complex, what is the manner of its complexity? Different possibilities, serious or playful, are explored in the *Phaedrus* and *Timaeus*. We do not need to infer any particular chronology in order to make sense of the turnings of Plato's mind, which we can understand as revolving within a circle already sketched out. The *Republic* is varied in another way: an initial bipartition between a rational and an irrational soul (4.439a9–e3), though immediately superseded by a tripartition (439e3–441c2), reappears unqualified in a different context (10.602c3–606d7). Plato's application of the same Principle of Non-Contrariety (cf. 436b8–c1, 602e8–10) justifies us in talking again of 'partition', though with a qualification: he writes as before of 'the reasoning' part (605b4–5), but never implies that what falls outside it has the unity of a single part. There is a still closer parallelism: in both contexts, reason or reasoning (*logos, logismos*) that quasi-verbally prescribes contrasts with feeling or affections (*pathos, pathêmata*) that quasi-mechanically pull (439c9–d2, 604a10–b1). Plato cannot simply have forgotten his earlier subdivision of the irrational soul; indeed, there is an allusion at least to its materials, notably sex and anger (606d1–2). But his new concern, not with justice and the state but with the impact of art, at last focuses his mind on those emotions, notably of grief, that elude tripartite classification; he now opposes to 'the naturally best' and 'reasoning' element (606a7, 605b4–5) merely 'the fretful' or 'senseless' one (604e1–2, 605b8). In the *Timaeus*, it suits his teleology and physiology to admit spirit as a separate part; in the *Laws*, he opts for fluidity, but with occasional reminiscences of tripartition, and no radically new way of conceiving of conflict.

One starting-point within the *Laws* has its parallel in the *Republic*: each man is his own enemy, and the best of victories is that over oneself (1.626d8–e3, cf. *Rep* 4.430e7–12). As before, the paradox is allayed by identifying the internal enemy with pleasures and desires (633c9–e6, cf. *Gorg* 491d7–e18), or with a multitude within the soul opposed to a better and more rational part (3.689a7–c1, cf. *Rep* 4.431a3–b2). To clarify how the good can rule themselves and the bad cannot (1.644b6–c1), and what it means to be 'stronger' or 'weaker than oneself' (645b1–3), Plato offers one of his best images:

> Let us suppose that each of us living creatures is an ingenious puppet of the gods . . . . These inward affections of ours, like sinews or cords, drag us along and, being opposed to each

other, pull one against the other to opposite actions; and herein
lies the dividing line between goodness and badness . . . . There
is one of these pulling forces which every man should always
follow and nohow leave hold of, counteracting thereby the pull
of the other sinews: it is the leading-string, golden and holy, of
reasoning, entitled the public law of the State; and whereas the
other cords are hard and steely and of every possible shape and
semblance, this one is soft since it is of gold. With that most
excellent leading-string we must needs co-operate always; for
since reasoning is excellent, but gentle rather than forceful, its
leading-string needs helpers to ensure that the golden kind
within us may vanquish the other kinds.

(644d7–645b1)

As readers of Plato we are already familiar with this conception of
conflicting desires as opposed forces, and its use to explain how it
can be that a man may fail to do what he reflectively thinks best.
Failure to act rationally is consistent with rational judgement just so
long as it is caused by motivating forces within the soul resistant to
reason. However, it may be that an intensification of pleasures, pains,
loves, and passions commonly goes with a dissipation of perceptions,
memories, beliefs, and judgements, as we are soon told that it does
during intoxication (645d6–e3, cf. 649d6–7 on the effect of pleasure
itself): we find in the passage no clear distinction between counteracting the pull of the golden cord by opposing reason, and sabotaging
it by silencing or corrupting reason. As I shall discuss in the next
section, it is typical of Plato not to give thought to distinguishing
different types of acrasia. Wholly faithful to the *Republic* is the
identification of our immortal part with intelligence, and of reason's
law with the law of an ideal state (4.713e8–714a2, cf. *Rep* 9.590c8–
d6). Strikingly absent, however, is any presumption that the forces
can be simply grouped within, say, a tripartition. Familiar, and
familiarly problematic, is talk of the agent as if he could operate from
outside his own desires, favouring some and restraining others. As
in the *Phaedo* and *Republic*, such talk must be played down; here its
sense is surely (as the plural 'helpers' confirms, 645a6) that rational
desires need to be supported by some non-rational desires if they are
to prevail against the rest. If we set the subject artificially apart from
the motive forces that inhabit his mind, he can only show up as
passive in relation to them: 'Pleasures, pains and desires are by nature
especially human; and from these, of necessity, every mortal creature

91

is, so to say, suspended and dependent by the strongest cords of influence' (5.732e4–7). But of course the artifice is distorting: according to Plato's conception, such internal motivations constitute the subject as an agent.

Can even knowledge fail of practical effect, or would the Athenian Stranger agree with Socrates and Protagoras that 'wisdom and knowledge is the mightiest of human things' (*Prot* 352d2–3)? When he later speaks of a man 'who does not love but hates what he believes to be noble and good, while he loves and cherishes what he believes to be evil and unjust' (3.689a5–7), he takes him to be subject to a state of 'ignorance' (or 'lack of learning', *amathia*), 'extreme' in that it involves a lack of harmony between feelings of pain and pleasure and rational judgement, 'greatest' in that it belongs to that within the soul which resembles the mass of the populace within the city (a1–b2). He remarks explicitly that the wise man is 'he who has his feelings of pleasure and pain in accord with the right dictates and following them' (696c8–10). This may appear both novel and confused: is harmony between judgement and desire simply being stipulated as a further condition for the possession of wisdom and avoidance of ignorance? If so, Plato is now putting a definitional full stop to the once interesting questions, answered and not silenced by Socrates in the *Protagoras*, whether wisdom implies the other virtues (notably temperance and justice), and whether it is possible to act against knowledge. In reality, as I see it, Plato is saying nothing new: as we already read in the *Republic*, the soul as a whole only possesses wisdom – or, equivalently, wisdom only possesses the soul as a whole – if reason exercises effective rule, so that the whole soul falls in behind it in judging and desiring (4.442c5–8, cf. 428d11–e9). Wisdom and friendship are really identical aims (*Laws* 3.693c3–4) in that a soul can only count as wise as a whole if its reason is happy, and it is happy with its reason. To 'live rationally' (689d7–8) is to live a life that displays a soul united in judgement and feeling behind the conclusions of reason, but a wise reason does not guarantee a wise soul.[25]

It is to be remarked, but not remarkable, that there are traces of tripartition. Most explicitly, Plato distinguishes three causes of wrongdoing: anger (or spirit, *thymos*), whether it be an affection (*pathos*) or a part (*meros*), is hard to fight against; pleasure operates by deceitful persuasion; there is also nescience (*agnoia*, by which he must have in mind a defect that in origin and in itself is purely intellectual, 9.863b1–c2). One may be stronger or weaker than pleasure or anger, but not than nescience (d6–11). Accordingly, there are three types (or causes) of wrongdoing: anger and fear, which are painful; pleasure and appetites; and 'expectations and false belief about the attainment of the highest good' (864b1–7). Generally, however, Plato does justice to the variety of passions without troubling himself about their grouping into factions.[26] In the very same passage he identifies injustice with 'the domination of anger and fear and pleasure and pain and envies and appetites in the soul' (863e6–864a1). All these are locatable within a tripartition (so long as they only form two factions), but he shows no concern so to place them. Thus voluntary murders may be caused by desire or appetite (*epithymia*), especially directed towards wealth, or by 'the state of the ambitious soul, breeding feelings of envy', or by 'fears bred of cowardice and injustice' (870a1–d4). Robbery and violence are to be punished more heavily when 'the man has done wrong owing to his own folly, because of his incontinence in respect of pleasures and pains and the overpowering influence of craven fears or of incurable desires, envies and rages' (11.934a3–6). It is tempting to read into such listings an awareness that the richness of the passions defies tripartition – though the point is better focused if it is aimed against the rigidity of the *Republic* (which defines spirit as a single tendency of mind) than against the fluidity of the *Timaeus* (which permits reconceiving it as a medley rooted in a single area of the body). In one respect, curiously, the discarding or neglect of tripartition produces a narrower view. I noted that the *Phaedrus* is strangely generous towards a love intermediate between those of the philosopher and the sensualist (256b7–e2). The *Laws* places it not in relation to spirit, but as an unhappy mixture of the other two loves (8.837b4–7); accordingly, it finds in it a more acute mental conflict (compare 837b7 with *Phdr* 256c6–7), and would even like to prohibit it (*Laws* 837d6–7). However, if I was right to explain away its more indulgent treatment as a sop to Phaedrus, there may be no actual change of mind.

What Plato ultimately thought of tripartition we cannot tell. Aware of its problems, we are tempted to suppose it still alive in the *Phaedrus* and *Timaeus*, but dead by the time of the *Laws*. However, three considerations give us pause: the *Laws* is a popular and non-technical work, of which we should expect a scientific psychology still less than of the *Republic*, and much less than of the *Timaeus* (cf. Saunders 1991: 177); it tells no more decisively against tripartition than did *Republic* Book 10, which Plato presumably took to be reconcilable in principle with Books 4, 8, and 9; and, as we shall see, tripartition remained the Platonist position, against which Aristotle and the Stoics reacted in their different ways. (History similarly tells against any inference from some late dialogues that Plato may have discarded the theory of Forms.) What we can more confidently learn from the *Laws* is how little really is lost when any definite partition is put aside: the mind remains a field of struggle between forces fundamentally alien to one another, and hence not easily accommodable within a single perspective constituted by rational reflection. If we now turn to consider acrasia more carefully, we may be struck by Plato's constancies.

11

Plato has a wide interest in the conflicted mind, its causes, condition, and cures, and a deep concern, at once philosophical and practical, to analyse what it is to succeed or fail in being master of oneself. Any failure will count for him as an instance of acrasia (literally, lack of power). We now apply the term more narrowly, and in this we are influenced by Aristotle, who was sharply to distinguish the self-indulgent (*akolastos*) from the acratic (*akratês*) man: 'The one is led on in accordance with his own choice, thinking that he ought always to pursue the present pleasure; while the other does not think so, and yet pursues it' (*NE* 7.3.1146b22–4). Plato uses *akratês* and related terms infrequently and less precisely. He applies them to anyone who fails to keep his appetites under control in that he is too given to pleasure (cf. *Laws* 1.636c7, 4.710a7, 10.886a9, 908c2). Just once, he applies *akratês* to the man who fails to control his anger (*akratês thymou*, 9.869a3). Temperance is the same as self-control (*enkrateia*) in respect of certain pleasures and desires (*Rep* 4.430e6–7, cf. 431b5–6). To be temperate is to be master of oneself (*kreittôn*, 431b7), while to be self-indulgent is to be a slave to oneself (*hêttôn*, 431b1–2), like the tyrant (who is '*akratôr* of himself', 9.579c9). An apparent contrast between self-indulgence and acrasia in the *Timaeus* is more likely elegant variation. Timaeus rejects talk of misconduct as being voluntary and due to *akrateia*, preferring to ascribe it to an involuntary *akolasia* whose cause is physical, the bad state of a body unskilfully nurtured (86d5–e3). Though Aristotle does make out that acratic action is still voluntary (e.g., *NE* 7.10.1152a15–16), he denies that it is paradigmatically so (9.8.1168b34–1169a1). He would count self-indulgent action as more clearly voluntary than acratic, and it is unlikely that, when Timaeus speaks as if the reverse were the case, he is making any real contrast between the two terms. Plato comes closer to making Aristotle's distinction when, in the *Laws*, he asserts that everyone is self-indulgent (*akolastos*) involuntarily, through ignorance (*amathia*) or acrasia (*akrateia*) or both (5.734b4–5). However, the most striking divergence here is not that he is using *akolastos* generically and *akrateia* specifically, but that he permits, and perhaps expects, acrasia and ignorance to be joint causes. If he ever paid attention to what we or Aristotle would count as acrasia, it was not through any interest in terminology.

In search of the nub of a problem, we need to make distinctions. I earlier (Chapter 1 §2) introduced a notion of 'hard acrasia', that is, of a conscious failure to live up to what I judge to be best in what I desire most, choose, and do. We need to distinguish this from 'soft acrasia': in cases of soft acrasia, the agent's perception is dimmed and his judgement deflected, so that he acts in a way that he would not have chosen in a cool hour, with judgement and perception un-impaired, and yet not with conscious contrariety to an occurrent choice; in cases of hard acrasia, his perception is clear, his judgement unequivocal – and yet, out of weakness, he acts otherwise. This second case is evidently problematic, and deserving of the attention of philosophers.[27] Platonic partition accommodates hard acrasia in this form: reason may decide what best serves soul and city, and yet its judgement may be inoperative because spirit or appetite is too strongly provoked or stimulated by some consideration that counts for everything in its book, but for less or nothing in reason's. This predicament looks much less of a problem, but is it acrasia? Plato invites the following objection. If my reason decides that I should act in a certain way, and I disregard it and act otherwise, this is indeed a failure on reason's part to be in control of me, but is it a failure on mine to be in control of myself? Disregarding reason may be dropping the pilot, but that is rather irresponsibility than weakness. Compare a committee that reaches a decision against the advice of its wisest and most experienced members: that is not the same as a committee that decides one way and acts in another. Plato appears to be overlooking the possibility of a failure to be irrational (of the kind, had von Aschenbach been an Englishman, that might well have prevented a death in Venice from occurring). Imagine this case: long schooled to act with tact and circumspection, I suddenly and irresponsibly decide, on reading a French existentialist novel, to perform the *acte gratuit* of trying out the echo in the reading-room of the British Museum; when it comes to it, my nerve fails me and my decision hangs fire. Plato could represent this as a failure of appetite (or whatever French philosophy appeals to), but how of the agent? The heart of this objection is not simply that certain cases of hard acrasia are inconceivable to him, but that the cases he does admit are admitted in such a way that they cease to look like acrasia. The problem of hard acrasia is not solved but suppressed.

This objection would be unanswerable if reason were just one faction among several in the soul, and its values just some among others. However, in Plato's thinking this is in a sense not so. Reason is what each of us fundamentally *is*. It was explicit in the *Phaedo* that each of us is his soul (e.g., 115c4–e4), and his soul is reason (e.g., 67c3). In the *Republic*, reason is likened to a man within each man (9.588d3–4, 10–11); if the best parts of the soul are in slavery, the soul itself is a slave (577d1–9). This conception rests on at least two grounds, one mythical in our eyes, the other empirical. Firstly, it goes deep in Plato's outlook – perhaps too deep to be a product of philosophy – to presume that our 'true' nature is our 'ancient' nature, before accretion (10.611d2, 612a3–4); hence, if reason is what we were before incarnation, it remains what we are fundamentally. Secondly, reason does not act as a special-interest group; rather (as I stated at the start of § 6), it has a double commitment, to acquiring the truth for itself, and to giving each part of the soul what it needs. While it supplies its own values, which we would otherwise lack, these respect the needs of the rest of the soul; its judgement is not partisan, but all-things-considered. It can indeed be corrupted, so as to assume and serve the values native to spirit or appetite (cf. 8.553d1–4, 560b7–561a1), but this is a corruption that comes of impressionability, not egocentricity. For these two reasons, what my reason decides is what *I* decide; hence its judgements are privileged, and a disregard of them is a kind of failure. Plato allows several diagnoses of my British Museum case. If my irresponsible impulse to test the echo only amounts to a momentary inclination (imagine that I say to myself, in the language less of Camus' Meursault than of Bertie Wooster, 'What a lark!'), that seems insufficient to identify what I really want with that impulse, and not with the more considered concerns that are so briefly eclipsed. However, it would be fairer to suppose that my reading impinges more deeply: like von Aschenbach reflecting before his journey on the constricting effect upon his imagination of his ancestral values, I am suddenly transported to a point of view from which my common preoccupations look unnecessary and inauthentic. A new self *confronts* the old: this cannot be appetite (which is non-confrontational), though it could be spirit. Then it briefly *supplants* the old: this can only mean a reason alienated from its customary reasonableness. If, at the moment of action, I relapse into my habitual character, not through feeling at home in it again but through a loss of nerve (perhaps prompted by spirit's concern to keep face or appetite's dislike of unpleasantness), this is indeed an acratic failure.

Thus Plato can hope to find room for an acrasia that is a possible form of failure. Both the possibility, and the failure, are evident in Plato's own initial case, that of a simultaneous desire and refusal to drink (*Rep* 4.439c2–7). If the ground of refusal is health, part of the goal is a flourishing thirst thereafter. Appetite is not being denied what it needs, but instructed in the ways of maximum satisfaction (9.586d4–587a1). If it disobeys, it defeats not only reason but itself: drinking wisely is not a sacrifice of appetite to reason, but an act of co-operation between them. However, this does not guarantee that appetite will comply. It is in its nature to take short views, and reason needs skill and patience if it is to succeed in making the future present to it. The accommodation of acrasia, in our sense and in its most problematic form, must look a success for Plato's theory to anyone who presumes that it is a possibility. Yet is this how he saw things? We might expect his writings to be rich in case-studies of hard acrasia. In fact, they contain few. We shall need to reflect why he expects reason to be more often suborned than subdued.

A clear candidate to count as a hard acratic ought to be Leontius, the victim of necrophilic impulses that he can neither accept nor resist; yet Socrates presents his situation with a degree of ambiguity. Catching sight of some corpses after execution, he simultaneously (as Socrates emphasizes) feels inclined, and averse, to looking at them. Though he fights his desire for a time, it masters him; rushing forward with staring eyes he cries, 'There, you wretches, take your fill of the fine spectacle' (4.439e7–440a3). Socrates generalizes: whenever a man is forced by his appetites against his reasoning, he is angry with that within which forces him (a8–b2). Which part of his soul prompts Leontius' words? Presumably it is his spirit, angry at appetite ('you wretches') even as it capitulates to it ('take your fill'); for all that Socrates infers at once is that spirit can oppose appetite as an alien (a5–6). However, it is next made clear that his spirit accords with his reason (a8–b4), and we may suppose that reason and spirit are speaking in unison. (Another possibility is plausible but not pertinent to Plato's immediate purpose, which is to distinguish spirit from appetite as reason's ally: if reason is too flexible, or spirit too intransigent, reason may well abandon spirit at its post, capitulating to appetite while spirit is still holding out.) Leontius is clearly suffering from a lack of self-control, which Plato counts as acrasia. Yet all this may leave open several interpretations of Leontius' words:

(a) The capitulation is ironic and idle, since spirit and reason recognize that appetite is carrying the day in disregard of their judgement; calling his eyes 'You wretches', they express impotent disgust.
(b) Knowing that appetite has won, spirit and reason keep face by changing sides, not hiding their irritation and yet approving action that they cannot prevent. (Cf. Freud, *PFL* xi. 364: 'Often a rider, if he is not to be parted from his horse, is obliged to guide it where it wants to go; so in the same way the ego is in the habit of transforming the id's will into action as if it were its own.')[28]
(c) Reason and spirit are stampeded into a decision to act appetitively that they once resisted making and already rue, keenly wishing that they had the power to decide otherwise (cf. Frankfurt 1988a).
(d) Spirit and reason deliberately decide to act on appetite, regretting the circumstances and desires that dictate the decision, but accepting that, given the way appetite is, they have no option. (This would be an unheroic reason, playing its role of serving the whole soul and all its parts along the line of least resistance, perhaps with an appeaser's hope that satisfying appetite may sate or quench it; cf. the reluctant compliance that the bad horse initially forces out of the driver and good horse at *Phdr* 254b1–3.)

Of these, (c) fits the passage but not Plato's purposes: it has reason divided against itself, a real possibility (we may think) but not one that he envisages. (d) is possible but unlikely: reflection can be rapid, but Plato's language tells against action on a deliberate decision. (b) is possible but strained: if that is their game, spirit and reason would be wiser to yield with a better grace. So (a) is the most likely, and it exemplifies hard acrasia.[29] Does Plato supply other instances?

Another possible case is that of the second-best lovers in the *Phaedrus*:

> When they are drinking or in some other moment of care-lessness their licentious horses catch the souls off their guard, and bringing them together take that choice which is called

blessed by the many, and carry it through; and once having done so, they [the souls] continue with it, but sparingly, because what they are doing has not been approved by their whole mind.

(256c1–7)

Since the lovers are not acting *with* their reason (so that Socrates can speak as if it is their appetites that are acting), we might expect them to be acting *against* it. If so, it may be that they are guilty first of weakness in decision (distracted from reflecting properly by drink and desire), and then of hard acrasia (wittingly doing, if only occasionally, what they disapprove of and are decided not to do). However, it is not clear that this is a case of acting against reason, for it may be instead that reason and spirit continue to affect the outcome through culpable inactivity, failing to bring their attitudes to bear at the moment of action. We may suppose that they were first taken unawares and out of action (say through the effect of drink), but are later half conniving, not approving and yet suspending their operations by failing to disapprove when it matters. If this is right, the lovers' lapses display appetite in action, but also reason and spirit in inaction, first unwittingly, later purposely, and so exemplify only soft acrasia. Action out of a divided mind must be a mixture of the exercise of thinking, and of the defeat or evasion of thinking.

The *Laws* contains a statement of acrasia that is only ascribed to common opinion: 'The worst of men are said, though they know that other things are better to do than what they are doing, not to do them, owing to their being somehow defeated by pleasures or pains' (10.902a8–b2, cf. *Prot* 352d5–e2). The Stranger does not endorse this, and it is strictly ambiguous: it could be that these men know, of the kind of act they are doing, that it is wrong, without clearly appreciating that the particular act they are doing is of that kind. Yet probably we should resolve this on the side of their knowing that they are acting wrongly (and the *Protagoras* parallel has it explicitly that many people 'are not willing to do' what they know to be best). Does the Stranger ever commit himself to an unequivocal case? Most vivid is the man (as I quoted in § 10) 'who does not love but hates what he believe to be noble and good, while he loves and cherishes what he believes to be evil and unjust' (3.689a5–7). Here hatred is provoked by moral approval, love by disapproval, so that passion (or what would be classed in the *Republic* as spirit) is parasitic upon reason, but in the mode not of respect but of reversal. We might interpret such a case as melodrama rather than acrasia: it may sound to us less like moral weakness (as when Macbeth is induced by his wife to murder Duncan in order to gain the crown) than like moral perversion (as when Iago hates what he has to admire in Othello). The immoralist finds value in morality, and yet a greater value in trampling upon his own moral values. An anti-hero, he is the converse of the moral hero who finds his supreme value in resisting the cosier values (which are also his own) of Milton's Belial, 'ignoble ease, and peaceful sloath'. If so, his mind is indeed divided, but within his reason, and he suffers from misdirected strength and not from weakness. However, it appears that Plato is conceiving the case differently. The Stranger finds in it a 'discord' not between some values and others, with moral values being trumped by immoralist ones, but between feelings of pleasure or pain and rational judgement (a7–8). The 'noble' is at the same time accepted as 'good', the 'unjust' as 'evil': the subject is accepting and not rejecting a coincidence between morality and self-interest (cf. 2.663d2–4). In hating morality, he hates himself; when he acts immorally, he will be his own victim. In opposing his own best judgement, he is resisting not only his better self, but a self that is wiser, and takes wider views, on his own behalf. So this does appear to be a definite instance of hard acrasia, though I know of none other in the *Laws*.[30]

Thus both the *Republic* and the *Laws* give prominence to one case that it seems right to interpret as exemplifying hard acrasia, while we might have expected to meet many more. One would think that, within Plato's theory, the simplest cases of the defeat of reason would be ones in which it is overridden, plainly losing out and losing face; and yet he more often envisages instead that, when defeat looms, it finds excuses for siding with the victor. In the *Republic*, courage is spirit's preservation through pleasure and pain of reason's pronouncements about what is or is not fearful (4.442b11–c3). This defines a possible sphere for a hard acrasia that might even be inveterate; however, within his description of a rake's progress from philosopher to tyrant, Plato expects a spirit that is habitually disobedient to take over the government of the soul (8.550b5–6). What this comes to is clarified by implication a little later (553d1–4): reason evidently becomes not impotent and inactive, but active on behalf of the ends that spirit supplies. Within this perspective, hard acrasia becomes the symptom of a state of transition. In the *Laws*, the Stranger resumes the old Socratic thesis that no one willingly does wrong (5.731c2–3, 9.860d5, cf. *Gorg* 509e6–7), but with an emphasis rather upon ignorance than upon lack of self-control. He makes a distinction between injuries and injustices (9.861e1–862b5): an act of injury can be voluntary or involuntary, but an act of injustice is always involuntary in that it implies a state of mind that the agent would never have acquired had he known that it was against his real self-interest (cf. Roberts 1987, Saunders 1991: 142–50). Here he assumes that, whatever is true of performing particular acts, a subject will not take upon himself lasting states that he knows to be damaging to himself; hard acrasia in respect of the latter appears to be excluded.[31] Pleasure, anger (*thymos*), and nescience (*agnoia*) have the same effect of 'often inducing each man, when he is being drawn towards his own wish, simultaneously towards its opposite' (863e2–3). This wording is careful and not clumsy: wish is most fully frustrated by failure not in execution but in conception, so that ineffectual wish is often half-conceived wish that one is only 'drawn towards'. According to Socrates, I may fail to get what I really want because, like an orator or tyrant, I do not realize how harmful it is to oneself to be unjust (*Gorg* 467a8–b7, 475e4–6); according to the Stranger, I shall gain through prayer the opposite of my desires if I lack the principal virtue of 'wisdom and intelligence and opinion' (*Laws* 3.688a6–c1). Nescience (*agnoia*) is not the sort of thing of which a man could manage or fail to be the master (9.863d10–11), for it is not a force but an intellectual failing. It is this, and not the element of error or ignorance, that marks it off from pleasure and anger as causes of wrongdoing. Pleasure owes its power to seduction: 'We assert that . . . it effects whatever its wish desires by persuasion with deceit' (b6–9). In this it is unlike anger, which 'overturns many things with irrational compulsion' (b4). If we confidently take this contrast to be between soft acrasia produced by pleasure and hard acrasia produced by anger, attention to the *Republic* makes us think again: sound opinions can be stolen from people not only when they are bewitched by pleasure, but also when they are compelled by pain or suffering (3.413b9–c2, cf. 4.429c7–d1, 430a1–b2, 442b11–c3). Pleasure may differ from anger not in the fact that it influences judgement, but in the manner in which it does so. I may slide into thinking well of what I find pleasant, with no inclination to hold back and be prudent, while I may be driven to think ill of what I find hateful, with no ability to hold out and be reasonable: judgement is seduced by pleasure, and rudely forced by anger. Reporting this risks proving too much: should we think again whether the divided mind of *Laws* 3.689a5–7 displays hard acrasia? More likely, it is only a generalization that pleasure and anger sabotage judgement; all the same, it is a generalization to give us pause.

So Plato is no more given to multiplying cases of hard acrasia than philosophers whose theories are inhospitable to it. Why should this be so? There would appear to be two main contributing factors within his own theory. One is reason's greater freedom and flexibility. In the imagery of the *Laws*, the cords of irrational desire are hard and steely, while the leading-string of reason is soft and golden (1.645a2–3). Appetite is passive, with no power of reflection because it has no power of self-movement (*Tim* 77b6–c5); indeed, all the mortal soul is subject to 'terrible and necessary affections' (69c8–d1). The philosopher views all pleasures other than reason's as 'the pleasures of necessity' (*Rep* 9.581d10–e4), and sharply distinguishes between the necessary and the good (cf. 6.493c5–6). Appetite and spirit are mental aspects of our metabolism: anger accompanies the swelling of the heart (*Tim* 70c1–4), appetite the depletion of the body (70d8, *Rep* 9.585a8–b1). Of course they are sensitive to psychological causes, such as the expectation of danger (*Tim* 70c1–2) or the sight of a sexual object (*Phdr* 250e1–5, 253e5–254a7), but their responses are regimented by physiology. The immortal soul brought to the body its own circuits (*Tim* 43a4–6); these were corrupted by incarnation, but may yet be corrected through attention to the orbits of the cosmos (90c7–d5). Reason's operations are never constrained by the brain in the way that spirit's are by the heart and appetite's by the belly and below. Consequently, reason is more concessive than its lower partners, both (for the best) in that it can take on a concern for their needs (*Rep* 4.442c5–8), but also (not so happily) in that it may concede too much to their demands. Thus, in the *Phaedrus*, a large concession by reason (to solicit the boy sexually, 254b1–3) is met by only a small one by appetite (to wait a little, d2). A second, perhaps fundamental, factor is that reason is the origin of the mortal soul (*Tim* 42e7–8), which it generates as it were by impregnating the body; whence a kinship (evident in the possibilities of reallocating the reserves of psychic energy, *Rep* 6.485d1–12) that underlies the concern and understanding that reason may display and appetite, especially, may exploit. This kinship is respected in the *Republic*'s combination, perhaps otherwise problematic (cf. Gill 1985), of an intellectualist conception of the ultimate goal of education (7.514a1–535a2) with an insistence upon the early training of the irrational soul in music and gymnastics (3.400c7–412b7). In the soul rightly nourished by rhythm and harmony, rationality arrives not as a stranger, but to be recognized through affinity (401d5–402a4). Lapses retrievable and irretrievable are part of the human condition (cf. 8.546a2–3), but it is generally true that reason knows what to command only within a soul whose lower parts are disposed to obey. The only two alternatives that Plato expects to take hold are the dominance both in thought and in action either of reason, or of some lower part. The man who has been sufficiently educated in respect of his whole soul for his reason to enjoy internal autonomy will both judge and act well. This should apply in a manner even to the natural producer lucky enough to be an actual producer lacking external autonomy and guided by the wisdom of another (9.590c8–d5): though the text mentions only that he, too, is taught the myth of the metals which underpins his subordination (3.414d3–4), he must be trained in what he can receive, and what he can accept, if the guidance is to constitute a form of friendship (590d5–6). By contrast, those who have been led into injustice by bad company (*Phdr* 250a3–4, *Rep* 8.550b4) hand over the rule within themselves to spirit or appetite (550b5–6, 553c4–6), making a slave of reason (553d1–4). Deposed reason has no ivory tower to retire to ineffectually; instead, the citadel of the corrupted soul is occupied by insurgency (560b7–8), so that it too thinks and acts according to base values. The hard acratic becomes a marginal character within Plato's moral melodrama.

As I said earlier (at the end of §5), I am postponing some discussion until much later (Chapter 4 §5). We shall find reason to deny that Plato does adequate justice to the unity of the soul, and yet it is evident that his partition throws up no very effective barriers. Even in conflict each mind remains single in a sense, with a longing for internal peace that may make for assimilation to the divine, or for appeasement and capitulation. Critical though one has at times to be in detail, at least of a tripartition that prefers a compelling picture to a working theory, one can more often admire a mapping of human nature which, like the Great Wall of China, sensitively adapts an idealized design to intricate terrain.

3

ARISTOTLE

1

Aristotle writes dismissively both of Socrates and of Plato: he complains of Socrates that, in denying that there is such a thing as acrasia, he 'plainly contradicts the appearances' (*NE* 7.2.1145b25–8); we have seen that Plato accommodates acrasia by distinguishing opposed families of desires, but Aristotle insists on the unity of desire, remarking, 'It would indeed be strange to tear this apart' (*DA* 3.9.432b4–5). In the light of my criticisms of both, this may seem a good start, but in fact Aristotle's own position is problematic because it combines dual loyalties: even though he complains that Socrates was wrong to exclude the possibility of acrasia, he concedes, 'The position that [he] sought to establish actually seems to result' (*NE* 7.3.1147b14–15); and yet he frequently writes of opposed desires in Plato's manner. It becomes hard to understand how, if he broadly followed Plato in distinguishing kinds of desire, which might have made acrasia easy, he also agreed with Socrates in finding it difficult. We must hope to interpret his implicit loyalty to Plato in a way that leaves room for his explicit loyalty to Socrates; his account of acrasia, elusive in detail but more deeply elusive in motivation, becomes the focus of his ambivalence.

2

Like Plato, Aristotle accepts the existence of conflicting desires that are multiple causes of motion:

> When desires arise that are opposed to each other, and this happens when reasoning and appetites are opposed, and arises in those who have perception of time (for intelligence pre-

scribes resisting because of the future, while appetite prescribes acting because of the present, for the presently pleasant appears also absolutely pleasant and absolutely good, because of not seeing the future), that which causes motion will be one in kind, the desiderative faculty *qua* desiderative . . . but numerically there will be several things that produce motion.[1]

(*DA* 3.10.433b5–13)

Appetites are one kind of desire, and liable to conflict with rational desires that are equally exercises of 'the desiderative faculty'. We meet the same way of thinking in the *Ethics*. Whereas the good man desires the same things 'in the whole of his soul' (*NE* 8.4.1166a14), the bad man's soul is in a state of faction, one element pleased while another is pained, one pulling one way, another another, as if they were tearing him apart (b19–22). 'Tear apart' is a strong metaphor which Plato applies to destroying the unity of his utopian city (*Rep* 5.462a8–b1, 464c7–8, *Laws* 9.875a7). Strictly speaking, a single soul, unlike a city, cannot be torn apart (*EE* 7.6.1240b29–30), and Aristotle's language strains expressively at the limits of possibility. Similarly, within divided minds that demand a self-control of which the 'encratic' are capable and the 'acratic' are not, reasoning and desire, being separate, push away (literally, 'knock out') one another (2.8.1224b23–4), with the victory going to the reasoning of the encratic and the desire of the acratic. In a different but equally mechanistic picture, we read that sometimes rational desire 'defeats and moves' other desire, and at other times is defeated and moved by it, like one ball hitting another, when acrasia occurs (*DA* 3.11.434a12–14). Such language puts one in mind of the 'inward affections' in Plato's *Laws* that 'being opposed to each other, pull one against the other to opposite actions' (1.644e1–3). It is clear that Plato and Aristotle both conceive of the divided mind as the battleground of antagonistic desires that determine action according to a play of forces.

Does Aristotle agree with Plato's use of the concept of mental conflict to yield a criterion of partition, that is, of a mapping especially of a mind's desires into families or clusters each of which tends to be in conflict with others, but has no inherent tendency to be conflicted within itself? The clearest evidence is of a kind of bipartition between a part of the soul that has reason, and another that may oppose it:

We praise the reason of the encratic and of the acratic, and the part of their soul that has reason, since it urges them aright and towards the best objects; but there is found in them also another natural element beside reason, which fights against and resists it.

(*NE* 1.13.1102b14–18)

It is implicit here that rational desires form a unity: that must be why Aristotle has to introduce irrational desires in order to find cases of conflict. However, there is no implication that the latter are unified as well, so as to constitute a 'part' in Plato's sense; hence to talk of 'bipartition' here is to talk inexactly. (Mention of bipartition below should be understood with this caveat.) Elsewhere, Aristotle quietly converts Plato's three parts of the soul into three species of desire, two of them non-rational: in a plurality of places, he gives the species of the genus of desire (*orexis*) as wish (*boulêsis*), anger or spirit (*thymos*, more rarely 'rage', *orgê*), and appetite (*epithymia*), unfortunately failing to spell out how these differ.[2] It seems that his thought is that they focus upon different concepts, and come to their desires differently. In a broad sense (as in those passages), wish is rational desire in general, and so subsumes choice (*prohairesis*, literally 'taking in preference', cf. 3.2.1112a16–17). In a narrower sense, it contrasts with it: wish is for a goal (1111b26, 3.4.1113a15) that one thinks *good* (5.9.1136b7–8), whereas choice is of something in one's power (3.2.1111b30) that one thinks *best* (1112a7–8). Ultimately, both derive from conceptions of *eudaimonia*, of what it is to live well not in some respect or for some time, but in every respect for a lifetime (cf. 1.2.1094a18–22, 1.4.1095a14–25, 1.5.1095b14–17, 1.7, 1.11.1102a2–4). As in Plato, appetites aim at pleasure (7.6.1149a34–b1, cf. *Rep* 4.436a10–11), and, more particularly, the pleasure of the moment (cf. *DA* 3.10.433b8–10, *NE* 7.3.1146b22–3, 8.3.1156a32–3). 'Pleasant' is *the* term in their vocabulary. It is debated whether 'good' belongs there also; it can be granted that it does, so long as it is given little work.[3] As we saw, Plato's spirit has a wide repertory. Aristotle usually focuses on anger, which is narrow, even when he needs a pair for appetite, which is wide (cf. 3.1.1111a30–1, *Rhet* 1.10.1369a4, both of which use the unambiguously specific term *orgê* or a cognate). Most illuminating is a passage within his treatment of acrasia:

Reasoning or appearance informs us that we have been insulted or slighted, and anger, reasoning as it were that anything like this must be fought against, boils up straightway; while appetite, if reasoning or perception merely says that an object is pleasant, springs to the enjoyment of it. Therefore anger obeys reasoning in a sense, but appetite does not.[4]

(*NE* 7.6.1149a32–b2)

Here Aristotle is considering the undisciplined responses of the mentally conflicted (the good-tempered and temperate are angry and desirous otherwise), but his contrast is instructive more generally. Even contrary-to-reason anger is more nearly rational and autonomous than appetite: while appetite has merely to hear that an object is pleasant and responds automatically, anger has to supplement the report of an insult with some moralizing of its own in terms of how it has to respond, and its conclusion is a passion. A crucial item of anger's vocabulary is a 'must' that is modal (implying derivability in principle from some exceptionless universal principle) and imperative (prescribing action): in anger a universalizable content assumes a peremptory emphasis. However, since it is the anger that generates the principle that would justify it, this is rationalization ('reasoning as it were'), and not rationality. No more than appetite does anger arrive at its responses through reasoning (cf. Cooper 1989: §3). Thus it seems that Aristotle distinguishes wish, anger, and appetite by their terminologies and modes of thinking, and sees their differences to be sources of conflict. How close does this bring him to Platonic partition? Though he often writes of conflict between wish and either anger or appetite, I do not know that he ever explicitly observes that anger and appetite tend to be in conflict with one another. Indeed, he strictly implies in the *Rhetoric* that anger cannot be self-directed, for there he defines the occasion of anger as 'an apparent slight' (2.2.1378a31), and then later remarks that it seems that one cannot slight oneself (2.3.1380a13–14). Yet one interesting remark is close to Plato: 'Appetite is opposed to choice, but not appetite to appetite' (*NE* 3.2.1111b15–16). This cannot be denying that a man's appetites may be contrary in a way (as when I cannot satisfy both my hunger and my thirst), and must rather be excluding either strong contrariety or confrontation between appetites (as I distinguished them in Chapter 2 §4). So it seems that Aristotle is willing to work with a division of desires that has much in common with Plato's central conception (paraphrasable in terms of conflicting clusters of beliefs and desires) of psychic partition.

Plutarch offers the interesting opinion that Aristotle changed his mind about the applicability of Plato's tripartition to species of desire:

> Aristotle made wide use of these principles, as is clear from what he wrote; but later he assigned the spirited part to the appetitive, on the ground that anger [*thymos*] is a kind of appetite, namely, a desire to cause pain in requital.
>
> (*DVM* 442b)

This is most easily understood as contrasting passages in his early work the *Topics* that propound ways of putting a tripartition of reason, spirit, and appetite to argumentative use (2.7.113a35–b6, 4.5.126a8–13, 5.1.129a10–16) with the bipartition that predominates in the later *Ethics* (as in *NE* 1.13). When Aristotle is playing along with tripartition, he has reason to extend the repertory of spirit to include more than anger. Thus fear may be placed within spirit (*Top* 4.5.126a8–9).[5] So perhaps may hatred, as accompanying anger – though, if it can, so also must its contrary, love (*philia*, 2.7.113a35–b3). This last extension is offered to a debater as a possible *reductio* (implying, on the supposition that love belongs within appetite, that hatred should *not* be ascribed to spirit); yet Aristotle can write in the *Politics* that spirit *is* the capacity by which we love (7.7.1327b40–1328a5).[6] If he changed his mind, and despaired of adapting tripartition to the phenomena, this could have been in imitation of a shift in Plato's own writings (whether or not this expressed a change of mind): as we saw, in the *Laws* Plato hesitates whether to count anger or spirit (*thymos*) as a certain passion or as a certain part (9.863b2–3). Aristotle may have come to suppose that anger was just one passion among many (as in his listing, at *NE* 2.5.1105b21–3, of 'appetite, rage, fear, confidence, envy, joy, friendship, hatred, longing, emulation, pity'), and not the kernel of a subdivision of the non-rational soul co-ordinate with appetite.[7]

In Plato, reason has a private passion, to discover the truth, and a partly altruistic concern, to exercise forethought on behalf of the entire soul. In Aristotle, it becomes moot (after a Platonizing remark at *Top* 4.5.126a13 that places all wish within the reasoning part, *to logistikon*) whether desires should be assigned to reason at all. In *Nicomachean Ethics* 1.13 we meet first within the non-rational part of the soul a vegetative element which is responsible for nutrition and growth, and irrelevant to ethics (1102a32–b12). Then comes another non-rational element, which can stand to the rational soul in relations of obedience and of resistance:

There seems also to be another non-rational nature in the soul, which, however, partakes of reasoning in a sense. For we praise the reasoning, and the part of the soul that possesses reasoning [*to logon echon*], of the encratic man and of the acratic, since it exhorts them correctly and towards the best objects; but there shows up in them also another part that is by nature beside reasoning, which fights and resists reasoning. For just as paralysed parts of the body, when we decide to move them to the right, turn aside on the contrary to the left, so it is with the soul; for the impulses of the acratic are in opposite directions. But while in bodies we see that which turns aside, in the case of the soul we do not see it. Yet presumably we must suppose none the less that in the soul also there is something beside reasoning that is opposed and resistant to it . . . . But even this appears to partake of reasoning, as we said. At any rate it obeys reasoning within the encratic man; and presumably it is still more attentive within the temperate and brave man, for it accords with reasoning in all respects. Therefore the non-rational part also is apparently two-fold. For the vegetative element in no way shares in reasoning, while the appetitive and (to generalize) desiderative element partakes of it in a way, inasmuch as it is attentive and obedient to it; this is also how we speak of taking account [*echein logon*] of one's father and friends . . . . That the non-rational element is in a way persuaded by reasoning is indicated also by admonition and all censure and encouragement. If one ought to say that this too possesses reasoning, the part that possesses reasoning will be two-fold as well, part strictly and in itself, part being a kind of listener just as to one's father.

(1102b13–1103a3)

Aristotle here makes a division between a part or element (I use the words colourlessly) that possesses reasoning, and another that falls within the non-rational soul (1102a28–2). This may be obedient to reasoning (b26, 31) and persuaded by it (b33); when it is, it may be described as partaking of reasoning in a sense, or sharing in it in a way (b13–14, 25–6, 30–1). Yet, being 'by nature beside reasoning' (b17), it can also be 'opposed and resistant to it' (b24–5). The desires of the encratic and acratic are divided, partly obeying reasoning and partly opposing it; in acrasia, the effect is to make reasoning inoperative in action. So much is clear, but in other respects Aristotle fluctuates. Firstly, he is undecided whether to use the phrases 'non-rational' and 'possessing reasoning' widely or narrowly: which applies to that part of the soul which shares in reasoning without possessing it? In general, he uses 'non-rational' widely and 'possessing reasoning' narrowly (as at b13–14, 28–31), so that to share in reasoning is not to possess it; yet he is willing instead to count sharing in reasoning as a way of possessing it (1103a1–3), even appealing, rather strangely, to the idiomatic use of 'to possess reason of' (*echein logon* with the genitive) to mean 'to take account of' (1102b31–2).[8] Secondly, he appears uncertain where to place rational desire, or wish (as he will later call it): does it fall within the rational or within the non-rational part of the soul? The innocent reader would surely suppose during most of this passage that wish belongs with reasoning within the rational soul: the unqualified assertion that the 'part that is by nature beside reasoning … fights and resists reasoning' (b17–18) naturally suggests that wish, which always follows reasoning, belongs upstairs in the reasoning part itself; and the remark that 'the impulses of the acratic are in opposite directions' (b21) most straightforwardly confirms the division between a rational and non-rational part if his good impulses belong in the first and his bad impulses in the second. Yet 'the appetitive and (to generalize) desiderative' element is explicitly placed within the non-vegetative subdivision of the non-rational part (b28–31).[9] It would be convenient if these two fluctuations simply cancelled one another out, so that wish fell outside the rational part in a narrow sense (only including the exercise of reasoning), and inside it in a wide one (also including obedience to reasoning). However, there are complications. There should be room for the thought that wish, which is rational by nature, belongs within the rational part in a sense narrower than that which also admits desires that only happen to accord with reason. Read without hindsight, b14–25 naturally convey that some impulses (*hormai*, b21, here meaning 'desires', cf. *DMA* 7.701a34–5) are to be ascribed to the rational part *qua* prescriptive (b16); and there are indications elsewhere to the same effect.[10] There is the further possibility that Aristotle would grant a special position to the desires that are needed to fuel intellectual enquiry, and are his equivalent of Plato's passion for the truth.[11] It is true that he proceeds in 1.13 plainly to place *all* desire outside reason in the narrow sense (1102b30–1103a3). I suggest that, while this is his standard view (cf. *EE* 2.4.1221b27–34, *Pol* 7.15.1334b18–20), he can be inconstant through a failure to distinguish clearly enough between reason as a faculty of the soul, to which perhaps all desire is extraneous, and reason as a faction of the soul, from which wish, which obeys reason automatically, cannot be sundered. To this I come next.

3

Famously, Aristotle was not only Plato's pupil but also his severest, and not his fairest, critic. It is difficult to apply a principle of charity both to Plato's theories and to Aristotle's criticisms, and this section may do nothing to confirm Aristotle's standing as the philosophers' philosopher. In the *Ethics*, he can make use of partition for local purposes (in *NE* 1.13, effectively in order to justify the table of contents of the *Nicomachean Ethics* as we have them, separating the moral virtues of Books 2–5 from the intellectual virtues of Book 6) without considering it critically as a contribution to a scientific psychology: precision would demand more effort than is called for, and what has been said in his popular writings suffices (1.13.1102a23–7). Of course, this could be why he appears not too concerned in the *Ethics* about consistency. With or without being more careful, he evinces a very different attitude in the *De anima* when he is enquiring about 'what it is in the soul that causes motion' (3.9.432a18–19). In this connection he raises the question of 'parts' of the soul separate either in reality or only in definition (a19–22). He commonly contrasts things separate only in definition, like the convex and the concave, with a thing with parts (*EE* 2.1.1219b32–6), or 'the parts of the body and everything that has parts' (*NE* 1.13.1102a28–32). How the contrast applies to 'parts' of the soul (1.13.1102a31–2, *EE* 2.1.1219b32) is irrelevant to ethics, but germane to psychology. An animal is a living organism, whose parts are the limbs and organs that serve together to enable it to live the kind of life appropriate to its species. Its soul is a hierarchy of capacities that may range from the digestion and growth of a plant, through the perception and motion of a beast, to the reasoning of a man. Hence it is natural for Aristotle to identify the parts of a soul with its various capacities. How should capacities be identified and differentiated? We shall find him saying, for example, that the capacity of perception (*to aisthêtikon*) is identical to the capacity of imagination (*to phantastikon*), though their 'being', that is, their definition, is different (*On Dreams* 1.459a15–17); as we might put it, they are two aspects of a single variety of living. Enquiry into the identity of capacities is an investigation of how psychic activities interrelate in virtue of the kinds of activity that they are. The parts of the soul that then come into focus will not be Plato's: 'For those who divide the parts of the soul, if they divide and distinguish according to capacities, very many show up, nutritive, perceptive, noetic, deliberative, and also desiderative; for these differ more between themselves than the appetitive and the spirited' (*DA* 3.10.433b1–3). Aristotle at once proceeds (in the passage that I quoted above at the beginning of §2) to accept a phenomenon that was salient for Plato:

> When desires arise that are opposed to each other, and this happens when reasoning and appetites are opposed ... that which causes motion will be one in kind, the desiderative faculty *qua* desiderative ... but numerically there will be several things that produce motion.
>
> (433b5–13)

This is a relation not of difference between psychic capacities, but of conflict between desires in virtue of their content. Aristotle does not – and it would be confusing in context if he did – identify these motivations with different 'parts'. Hence it is unsurprising that, in his discussion of Platonic partition within the previous chapter of *De anima* (3.9), there is no meeting of minds:

> We must enquire what it is in the soul that causes motion, whether it is a single part which is separate either spatially or in definition, or the whole soul, and, if it is a part, whether it is a special part beside those commonly spoken of and those mentioned by us, or is one of these. A problem arises at once, in what way we should speak of parts of the soul and how many there are. For in some way they seem to be indefinite in number, and not only what some people mention in distinguishing them, the reasoning, spirited, and appetitive parts, but others the rational and non-rational parts. For according to the differentiating features through which they separate these, there emerge other parts too that contrast more than these we have just mentioned: the nutritive, which also belongs to plants and all animals; and the perceptual, which one could not easily set down as either non-rational or rational; further there is the imaginative part, which is different from them all in what it is to be such, although to which of them it is identical or non-identical presents a great problem, if we are to posit separate parts of the soul; in addition to these there is the

desiderative part, which would seem to be different from them all both in definition and in potentiality. And it would indeed be strange to tear this apart, for in the reasoning part there will be wish, and in the non-rational part appetite and anger; and if the soul is three, there will be desire in each part.

(432a18–b7)

Admirably, Aristotle raises and faces the question 'in what way we should speak of parts of the soul', and raises but leaves hanging the question 'how many there are'. However, his assumption, natural in the context of his present enquiry (into the capacity for motion), that parts are capacities makes it impossible for him to do justice to Plato. When he speaks of 'the differentiating features through which they separate these' (a26–7), he apparently supposes that it is the same features by which some distinguish the reasoning, spirited, and appetitive parts, but others the rational and non-rational parts, and this threatens some confusion. His uncertainty in *Nicomachean Ethics* 1.13 about the location of rational desire suggests a failure to keep apart two different types of distinction: the Platonic one, call it (a), between different *factions*; and a different one, (b), betweeen different *capacities*. Within (a), there is simply no sense in putting wish in a different part from reason: they can never diverge. And yet it may be that within (b) wish belongs apart from reason just because it is a species of desire, and hence conceptually distinct from any kind of opinion (cf. *NE* 3.2.1111b34–1112a13). Here, in *De anima* 3.9, it is the allusion to a bipartition into the rational and non-rational that imports confusion, for *Nicomachean Ethics* 1.13 shows that this can take two forms: (a) opposes a rational faction (including wish) to irrational powers that can resist it, while (b) distinguishes a rational capacity (excluding all desire) from non-rational capacities that are different. It is a fair objection to this application of (b) that other capacities display greater differences: notably, the nutritive, perceptual, imaginative, and desiderative. Is this a fair objection to the bipartition of *Nicomachean Ethics* 1.13? The vacillations of that chapter exclude any simple answer, but two possible targets are not hit: firstly, whatever uses of bipartition in the *Ethics* accord with distinction (a) (e.g., *NE* 5.11.1138b8–13); secondly, Plato's tripartition between reason, spirit, and appetite – for that at least derives from (a).[12]

Aristotle's unclarity emerges particularly when he suggests that a division of the soul into separate parts (and not just, say, various aspects) produces the same kind of problem in relation to imagination as in relation to the different species of desire. The imaginative part is distinct in definition; that is, a capacity to imagine is not analytically given in the ascription of any of the other capacities. But where we should locate it becomes a problem 'if we are to posit separate parts of the soul'. Suppose that perception and reasoning are parts that work independently of one another (which is one possible sense of 'separate'):[13] then imagination can only belong with perception (for it is a motion produced by the activity of perception, and similar to it, *DA* 3.3.428b13–14), and yet it must also belong with reason (for thinking is impossible without images, 3.8.432a13–14). Separation is similarly problematic, Aristotle appears to be thinking, in the case of the desiderative part: 'It would indeed be strange to tear this apart; for in the reasoning part there will be wish, and in the non-rational part appetite and anger; and if the soul is three, there will be desire in each part' (432b4–7). Yet Plato need have no difficulty with the conclusion of this *reductio*: parts of the soul that differ according to (a) may very well – according to Plato, *do* – share certain capacities. Indeed, it is only for this reason that there can be a danger that one part may usurp the functions of another (*Rep* 4.443d1–3, cf. Moline 1981: 58). Aristotle appears to be assuming that the criteria of partition that we accept must all yield the same parts, so that (b) excludes (a) if the effect of (a) is to fragment the parts that (b) recognizes. Hence (a) is not to be judged on its own merits as one possible scheme of classification among others (and Aristotle fails to identify any part-like feature of Plato's parts that independently generates embarrassment). Instead, Plato's partition has to be rejected in favour of his own, and can be admitted within his *Ethics* only with the excuse that ethics does not demand the precision of psychology. Happily, indeed all too conveniently, he is willing to play along there with ways of thinking that he views as popular. His injustice to Platonic partition in his philosophy of mind does not prevent him from making use of it (with real differences that I have only partly touched on yet) within what we call 'moral psychology'.[14]

4

To discover more fully how Aristotle relates appetite and such emotions as anger to reason and rational desire, we need now to investigate his conception of the *pathê* ('affections' or 'passions') as constituting part of the interface between mind and body. We shall find, I think, that a pattern of thought that remains obscurely intelligible within his philosophy of mind lends itself to a coherent position within his moral psychology.

Etymologically, a *pathos* is something undergone (from *paschein*, 'to suffer'). Among the soul's contents, it is something accompanied by an alteration of the body:

> It seems that all the affections of the soul involve the body – anger, good temper, fear, pity, confidence, and, further, joy and both loving and hating; for at the same time as these the body is affected in a certain way.

(*DA* 1.1.403a16–19)

Aristotle is aiming rather to make a point than to define a class: he writes briefly, 'The affections are principles involving matter' (a25), but this holds, in his view, of most of the mind, certainly of perception, and largely of thought. Yet he at once gives an example that concerns us more precisely: 'Being angry is a particular motion of a body of such and such a kind, or a part of potentiality of it, as a result of this thing and for the sake of that' (a26–7). This definitional schema aims to accommodate the two aspects of anger, mental and physical, formal and material: there is 'a desire for retaliation or something of the sort', which interests the dialectician as the form of anger, and 'the boiling of the blood and hot stuff round the heart', which interests the student of nature as its matter (a29–b2). Unfortunately, the accommodation has the air of a forced marriage: the materiality of boiling blood and the intentionality of revenge as a goal are not happily united by saying that the former is 'for the sake of' the latter. Observing that the phrase 'for the sake of' often conveys not goal but result (even in the *Ethics*, cf. Müller 1982: 50–2), or that revenge may be not the blood's goal but nature's (within a teleological explanation of natural processes that has them serve purposes of which *they* may have no conception), removes evident nonsense without producing evident sense. Aristotle's concern here is to illustrate *that* mind and matter interrelate, but not to explain *how*.

For a fuller account of the affections (or passions) that concern us, we turn to the *Ethics* and *Rhetoric*. Unfortunately, it is relevant to neither to clarify how mind and body come together within them. The *Rhetoric* defines the affections as 'those things whose changes make men differ in their judgements, and which are accompanied by pain and pleasure, such as anger, pity, fear, and the like' (2.1.1378a19–21). The orator has to persuade his audience into those feelings and emotions that will predispose them to the beliefs and expectations that suit his purposes, forensic or political (cf. 2.1.1377b31–1378a5). His means are not exclusively verbal: to excite pity he may supplement his words by suitable gestures, get-up, and presentation in general (2.8.1386a32–3). Still less need they be logical: he may use the language of indignation to heighten the severity of the crime without proving that the defendant was the criminal (2.24.1410b3–5). Yet the medium of persuasion, like its object, must primarily be thought. Unlike the doctor (cf. Plato's comparison, *Phdr* 270b1–9), the orator has no drugs to act upon emotion through its physiology. It may help him to know which emotions are fuelled by which metabolisms (for example, that warm blood inclines the young to hope, while a chilly temperament inclines the old to fear, 2.12.1389a18–19, 2.13.1389b29–32), but metabolism is not his affair. Thus the rhetorical viewpoint upon the affections is one-sidedly dialectical, in the sense given above, attending to their intentional content (for example, on retaliation as the goal of anger) and ignoring their physiology.[15] The best articulated definition is of anger as a kind of desire (*orexis*): it runs, 'desire accompanied by pain for an apparent retaliation on account of an apparent slight to oneself or a friend by someone from whom the slight was inappropriate' (2.2.1378a30–2). Two elements that recur through (though not throughout) the series of definitions are pain, and appearance. Many of the affections are actually defined as species of pain (*lypê*): this is true of fear (2.5.1382a21–2), shame (2.6.1383b12–14), pity (2.8.1385b13–16), indignation (2.9.1387a9), envy (2.10.1387b23–5), and emulation (2.11.1388a32–5). The pains that constitute fear and shame are, or may be, accompanied by 'disturbance' (*tarachê*, 2.5.1382a21, 2.6.1383b13), while the pain of envy is itself characterized as 'disturbance-like' (2.9.1386b18); with an eye to what we read elsewhere, we may generalize that affective pains tend to run to states of turmoil and distress. Then the occasion of the affection must *strike* its subject in the relevant way, as is emphasized by the recurrent qualification 'apparent' (*phainomenos*, 2.2.1378a31, 2.3.1380a11, 2.6.1383b13, 2.8.1385b13, 2.9.1387a9, 2.10.1387b23, 2.11.1388a32). 'Apparent' does not merely convey that the occasion may, in actual fact, be inappropriate. When at one point Aristotle writes of 'an appearance [or imagination, *phantasia*] of future misfortune' (2.5.1382a21–2), he may have in mind passive appearing or active imagining, but in either case must mean a vivid mode of presentation. To borrow a graphic phrase (from 3.11.1411b22–5), oratory has to 'bring things before the eyes' of its audience. When he defines friendly feeling (*philêsis*) as a kind of wish, so implying that it is more rational than most affections, he says, rather differently, that it involves wishing what one 'thinks' to be goods (2.4.1380b36–7), presumably because wishing depends upon the content of thought, and not upon the mode of presentation. One might infer that friendly and hostile feeling depend only on beliefs (cf., of hatred, 1382a4–5), while the other affections depend only on appearances, but this would be a false contrast. Even the thinking good on which wishing depends involves appearance, for its object is the 'apparent' good (*NE* 3.4); indeed, all thinking involves images (*DA* 3.8.432a13–14). And even where not only the fact but the mode of appearance matters, the subject must accept the appearances: if he is to be affected seriously, and not to be pretending or playing a game, he must believe that things are as they strike him (cf. *Rhet* 2.1.1377b31–1378a5, 2.2.1379a39, b5–6, 2.3.1380b17–18, 2.5.1382b29–1383a12, 2.8.1385b34–1386a1).[16] It is particularly clear from the goals of the affections that the type of action that they prompt is no mere acting out or make-believe. When we read that the aim of anger is 'an apparent retaliation' (2.2.1378a30), we must understand not that the agent desires a simulacrum of revenge – or need *retaliations* be transmuted to become *Aristotelian*? – but that he desires a revenge evident to the recipient (cf. 2.4.1382a8–9). Again, emulation makes one act not merely upon one's own perceptions, but to secure goods for oneself, just as envy makes one act to deprive another of them (2.11.1388a36–8). In a single phrase, confidence involves 'expectation together with appearance' (2.5.1383a17–18). Aristotle finds within the affections an acceptance of propositions and projects as well as the presentation of a gestalt.[17]

We need not suppose that the *Rhetoric* contradicts his general distinction between the rational and non-rational soul in insisting upon the connection between affections and beliefs. An affective experience will presuppose some beliefs (as anger presupposes that one has been slighted, and appetite that a thing is pleasant, cf. *NE* 7.6.1149a32–b1), and may then generate others (as anger generates the thought that such a thing should be fought against, a33–4). Presupposed beliefs may be supplied by reason, and be wholly rational; they may also be generated by a disposition towards the affection (as when the irascible are too quick to detect an injury). Beliefs generated by affective states or dispositions are propositional, of course, but not cognitive: they are not states of knowledge, for they do not amount to reliable ways of apprehending reality.[18] In *Rhetoric* Book 1, Aristotle remarks that to induce emotion in a juror is to 'pervert' him, likening it to bending the mason's rule that one is about to use (1.1.1354a24–6); elsewhere he applies the same term 'pervert' (*diastrephein*) to the effect of anger upon even the best rulers (*Pol* 3.16.1287a31–2), and of wickedness upon one's conception of the end of action (*NE* 6.12.1144a34–6). Later in the same book of the *Rhetoric*, he distinguishes anger and appetite, as irrational desires, from wish, which is rational and presupposes judging its object to be good (1.10.1369a1–4); he opposes affection (*pathos*) to reasoning (*logismos*, a17–18).[19] It is true that he is silent about partition throughout his treatment of the affections in *Rhetoric* Book 2, and fails to make explicit a contrast that he might have emphasized: friendly feeling, hatred (which is without pain, 2.4.1382a12–13, *Pol* 5.10.1312b33–4, as is true of all wishing, cf. *Top* 6.146b2) and probably kindness (since *Rhet* 2.7.1385b1–2 imply that it involves goodwill, which is a kind of wishing, cf. *NE* 8.2.1155b32) belong within the non-rational soul only in the broad sense in which all desire does so, whereas the other affections there treated belong, together with desires other than wish and choice, more narrowly within 'the affective part' (*to pathêtikon morion*, *Pol* 1.5.1254b8).[20] (From now on, I shall use the phrase 'the affective soul' to mean the non-rational soul in the sense that excludes wish.) Yet we could as well suppose that, within the *Ethics*, he shifts to a different psychology whenever he focuses on ethical virtue and the ethical virtues, for there he asserts partition when contrasting ethical with intellectual virtue (e.g., *NE* 1.13.1102a18–1103a10, *EE* 2.1.1219b26–1220a12, 2.4.1221b27–34), but not when defining ethical virtue either in its generality (cf. *NE* 2.6.1106b36–1107a6, *EE* 2.5.1222a6–12) or in its varieties. There is no secure inference from the silence of *Rhetoric* Book 2 to any change of mind about the relation of the affections to a partition of the soul.

The *Nicomachean Ethics* glosses the affections as follows: 'By the affections I mean appetite, anger, fear, confidence, envy, joy, love, hatred, longing, emulation, pity, and in general things that are accompanied by pleasure or pain' (2.5.1105b21–3). This is rather a characterization than a definition, for Aristotle has just said that pleasure and pain accompany not only every affection but every action (2.3.1104b14–15). Why does he focus here on just one element (the presence of pleasure or pain) within the dialectical definition of the affections in the *Rhetoric* (2.1.1378a19–21)? Surely because of his emphasis upon acquiring the moral virtues through habituation, as here:

> Moral virtue is concerned with pleasures and pains; it is on account of pleasure that we do bad things, and on account of pain that we abstain from noble ones. Hence we ought to have been brought up in a particular way from our very youth, as Plato says, so as both to delight in and to be pained by the things that we ought; for this is the right education.
>
> (*NE* 2.3.1104b8–13)

Oratory works on and through what one believes; so the *Rhetoric* stresses the propositional aspect of the affections. Habituation works on and through what one enjoys; so the *Nicomachean Ethics* mentions only their pleasure–pain aspect (which features more in the *Rhetoric*'s initial definitions than in its ensuing descriptions). It is needless to infer any change of mind. Elsewhere in the *Ethics*, when Aristotle is discussing the intimate relation of moral virtue to practical wisdom, he does more justice to the propositional aspects of moral education, recognizing that habituation is a source of right thinking about the starting-point (*NE* 7.8.1151a18–19), and that virtue gives us the right goal (6.12.1144a7–8), of which vice distorts our apprehension (a31–6); if he had made the affections a topic in such passages, he might well have written of them as in the *Rhetoric*. The *Eudemian Ethics* offers a variant: 'By the affections I mean such things as anger, fear, shame, appetite, and in general things that, as such, give rise for the most part to perceptual pleasure and pain' (2.2.1220b12–14). What is the force of the epithet 'perceptual' (*aisthêtikos*)? It might just mean 'perceptible' and so be redundant (since Aristotle envisages no unconscious pleasure), with the qualification 'for the most part' sensitive to the point that, among the affections, hatred – though not mentioned here – is not accompanied by pain at all (*Rhet* 2.4.1382a13); however, the *Nicomachean Ethics* does list hatred (2.5.1105b22), and yet omits the qualification. It is hard not to connect the unusual appearance of 'perceptual' with that of 'for the most part', and then the former must be restrictive rather than redundant, conveying some special relation to the senses. This is supported by a striking passage in the *Physics*, where Aristotle identifies the affections with changes in the soul's sensitive or perceptual part (*to aisthêtikon meros*) that involve bodily pleasures and pains excited by action, memory, or expectation (7.3.247a3–9);

such pleasures and pains are excited by sensible things through sense-perception (a9–17). As we read in the *De anima*, 'To feel pleasure or pain is to be active with the perceptual mean towards the good or bad as such' (3.7.431a10–11), that is, I suggest, as perceptible. The pleasures and pains of most of the affections arise from their location within that part of the soul which Aristotle calls 'the perceptual and desirous' (*EE* 2.2.1219b23): they are not merely sensible because conscious, but sensory in that they connect closely with sense-perception and imagination within the affective soul. Many of the affections involve imagination (*phantasia*) in the service of memory and expectation; this connects them with the pleasures that follow on imagination as a form, if a weak one, of perception (*Rhet* 1.11.1370a27–32). Exactly how mind interacts here with body is not explained, and to that extent the unity of the affections, so barely asserted in the *De anima*, remains mysterious; but we need not doubt that the *Rhetoric* is alluding to the same pleasures and pains (2.1.1378a20–1), and that the same conception of the affections is receiving different emphases in different contexts.[21]

So the soul's affections (in the sense of 'affection' that covers emotions but also appetites) belong mostly within the affective soul, and connect closely with its operations and pleasures. How then should they relate to reason? *Nicomachean Ethics* 1.13 demands that they be *obedient* (1102b26, 31), and this is often repeated elsewhere. Perhaps most suggestive are social analogies: reason may stand to desire like a father (1103a3), a king (*Pol* 1.5.1254b5–6), or a tutor (*NE* 3.12.1119b13–15). Sharing in reason 'in so far as it listens to and obeys it' (1.13.1102b30–1), desire resembles the natural slave who 'participates in reason to the extent of apprehending but not possessing it' (*Pol* 1.5.1254b22–3). Such obedience comes of persuasion. Simply commanding slaves gives them no opportunity to apprehend the reason, though they need admonition (*nouthetêsis*) more than children (1.13.1260b5–7); admonition, censure, and encouragement all indicate that the non-rational soul is persuadable by reason (*NE* 1.13.1102b33–1103a1). Although there is no being persuaded not to feel hot or hungry (3.5.1113b26–30), a temperate appetite is readily persuaded by the ruling principle (cf. 3.12.1119b7), and appetite differs from reason in that it acts without persuading (*EE* 2.8.1224a38–b2). All this confirms that we need not take the *Ethics* and the *Rhetoric* to be at odds: Aristotle can simultaneously house the affections within the non-rational soul, and leave them exposed to rational persuasion. That, after all, is why they can be said to be rational, in a way (e.g., *NE* 1.13.1103a1–3). What it is for them to be persuaded must depend on how they involve thoughts. Hunger as a mere sensation demands no grasp of a possible object; hunger as an appetite requires the conception of an object, particular or general, as pleasant. Hence there are various ways in which, even when hunger is present as a sensation, reason may inhibit the formation or retention of hunger as an appetite: it may hinder a man from thinking of a general object, or from searching for a particular one; even when an object offers itself, it may hinder him from thinking of it with pleasure and as pleasant. Appetites are affections not merely *in* but *of* the sensitive soul, and may be inhibited by its apprehensions: if it is too vividly aware that, say, indulging in another slice of cake will produce indigestion, it will follow reason in being unable to enjoy the prospect, or to focus upon its pleasant aspect. Other affections require richer thoughts, and offer reason a larger target. One point that lies behind a remark that not only the rational part but also the perceptual and desirous part are peculiar to men (*EE* 2.1.1219b37–8)[22] may be that animals lack the universal judgements that are integral to many human passions (*NE* 7.3.1147b4–5). Uncontrolled anger apes reason in 'reasoning as it were that anything like this must be fought against' (7.6.1149a33–4); 'in a sense', Aristotle says twice, it obeys reasoning or is overcome by it (b1–3). Anger is a sententious emotion, and naturally translates a particular response into a universal principle. Its moralizing pretensions make it sensitive to true morality, so that to resist rational persuasion it may need to mishear reason's commands (a25–32). In anticipating revenge with pleasure (*Rhet* 2.2.1378b1–9), it takes on a resemblance to appetite, but its own intentionality compels it to trespass rather upon reason's domain, pronouncing and applying a categorical 'must'. Though children and animals are capable of anger of a kind (cf. *NE* 3.2.1111b8–13), adult anger is a child of the language of morals, to which it is faithful in its fashion.

It is a further question *how* the affective soul can be persuaded by reason. To the extent that affections are partly constituted by patterns of belief and desire, there is no special problem: if one person's system of beliefs (say) can change in response to another person's, so may one subsystem of his beliefs (however we draw its boundaries) in response to another subsystem. But there must be a more complex and distinctive story to be told given the double aspect of the affections, and their location within the composite of soul and body (*NE* 10.8.1178a19–20). A physiological precondition of obedience is that the body should be in a state of balance, waiting to be swayed, as it were, by the mere breath of reason. This state is typically denied to the young and the old: the young are heated by their nature as though by wine (*Rhet* 2.11.1389a18–19), so that they overdo everything, loving and hating too much (b4–5); the old have been chilled, so that their age is a seed-bed of cowardice, since fear is a chilling (2.12.1389b31–2, cf. *PA* 4.11.692a23). That the affections involve the body is confirmed by inappropriate reactions whose causes are internal and not external:

> Evidence of this is that sometimes on the occasion of severe and striking misfortunes we feel no irritation or fear, while at other times we are moved by minor and indistinct ones, when the body is swelling and is in such a state as when we feel anger. Here is a still clearer case: on the occasion of nothing fearful we become subject to the affections of a man in fear.
>
> (*DA* 1.1.403a19–24)

Aristotle avoids saying that one could actually *be* angry or afraid without the appropriate thoughts (say about outrage or danger); the affections are never purely physiological. Yet we may take him to suppose that an excessive bodily state will preclude certain thoughts, while predisposing one to others. Just as affections fuel perceptual delusions, as when fear makes the coward think he sees the enemy approaching (*On Dreams* 2.460b3–11), so bodily imbalance fuels affections whose thoughts are false. Too watery a mixture in the heart 'paves the way' for fear, since water is congealed by cold and fear chills (*PA* 2.4.650b27–30, cf. 4.11.692a22–4); too large a heart makes blood cold, and so already in the state that comes of fear (3.4.667a15–18). The famous doctrine of moral virtue as a mean between extremes can be applied not only to virtue itself, but to its underlying physiology (cf. Tracy 1969). We may suppose that the 'natural' virtues of *Nicomachean Ethics* 6.13 (1144b1–17) are realized in a physical predisposition to develop correct responses sensitive to situations (though this sensitivity must transcend the bare demands of a balanced metabolism). So much for the physical preconditions of obedience; what of its mechanism? As we saw in the *Rhetoric*, a crucial role is played by *phantasia* (literally, 'appearance'), whether one is seeing actualities a certain way, or visualizing possibilities (cf. 'as if seeing', *DA* 3.7.431b7, 'putting before the eyes', *Mem* 1.450a5). This capacity is needed, within a soul that animates a body, for thinking (*DA* 3.8.432a12–14, *Mem* 1.449b31–450a1) and desiring

(*DA* 3.10.433b28–9) in general; but more particularly it acts, through the affections, on the organic parts (*DMA* 8.702a17–19). Causation plays both ways across the dual aspect of affection: while an excess of water predisposes one to fear and one of natural heat to anger, 'fear chills the body' and 'anger is productive of heat' (*PA* 2.3.650b27–35). It also plays both ways between judgements and feelings: things appear good because they are pleasant (*NE* 3.4.1113a33–b1); equally, the memory or expectation of a good or of an evil becomes, through imagination, a felt pleasure or pain (*Rhet* 1.11.1370a27–32, 2.2. 1378b9–10, 2.5.1382a21–2). I take it to be in this way that the fine or *to kalon* can become a target even of appetite (*NE* 3.12.1119b15–16): the fine puts on the appearance of being pleasant (2.4.1105a1), and in this guise it attracts appetite as well as wish, for its lack is felt as a pain. It is true that mere imagining has no such effect: it is *believing* that something is terrible or alarming that produces affection, while just *imagining* it is like looking at it in a picture (*DA* 3.3.427b21–4). Yet, if imagining without believing is frivolous, believing without imagining (if it were possible) would be ineffectual. Among imagination's many roles is precisely to translate thought into feeling, and passion counts as 'obedient' to reason when the translation takes place and is fully effective. Acratic agents follow appearances and disregard knowledge (3.10.433a10–11), while virtuous ones have hearts and minds suffused with knowledge through the medium of the imagination.

Aristotle demands that reason permeate passion, but how demanding is that? The rule is that one should act *and feel* as right reason prescribes (cf. *NE* 3.12.1119b15–18, *EE* 3.4.1231b29–33) – which is how? Most strongly, it might require (a) that one *have no desire* to act in ways that reason forbids (so that, say, my appetite for a piece of Roquefort evaporates when I see its price); more realistically, it might require (b) that one *should not want* to act so, that is, that one should not feel set on so acting. (Here I resume the distinction that I drew in Chapter 2 §4 in relation to weak and strong contrariety.) At times Aristotle seems unconcerned to make the distinction, as when he writes,

> The intemperate man is so called because he is pained more than he ought at not getting pleasant things (even his pain being caused by pleasure), and the temperate man is so called because he is not pained at the absence of what is pleasant and at his abstinence from it.
>
> (*NE* 4.11.1118b30–4)

On the face of it, this leaves an awkward gap between the temperate man, who feels no pain at all, and the intemperate one, who feels too much: Aristotle appears to be blaming the intemperate man for failing to meet requirement (b), while praising the temperate one for meeting requirement (a). However, we need to read further:

> The intemperate man, then, desires appetitively all pleasant things or those that are most pleasant, and is led by his appetite to choose these at the cost of everything else; hence he is pained both when he fails to get them and when he desires them appetitively (for appetite involves pain); but it seems strange to be pained for the sake of pleasure.
>
> (1119a1–5)

Perhaps 'appetite involves pain' just as most affections do (and hatred is unusual in not doing, *Rhet* 2.4.1382a13). However, then the final claim is equivalent to one that it seems strange to have any appetite for pleasure, which is an austere view, and not Aristotle's. So I would rather diverge from the Oxford Translation and write '*his* appetite involves pain' (1119a4), that is, the excessive and impatient appetite of the intemperate man. If we distinguish, more lucidly than Aristotle, between the pain that accompanies any appetite, call it pain$_1$, and that which is a corollary of excessive appetite, call it pain$_2$, we may clarify the preceding lines to the effect that pain$_1$ affects both the temperate and the intemperate man, while pain$_2$ affects only the latter. The same clarification is invited by a later passage:

> We have pointed out in what sense pleasures are good without qualification and in what sense some are not good; now both the brutes and children pursue pleasures of the latter kind (and the man of practical wisdom pursues freedom from pain in regard to that kind), namely, those which imply appetite and pain, i.e. the bodily pleasures (for it is these that are of this nature) and the excesses of them, in respect of which the intemperate man is intemperate. This is why the temperate man avoids these pleasures.
>
> (*NE* 5.12.1153a29–34)

Here Aristotle makes the goal of the temperate man in respect of bodily pleasures to be a state of insensibility; yet he has denied that such a state is human (3.11.1119a6–7). Happily, there is an explanation to be retrieved (from 2.9.1109b1–13): since we are naturally tempted by an excess of pleasure, we are more likely to hit the mean if we aim at the opposite extreme, dismissing pleasure as the elders did Helen. Accordingly, we may understand that the temperate man aims at insensibility (i.e., 'freedom from pain$_1$', which excludes appetite) in order to achieve the mean (i.e., 'freedom from pain$_2$', which comes of a moderate appetite). Such an interpretation is confirmed, I think, by Aristotle's account of courage. The popular view that the brave man is 'fearless' (3.6.1115b16) is qualified by observing not merely that he should feel fear when he ought to run away, but also that he will fear some things that he has to endure (3.7.1115b11–13), always to a degree that leaves him undisturbed (*atarachos*, 3.8.1117a19, 31).[23] Disturbance is also alien to the mean in respect of anger (4.5.1125b33–4); we may take good temper to be manifest, like proper pride, in an even step and a level voice (4.3.1125a12–16). Thus moral virtue requires not that every desire should fall in line behind choice, but, less impossibly, that no restive desire should impede its formation and execution. Theory has promoted phlegmatism from a temperament to a norm.

It has become evident how physiology and psychology come together in Aristotle's treatment: moderate affections supervenient on a balanced metabolism maintain the affective soul in a state of equilibrium in which it can heed the still small voice of reason. So far, his account of the soul's workings is complex but coherent.

5

However, there are uncertainties, some of which (I believe) relate closely to the underlying motivation of that account of acrasia to which we shall be coming in my next section. To appreciate how close Aristotle remains to Plato, and yet that he must view the possibilities of acrasia differently, we need to reflect further upon his conception of the contents of the non-rational soul, and their relation to reason.

I have urged that there is no incompatibility between the ascription of most affections to the affective soul (as in *Rhetoric* Book 1), and a conception of them as closely connected to beliefs (as in *Rhetoric* Book 2). The beliefs associated with an affection may be supplied by reason, or arise irrationally. When they arise irrationally, they may infect reason (interacting inferentially with rational beliefs and desires), or operate outside reason, fuelling irrational desires and causing acratic action. Whether they can survive conscious contradiction with rational belief is a variant upon the problem of hard acrasia (cf. notes 26, 35). So Aristotle's affective soul, like Plato's, should be taken to contain irrational beliefs. We may speculate that this may be stated less explicitly because desires are partitioned as kinds, but beliefs as particulars: it may have been evident to him that, apart from beliefs that are wedded to desires (e.g., those about the outrageous or the sensually pleasant, cf. *NE* 7.6.1149a32–b1), beliefs count as rational or irrational in virtue not of their general content, but of the manner in which they individually arise. However, it was probably a sufficient factor in his silence that his partition within faculties (in *NE* 1.13, *EE* 2.1) is intended to serve ethics rather than psychology, and it is the reference to desires that does the work in distinguishing ethical from intellectual virtues. Yet some may doubt the extension of partition to beliefs not just because this is at best implicit in his account of the affections, but on the ground that it gives rise to a difficulty. He ascribes to non-rational animals anger (*NE* 3.2.1111b12–13, *EE* 2.10.1225b26–7), but not belief (*DA* 3.3.428a20–4). In this respect, he does not view beliefs and desires on a par. If men have an affective soul that is much like that of animals (as they have a nutritive soul that is somewhat like that of plants), it would seem, after all, that beliefs should not be located within the affective soul; but then beliefs connected with the affections but rejected by reason will inhabit a no man's land. The solution, I think, is to differentiate between the affective soul human and non-human, as Aristotle does implicitly when he remarks that *both* parts of the soul that partake of reasoning, whether their role is to prescribe or obey (and so passion and desire as well as reason), are peculiar to the human soul (*EE* 2.1.1219b37–8). He states his reason for denying belief to non-rational animals in a passage of the *De anima* in which he is arguing against identifying appearance or imagination (*phantasia*) with belief (*doxa*):

> Belief is accompanied by conviction (for it is not possible to hold a belief without being convinced of what one believes), while no beast has conviction, though many have appearance. Further, every belief involves conviction, which involves being persuaded, which involves reason; but some beasts have appearance, but not reason.[24]

(3.3.428a20–4)

Unfortunately, this gives us pause. The two sentences read like alternative presentations of the same argument, and the second is doubly infelicitous: its syntax permits the impossible reading that other beasts (that is, lower animals) do have reason; what is worse, it appears to be stating that all beliefs are rational. Presumably what Aristotle means is that only rational creatures can have beliefs, since belief entails conviction, and only creatures capable of rational conviction are capable of conviction. (As he might have expressed it, a capacity to be convinced and a capacity to be rationally convinced are one and the same capacity, even though it is possible to be convinced irrationally, much as a capacity to perceive and a capacity to perceive veridically are one and the same capacity, even though not all perception is veridical.) Why does he make persuadability a condition of having beliefs? I take his ground to be the double role of reason in supplying concepts for all beliefs, and in reaching rational beliefs. A creature without any rational beliefs is not a possible subject of persuasion: it can neither persuade itself (for that demands the exercise of reason, cf. *EE* 2.8.1224b1–2), nor be persuaded (for that demands the comprehension of reason through the grasp of concepts). Non-human animals are at once incapable of universal judgements (which are required for inference), and of more than the seeds of concepts. What denies them acrasia is that 'they do not have any supposition (*hypolêpsis*) of universals but only imagination and memory of particulars' (*NE* 7.3.1147b4–5). Memory grants them a little 'experience' (*empeiria*, *Met* 1.980b27), which Aristotle can equate with 'the whole universal stabilized in the soul' (*Post Anal* 2.19.100a6–8); yet, lacking a language, they cannot advance to 'skill and understanding' (100a8), which involve two things that go together, an understanding of concepts, and a deployment of universal propositions. They are incapable of 'thought' (*dianoia*, *PA* 1.1.641b7–8), which can be paired with calculation (*logismos*, *DA* 2.3.415a8), and contrasted with experience (*NE* 10.9.1181a1–3). Appearance has a complex content (and one not exhausted by the 'proper sensibles' like colour and sound), and so, in men, serves the emergence, and invites the application, of concepts; but it is too imagistic and inarticulate to constitute an 'interweaving of concepts', and so is neither true nor false (*DA* 3.8.432a10–12). Here appearance falls short of belief, and even to act on an appearance is not to act on a belief. Supplementing Aristotle by a little jargon, we can say that beasts 'accept' the appearances upon which they act: when the lion 'perceives' that an ox is near by its lowing (*NE* 3.10.1118a20–1), it accepts the appearance; when Aristotle writes that all remembering involves 'asserting' something in the soul (*Mem* 1.449b22–3), he can only have humans in mind (or be using 'assert', *legein*, metaphorically), but invites us to say that non-human remembering involves accepting. Yet animal acceptance falls short of human belief in that it is an aspect of appearance in creatures that lack concepts, and cannot discriminate between veridical and non-veridical appearances. Things can look frightening to men without their being frightened, for they may not believe that they are frightening (*DA* 3.3.427b21–4), but the inarticulacy of beasts excludes any criterion of their perceiving a thing as having a certain quality while disbelieving that it does so (for example, of their seeing the sun as being a foot across while believing it to be huge, cf. 428b2–4).

So much for the lower animals, from whom we differ not only in our rational but also in our affective soul. We can infer (on the basis of the same passage 428a20–4) that the human affective soul is capable of forming beliefs when we learn that it is capable of being 'persuaded' by reason (cf. *NE* 1.13.1102b33–4, 3.12.1119b7).[25] It partakes of reason's reasoning in a way (1.13.1102b13–14) when it respects it in forming its beliefs and desires (though without the automatic accord that attaches essentially rational desires and beliefs to reasoning); it remains reason's parasite when it uses concepts borrowed from reason in order to reject reasoning, as it were biting the hand that feeds it. So Aristotle can both place most affections within the affective soul, and define them, in the human context of the *Rhetoric*, as involving judgements or *kriseis* (2.1.1378a19–21, cf. *Top* 4.6.127b30–1). When he allows affections like anger to the lower animals (*NE* 3.2.1111b12–13), he must be using the terms somewhat differently, so that they do not imply beliefs. I conclude that *our* affective soul is a habitat of beliefs as well as of desires. If its beliefs resist correction by reason, conflict will result. Such an extension of the field of mental conflict is evidenced when he describes angry acratics as 'reasoning as it were that anything like this must be fought against' (7.6.1149a33–4). In a man, unreason can ape reason and pretend to be applying a moral principle reflectively, though the thought 'Anything like this must be fought against' is really a child of passion and not a tool of reflection. It is still a thought (cf. *Pol* 3.15.1286a33–5 on the perversion of judgement by passion), and one that conflicts with a better thought recommending prudence or a sense of proportion. To dismiss the example as involving no genuine belief, but rather a desire (to fight back) masquerading as a proposition (that resistance is right), would be to import Hume into the interpretation of Aristotle; it is better to accept the appearances and allow that belief, as well as desire, can arise contrary to reason. Here

Aristotle is faithful to Plato: in describing how the mind can be divided against itself both emphasize conflicts of desire, but also envisage conflicts of belief. (However, following Aristotle's emphasis, which is restrictive, I shall focus upon conflict of desire below, with only occasional speculation about how his treatment of that might carry over to conflict of belief.)

Yet I believe that in another respect Aristotle coincides verbally with Plato in a manner that obscures a deep divergence that underlies their differing accounts of acrasia, and helps explain why Aristotle turns out at the last unexpectedly Socratic. As I have noted, both convey the proper relations between reason and desire by the language of command and obedience. When reason has been properly educated to command, what is the source of its authority? In Plato, theoretical and practical wisdom are indissoluble, for both are achieved through the same grasp of the Forms. Intellectual aspirants cannot choose, say, whether to pursue mathematical and geometrical Forms up one ladder, or moral and aesthetic Forms up another, for the world of Forms is unified (ultimately, through the Form of the Good, *Rep* 6.509b6–10), and a thorough grasp can only be synoptic (7.537c1–7). Once the soul has become incarnate, discovery is recollection and progress retrieval. The senses provide our clouded reason with necessary reminders (*Pdo* 75a5–b2), but the goal is a kind of understanding that is no longer guided by the senses (*Rep* 6.511b3–c2). Similarly, we are to be trained in enjoying the right activities unconflictedly, but the goal is a kind of motivation that owes nothing to bodily desires. Rhythm and harmony prepare the young soul to feel an affinity with reason when she emerges (3.401e4–402a4), and it is the child (2.377a12–b3), indeed the infant (*Laws* 7.792d8–e2), who is most malleable towards that end; yet in no Wordsworthian sense is the child father of the man (cf. Gill 1985: 16–17). When we are fully educated, reason models our values and principles on the Forms (cf. *Rep* 6.500b8–d1), and then imposes them throughout the soul like a benevolent despot who is concerned for the welfare of his subjects but has nothing to learn from them. An apt simile likens reason to 'a farmer who cherishes and trains the cultivated plants but checks the growth of the wild' (9.589b2–3). Reason will stand to the other parts of the soul like a condescending altruist (cf. 4.441e4–6, 442c5–8), bestowing care but keeping its own counsel. In Aristotle, by contrast, theoretical and practical reason are separated, and only the former retains its Platonic privileges. It is intellect (*nous*) that seems to exist within the body as an independent substance, and not

129

to be destroyed (*DA* 1.4.408b18–19); it seems that it 'alone can be separated, as the eternal from the perishable' (2.2.413b26–7). Yet it is separate from matter only to the extent that its objects are immaterial (cf. 3.4.429b21–2): contemplation alone exercises something divine present in us, and by thinking of immortal things we identify ourselves with immortality (*NE* 10.7.1177b26–34). Grasp of the right practical starting-points is a kind of exercise of intellect (6.11.1143a35–b5), but practical intellect does not only put psychological data to its own uses (as even contemplation makes use of images, *DA* 3.8.432a13–14), but serves their importunities: we owe to the contingencies of our composite nature only our *means* of theorizing, but much of the *content* of our moralizing. It is true that Aristotle is not a relativist of the kind who assesses each man's success in life by reference to his own choices and projects, for only the practically wise man is the measure (e.g., *NE* 7.11.1152b1–3). Yet he appears to envisage that right desire is not dictated by a transcendent grasp of rational values and demands, but emerges out of a reflective development of natural desires. Practical wisdom (*phronêsis*) is not solely a rational state, for it can neither be forgotten (6.5.1140b28–30), nor be turned to perverse uses (*EE* 8.1); it is rather the rational aspect of a correct practical orientation. Inasmuch as we are creatures of desire, our goal is characterizable as a life in which desires are maximally satisfied: a way of life is choiceworthy if it is 'such that one who obtains it will have his desire fulfilled' (1.5.1215b17–18). The good man 'desires the same things with all his soul', and 'grieves and rejoices, more than any other, with himself', so that 'he has just about nothing to rue' (*NE* 9.4.1166a13–29). Of course, this ideal is not to be achieved by taking one's desires however they happen to stand, and contriving situations to suit them: anyone who elects to be passive in the face of whatever desires possess him will find himself the plaything of the shifting intensities of contrary desires; acting on choices that turn out to be expensive, 'he could have wished that these things had not been pleasant to him' (b23–4). The wiser course, which goes through a training in pleasures and pains, is to let one's desires develop in two directions: on the way up, they will unite, with adjustment and revision, to achieve a focus upon a feasible life plan (as Aristotle puts it, a conception of *eudaimonia*); on the way down, they will be highlighted or eclipsed by that focus in such a way that nothing within one rebels against one's choices, and one's acts leave no serious frustration in their wake. Special status will attach to theoretical reason's natural *nisus* towards pursuing and enjoying the higher truths: assuming the superiority of its objects (6.7.1141a20–2, a33–b3), this 'would seem, too, to be each man, since it is his authoritative and better part' (10.7.1178a2–3). However, rational choice arises not through some special, celestial motivation, but as the summation of ordinary appreciations. In the broader sense that links 'each man' (*hekastos*) to his practical rationality, each man is identified not with some privileged subsystem, but with the intelligent focus of the whole. Though not all voluntary acts are chosen (3.2.1112a14–15), acts done from reason are 'especially' one's own and voluntary, for reason is what each man is 'especially' (9.8.1168b34–1169a2; cf. *Protrepticus* B62 Düring): responsibility paradigmatically involves not just internal causation, but causation by the summation of desire. We can further distinguish the two ways, the way up and the way down, by noting that on the way down practical reason is directive, while on the way up it is emergent. The Platonic metaphors of command and obedience are only apt in Aristotle to half the process of putting one's mind in order.

Let me anticipate how this is crucial for Aristotle's unexpected combination of a largely Platonic moral psychology with a partly Socratic account of acrasia. In mature Plato, practical reason properly stands at a distance from non-rational desire. Since its attitude is altruistic, it can hope to persuade it (offering it what it really wants, or warning it of dangers ahead); alternatively, it may be corrupted or disregarded. When disregarded it may be overridden in action through a conflict of forces that leaves it intact but impotent. It appears that, for reasons that I tried to explain (at the end of Chapter 2), Plato expects this mode of defeat to be rare; yet accommodating it is not for him a problem. In Aristotle, practical reason does not achieve the same distance from passion and appetite, but forms a conception of its goal through the reflective mingling of motivations; hence an overstrong affection (*pathos*) must upset not just action but also decision and judgement. Rather as orderly affections are the mental aspect of a properly balanced physiology, so true and sincere practical judgements are the cognitive aspect of adequately ordered desires. Within the virtuous soul an all-things-considered judgement is the expression of a general consensus of desire (with some desires disappointed, maybe, but none making trouble); if the soul is self-controlled but not fully temperate, the judgement expresses a preponderance of desire. While the good of theoretical reason is just truth, the good of practical reason is truth in agreement with right desire (*NE* 6.2.1139a27–31). The encratic approach this ideal closely enough for practical purposes, but the failure of all their motivations to fall into place within a single perspective incurs some lack of appreciation of the full value of the right option (cf. Woods 1986: 150–2). When desires are so disorderly as to make choice ineffectual, practical judgement can still be true, but it loses contact with one's psychology and becomes the hypocritical mouthing of an actor (*hypokritês*, cf. 7.3.1147a18–24). Hence there is no real possibility of grasping practical truth while pursuing practical error, for disobedient desire that prevails in action also subverts judgement, reducing the rational assessment to a memory that speaks of an all-in perspective that is temporarily clouded. True judgement answers to all the relevant features of the situation, while sincere judgement reflects a marriage between reason and desire. Acrasia is a form of transient insincerity.[26]

Just how the detail of Aristotle's text in *Nicomachean Ethics* 7.3 spells out such a position is debated and inescapably debatable; even the best readings are only possibly correct. I have chosen to state his presuppositions, as I understand them, before I set out what he says. Interpreters insensitive to his motivation (which his text leaves unhelpfully implicit) have tended either to focus narrowly on what he says, with little concern to make it plausible, or to rewrite what he says for the sake of plausibility. My hope now is to be able, without embarrassment, to identify what Aristotle is really saying with what he is apparently saying.[27]

6

Over the centuries, no work of Aristotle's has been more generally studied than the *Nicomachean Ethics* (as we have it);[28] in recent years, no chapter has been more intensively scrutinized than 7.3, and yet numerous uncertainties of interpretation remain. Happily, many of them are more intriguing than important, and leave nothing of significance in suspense. To speak only for myself, I do not believe that I have any more ability to resolve them than many others whose views have not been widely accepted. In default of any confidence that I can confute alternative views, I shall now state my own (in the hope that they are as plausible as any), quoting texts fully but relegating controversy to notes. Every critical reader will disagree with me over some details; reflective readers will reflect what difference these make.[29]

Aristotle refers to Socrates in two passages. It already clarifies their relations to take the references together:

> It would be strange – so Socrates thought – if when knowledge is in a man something else masters it and drags it about as if it were a slave. For Socrates wholly combated the view in question, holding that acrasia does not exist; no one, he said, acts against what he believes best, but acts by reason of ignorance. Now this view plainly contradicts the appearances, and we must enquire about what happens to such a man: if it is by reason of ignorance, what is the manner of the ignorance?
>
> (7.2.1145b23–9)

> The position that Socrates was seeking to establish actually seems to result; for it is not so-called knowledge proper that the affection overcomes (nor is it this that is dragged about as a result of the affection), but perceptual knowledge.[30]
>
> (7.3.1147b14–17)

One ambiguity here is real but immaterial: are 'the appearances' (*ta phainomena*) the manifest facts, or common opinions? The phrase can signify either. The view that contradicts them conjoins three claims: (a) acrasia does not exist; (b) no one acts against what he believes best; (c) the cause of acting wrongly is always ignorance. Of these Aristotle will deny (a) and (c), and indeed (b): the acratic agent acts contrary to his choice and judgement (7.4.1148a9–10, 7.8.1151a6–7). Hence he will endorse 'the appearances' whatever status we give them. And yet his eventual half agreement with Socrates is already anticipated: he will define 'the manner of the ignorance' compatibly with his denials, agreeing that the acratic agent lacks knowledge of a kind, but distinguishing that from what Socrates counted as 'knowledge', and treating the ignorance as a condition of his action but not its cause. Aristotle intends to advance beyond Socrates, but not to turn his back on him.

So the crucial question becomes 'whether the acratic act knowingly or not, and in what sense knowingly' (7.3.1146b8–9). To answer this, Aristotle introduces four distinctions, which he will next put to work in identifying the form and content of an ignorance that plays a role in explaining acrasia without explaining it away:

(a) The first (1146b31–5) is between merely possessing some piece of knowledge, and actually rehearsing or exercising it (most often for some inferential or practical purpose).[31]

(b) The second (1146b35–1147a4) is between two types of premiss, one universal, the other particular: one may well act contrary to one's knowledge if one is making use of the universal, but not of the particular.

(c) The third (a4–10) is between the two halves of a universal principle, of which one specifies the subject, the other the object, as in this example (which I set out after the model of *DA* 3.11.434a16–19):

> Dry food is good for every man (major premiss).
> I am a man, and such and such food is dry and this food is such and such (conjunctive minor premiss).

(d) The fourth (a10–14) is between two ways of possessing knowledge (later labelled by the scholastics 'habitus solutus' and 'habitus ligatus'): I fully possess my knowledge if it is ready to be activated (it is 'solutus' or free); I possess it only in a sense if, say asleep or raving or drunk, I am temporarily unable to put it to use (it is 'ligatus' or bound).

Of these, (b) and (c) are the distinctions necessary for the construction of the practical syllogism (a phrase that Aristotle gets close to coining when he writes 'syllogisms of things to be done', 6.12.1144a31–2), which is a kind of reasoning that necessitates action, if all goes well. These distinctions will help Aristotle to identify elements of thinking that the acratic agent may be exercising or possessing or not, and in respect of which he can count as knowing *in a way* that he is acting wrongly (cf. 7.3.1147b18, 7.10.1152a15–16). (d) is a refinement of (a) that more particularly applies to this agent in two ways: it brings out how acrasia is an affective state in which his intelligence is sabotaged by the joint workings of his mind and body, and it allows him to use the words of knowledge while still not counting as exercising it.

Aristotle at once applies (d) to his topic by asserting that the acratic only half possess the knowledge they need: anger or sexual desire or the like so alter their bodily state that they are temporarily incapable of putting it to use (7.3.1147a14–18). Times when they *say* the right things prove nothing: think of a drunkard reciting temperance verses, or a child parroting what he has just been told – the acratic are like actors (a18–24). I give what follows in full, with glosses between square brackets:

Again, one might scrutinize the cause scientifically as follows.

134

The one opinion is universal, while the other concerns particulars, of which perception is determinant. Whenever a single opinion results from them, the conclusion must in the one case [theoretical reasoning] be asserted by the soul, and in the other [practical reasoning] be immediately enacted; e.g., if everything sweet should be tasted, and this is sweet (which is one of the particular premisses), the man who is able and not prevented must at the same time [sc., as he asserts the conclusion] also enact this. So whenever the universal opinion is in a man forbidding him to taste, and the other opinion [the composite particular premiss] is that everything sweet is pleasant and this is sweet (and this opinion is active), and appetite happens to be in him, the one tells him to avoid this, but appetite leads him on; for each of the parts [sc., of the soul] can cause motion. So it comes to pass that he behaves acratically under the influence in a way of some reasoning and an opinion, but of an opinion that is opposed not in itself but only incidentally; for it is the appetite and not the opinion that is opposed to the correct reasoning. Thus it is also because of this that non-human animals are not acratic, because they do not have any supposition of universals but only imagination and memory of particulars. Of how the ignorance dissolves and the acratic man again regains his knowledge the account is the same as about the man drunk or asleep and is not peculiar to this state; we must hear it from scientists. Since the last premiss is a perceptual opinion and determinant of actions, the man in this state either lacks it, or so possesses it that the possessing is not knowing but speaking, like the drunkard speaking the verses of Empedocles. And because the ultimate premiss is taken not to be universal nor equally cognitive as the universal premiss, the position that Socrates was seeking to establish actually seems to result: for it is not so-called knowledge proper that the affection overcomes (nor is it this that is dragged about as a result of the affection), but perceptual knowledge. About acting acratically with knowledge and without, and with what kind of knowledge it is possible to act acratically, let so much be said.

(1147a24–b19)

Standardly, Aristotle begins, to draw a practical conclusion is at once to make an assertion (say, 'I should taste this') and to perform an act (of tasting it). Assertion without action has to be explained by incapacity or interference, which make for asserting the conclusion without enacting it (1147a29–31), and not for failing to draw the conclusion or to keep it in mind. We are to think of factors, like paralysis, that are external to the desiring faculty, and only analogous to the passions of acrasia (cf. 1.13.1102b18–21). Acrasia works differently, and affects thinking as well as action. In Aristotle's example, the syllogism on which the acratic agent ought to be acting might be filled out like this:

> No man should pursue pleasures to excess.
> I am a man, and everything sweet is pleasant and this is sweet,
> but tasting this would be excessive.
> So: I should not taste this.[32]

Whether the conclusion is initially drawn and asserted is not made clear: is 'the correct reasoning' to which appetite is opposed actual or only potential? Has the acratic agent already thought it through, or is it merely available to him if he stops to think? To this extent, the description covers a variety of cases. In those to which we are to apply a later remark that the acratic man 'is not wicked since his choice is good' (7.10.1152a16–17, cf. 7.4.1148a9–10, 7.8.1151a6–7) we must suppose him to make a judgement and choice, though in vain: immediate action is prevented in a manner that subverts them also. Appetite awakens to reason's implicit inference to 'This is pleasant.' This opinion is not opposed to 'the correct reasoning' in itself (indeed, it is part of it), but only incidentally – indeed accidentally – in that it triggers an appetite that, being unruly, not only regrets the prohibitive conclusion but resists it. This so changes the agent's physical condition that the conclusion shifts, perhaps imperceptibly, from being meant to being mouthed; nothing then obstructs the causation of action by appetite alone. It may be that the agent's assent was never complete: his dominant appetite even for excessive pleasure may just have been dormant, and never party to reason's attempt at an all-in decision. Alternatively, his appetite may have consented when its only stimulant was imagination, and revoked under the impact of perception. To either possibility we can apply a remark that Aristotle makes about learners: if a judgement (or, when each judgement is particular, a pattern of judgements) is to be reliably within their repertory, it 'has to become part of themselves, and that takes time' (7.3.1147a22). Without such training, the best motivations can slacken: practical judgement, drained of the effective desire that alone gives it life, survives only vestigially as the echo of a voice in the wilderness of the heart. Where knowledge is practical, a failure of desire brings with it a kind of ignorance.

When appetitive desire undoes the conclusion, through what weak point in the syllogism does it initially break through? Aristotle asserts that it is 'the last premiss' (1147b9).[33] On my speculative reconstruction, this is plausible enough: no element can more credibly decline from a mandate to a murmur than 'This is excessive', which is the final element of the minor premiss. This can still count for Aristotle as a 'perceptual opinion' (b9–10), for he has a wide conception of practical 'perception', extending beyond plain matters of fact to matters of evaluation, either commonplace (whether bread has been baked as it ought to be, 3.3.1112b34–1113a2) or tricky (when deviations become blameworthy, 2.9.1109b20–3). However, in another respect this is problematic: since excess and deficiency are the two species of wrongness, there seems to be no distance between 'Tasting this would be excessive' to 'I should not taste this' that a universal prohibition is needed to traverse. If we avoid this objection by rewriting the universal premiss, after Aquinas, as 'Nothing pleasant should be tasted between meals', we shall have Aristotle insisting implausibly that it is 'It is now between meals' that gets repeated without being meant. A happy compromise might be to permit a final predicate neither so prescriptive as 'excessive' nor so neutral as 'between meals': perhaps the universal premiss could be 'No man should pursue unhealthy pleasures', and the final premiss 'This is unhealthy', an evaluation (since health is a good) that falls short of a decision (since health may, on occasion, have to be sacrificed to other goods, e.g., politeness to one's host; cf. Wiggins 1991a: 95–6). Applying Aristotle's two disjuncts (7.3.1147b10–12) to different cases, we may suggest that 'It is now between meals' becomes overlooked, while 'Tasting this would be unhealthy' may still be said but ceases to be meant. Assent to such an evaluation involves an attitude of which the acratic are hardly capable, while a trivial fact has only to be noticed and kept in mind, which they can hardly avoid doing while they are repeating it. (To keep saying 'This is whisky' without meaning it is only possible for the deeply drunk.) However, it remains problematic why Aristotle wishes to generalize to a claim that it is always the last premiss that goes under: why does he not simply say that in acrasia the practical syllogism is invaded by appetite through *whatever* point its content, or the context of action, or the agent's character, makes most vulnerable? Is it simply deference to Socrates that precludes him from envisaging that what might, on occasion, be dragged about like a slave is what Socrates would count as a state of knowledge, namely, a grasp of the major premiss? After all, outside 7.3 (and *DA* 3.11.434a16–21), it is his own practice to restrict the term 'knowledge' honorifically to a grasp of propositions that are not only universal but necessary (cf. *NE* 6.6), and *their* maltreatment by appetite is not in question. The easiest suggestion I have is that he feels bound by one of the common opinions surveyed in 7.1: the acratic agent does things that he knows are bad as a result of passion (1145b12–13). Even while I have lost the thought that the tasting is unhealthy, I may still know that eating unhealthily is wrong in such circumstances, and hence, in a sense, that what I am doing is wrong. This is the upshot that Aristotle intends: when I act acratically, it is 'knowing in a manner both what I am doing and its result' (7.10.1152a15–16). By contrast, if I keep the thought that the tasting is unhealthy, but mislay the knowledge that eating unhealthily is wrong in such circumstances, there is no sense in which I concurrently know that what I am doing is wrong. If this suggestion is right, the connotations of the term 'acrasia', requiring knowledge in a sense that one is acting wrongly, are restricting Aristotle's attention (quite reasonably, perhaps) to a fraction of the phenomena.[34]

The same feature yields an apparent inconsistency. Aristotle claims in his discussion of responsibility that, while men are blamed for ignorance of the universal, 'ignorance of the particular circumstances of the action and the objects with which it is concerned' makes an act involuntary (3.1.1110b32–1111a2), so long as it is later rued (1110b18–24); so acratic loss of 'the last premiss', which *is* rued (7.8.1150b30–1), should preclude voluntary action. Yet we also read that action is voluntary whether it be chosen or passionate (*Rhet* 1.13.1373b33–6). Now it is possible that Aristotle escapes this difficulty through imprecision: when he writes that the acratic agent 'acts voluntarily (for in a way he knows both what he does and its result)' (*NE* 7.10.1152a15–16), he may be supposing, rather severely, that partial knowledge of the nature of the action is sufficient for total responsibility. For precision, he might have relativized the voluntariness of an act to its various descriptions (e.g., by saying that Oedipus voluntarily married an older woman but involuntarily married his mother); but he never quite does that (cf. 3.1.1111a15–19), and would hardly wish to say that his acratic agent voluntarily tastes something pleasant and involuntarily tastes something excessive or unhealthy, since this would absolve him of blame (*pace* 7.4.1148a2–3). However, he has a better point to appeal to:

> Acting *because of* ignorance seems also to be different from acting *in* ignorance; for the man who is drunk or in a rage is thought to act as a result not of ignorance but of one of the causes mentioned, yet not knowingly but in ignorance.
>
> (3.1.1110b24–7)

Though the ignorance is particular, and rued, it is not the cause of the action, for the cause of the action is also the cause of the ignorance, namely, the affection; and 'presumably acts done by reason of anger or appetite are not rightly called involuntary' (1111a24–5). It is true that the paradigm of the voluntary is the chosen (9.8.1168b35–1169a1); acratic action is a perversion of the voluntary.

<h1 style="text-align:center">7</h1>

There are varieties of acrasia, to some of which the account in *Nicomachean Ethics* 7.3 applies as it stands, to others only with modification. One important distinction is between the weak, who 'after deliberating fail, owing to their passion, to stand by the conclusions of their deliberation', and the impetuous, who 'because they have not deliberated are led by their passion' (7.7.1150b19–22). I take 7.3 to be neutral between these two: the weak agent draws a conclusion, and makes a choice, which are then together subverted by passion (through the weak point of his final premiss) before action follows; the impetuous agent is carried away by passion so that he fails to detect the salient feature of the situation (statable in a final premiss) in the first place. Their different failures are very briefly indicated at 1147b9–12: the impetuous agent simply does not possess the final premiss, while the weak agent possesses it in the sense of mouthing but not of knowing it. Now it is very often only detection of the salient feature that brings the major premiss into actuality (as when remembering that a woman is another man's wife puts one in mind of the Seventh Commandment); so 7.3 only applies plausibly to impetuous acrasia if the principle against tasting counts as 'being in' a man (1147a32) even when it is possessed but not exercised – as surely it may. We need not worry that often in impetuous acrasia, when universal knowledge remains unactualized because appetite has obscured its relevance, it is, after all, being 'dragged about as a

139

result of the affection' (b16–17): innumerable factors (such as our finite attention) keep most of our knowledge unactualized most of the time, and this cannot count as its being 'dragged about'.

Another difference is between kinds of acratic motivation. Acrasia so called without qualification involves the same objects as self-indulgence, namely, the pleasures of touch and taste of which food, drink, and sex are the prototypes (cf. *NE* 3.10). The acratic in respect not of bodily pleasures, but of money, honour, or anger, are so called not 'simply', but 'according to similarity' (7.4.1147b34–5, cf. 7.5.1149a1–3), or 'with an addition' (7.4.1148a10, cf. 1147b33–4). It is true that these all fit the characterization of the acratic as 'those who go to excess . . . contrary to the correct reasoning that is within them' (1147b31–2). However, Aristotle is concerned with real natures and not nominal definitions. The reality of acrasia is constituted by its mechanism, and that varies with the nature of the temptation: honour and money do not act through one's natural responses in the manner of objects of hunger or sexual desire. The objects of acrasia proper are bodily and 'necessary' (b25–6), and intermediate between two classes of object of qualified acrasia: 'things generically fine and good' which are 'pleasant things by nature worthy of choice' (1148a23–4), for example, wealth, gain, victory, honour (a25–6), and opposite things (a24) that 'are not pleasant by nature', but through disabilities, corrupting habits, or bad natures (7.5.1148b17–18). (Aristotle touches here on an aetiology of the perversions: cannibalism comes of a brutal nature, or else madness; nature or habit can produce nail-biting or sexual inversion, b18–34.) Both these varieties of qualified acrasia differ in their operations from acrasia proper: love of money may cause selective attention, but it does not transport the miser like a fit of madness; love of human flesh is likely so to brutalize the cannibal that he cannot count as knowing that cannibalism is wrong (though he will not be up to moralizing in its favour either). Acrasia in respect of anger is a kind of qualified acrasia that seems to fall outside this classification of pleasures: even if the angry man views revenge with pleasure (*Rhet* 2.2.1378b1–9), what fundamentally motivates him is not pleasure but pain (cf. *NE* 7.6.1149b20–3). The most interesting difference between acrasia proper and acratic anger is one that I have often cited already: anger erupts through 'reasoning as it were that anything like this must be fought against', while appetite springs to action 'if reasoning or perception merely says that an object is pleasant' (1149a33–b1). A common feature is that 'each of the parts' (sc., of the soul) 'can cause motion' (7.3.1147a35), but anger and appetite operate differently. Appetite merely overhears, understands, or perceives that some prospect is pleasant (as may be explicit or implicit within the prohibitive syllogism itself), while anger generates a rival practical syllogism. Angry action obeys a prescriptive conclusion (though the wrong one), while appetitive action ensues on descriptive perceptions or premisses that it misappropriates; so anger's reasoning is in itself opposed to good reasoning, while an opinion exploited by appetite is opposed only incidentally. 'Therefore anger obeys reasoning in a way, but appetite does not', and is more disgraceful (7.6.1149b1–2).[35]

Among objects of attraction, one would welcome more discrimination between 'things generically fine and good' (7.4.1148a23). Towards the end of the *Eudemian Ethics*, Aristotle distinguishes between the good and the 'fine-and-good' (8.3.1248b16–18): things 'naturally good', for example, 'honour and wealth and bodily excellences and good fortune and capacities', are good for the good man but may be harmful for the foolish or vicious (b26–32), and so are fine not by nature but only when put to fine ends (1249a5–14); only things commended for themselves are fine by nature, notably virtuous states and acts (1248b18–23). His conception of virtues of character is that they are not merely patterns of desirable motivation but dispositions to feel and to act 'as one ought' (e.g., *NE* 3.7.1115b12), that is, as right reason directs (cf. 3.12.1119b17–18, *EE* 3.4.1231b33); consequently, there can be no question of displaying acrasia by exercising some virtue to excess. But what of other things fine by nature? Aristotle concludes the *Eudemian Ethics* by defining the 'best' or 'finest' criterion for the choice of natural goods: it is whatever maximizes contemplation of the divine, and minimizes awareness of the non-rational part of the soul (8.3.1249b16–23). He does not imply that contemplation is the only proper ultimate goal of action (for the best and finest criterion may well not be the only one); he does imply that contemplating is fine by nature *par excellence*. Now he cannot sensibly hold (and there is no sufficient evidence for taking him to hold) that in all circumstances even a little contemplation is to be preferred to any amount of virtuous action;[36] hence he ought to allow (though one senses that he would prefer not to) that a man might display acrasia in contemplating when he ought to be acting, say by pursuing a mathematical proof that can wait when he ought to be helping a friend who cannot – itself an act that remains an object of wish, through answering to friendly feeling, even when it is not choiceworthy (*Rhet* 2.4.1380b36–1381a1). Here Plato and Aristotle are contrasted: in Plato moral action is an aspect of thinking through the moral Forms, while in Aristotle action is divorced from contemplation. Plato identifies rational choice with the choice of reason, which has its own activities, but ones that connect closely with the good of the whole soul; Aristotle (if I am right) identifies rational choice with the choice that emerges reflectively out of the motivations of all parts of the soul. Plato must view a sacrifice of morals to mathematics as an intellectual aberration, a sensitivity to one claim of reason that goes with a failure to think through another; Aristotle should view it as an instance of acrasia of a kind, whereby one pleasure escapes and subverts a balanced summation of pleasures. Reflection upon this would have helped him get clear about the distinction between parts as factions and parts as faculties: practical deliberation and theoretical contemplation belong together as putting language at the service of truth, and are to that extent ascribable to the same faculty; but a desire to contemplate may find itself at odds with deliberated choice, so that they become points of friction between two intelligent factions.

8

My understanding at least of the details of Aristotle's account of acrasia has been traditional. Many recent writers are unhappy to understand Aristotle so, for two different kinds of reason: they think that talk of acting in ignorance applies only to 'soft' cases of acrasia, and not the most illuminating ones, which are of 'hard' acrasia and involve an unclouded awareness that one is acting wrongly; and they find evidence of a recognition of hard acrasia in Aristotle elsewhere. Let us first consider this other evidence: does it indeed conflict with *Nicomachean Ethics* 7.3 traditionally understood?

The comparison with physical paralysis in 1.13 may put us in mind of a more open conflict: 'Just as paralysed parts of the body, when we decide to move them to the right, turn aside on the contrary to the left, so it is with the soul; for the impulses of the acratic are in opposite directions' (1102b18–21). But how is the analogy exact? We need not take Aristotle to be pronouncing one way or the other upon whether acratic action ever occurs contrary to occurrent choice. As physical paralysis is a failure within the body that breaks the usual connection between choice and motion, so mental acrasia is a failure within the mind that breaks the usual connection between being resolved upon an end and attempting to realize it in action. What gets paralysed here? We shall learn that it is practical reason, which (either in the form of weakness or of impetuosity) loses its capacity to think through goals into acts. There is no ground here to take choice as itself one of the conflicting impulses: for all that is said, these may have general objects, say fineness against pleasure, and 7.3 allows the appeal of both of these still to be felt as the acratic action occurs. Nothing here contradicts what will be spelt out later.[37]

More troublesome are two remarks in the *Eudemian Ethics*: we read that the acratic agent enjoys getting what he desires, but is pained by the expectation that he will fare badly (2.8.1224b19–21), which implies a simultaneous awareness that he is not acting well; also that he finds fault with himself not just later (as in contrition), but at the moment of acting (7.6.1240b21–3).[38] It looks as if Aristotle is failing to maintain consistency on a delicate matter between different contexts. Do we have to say more than that even philo- sophers can lapse, on occasion, into common sense? He more often leaves open the focus of conflict. It is less troubling that the acratic have appetites for some things and wishes for others (*NE* 9.4.1166b7–8), for this is a kind of dividedness, directed at types rather than instances, that particular ignorance does not remove. As I noted in §2, there are two particularly vivid sentences (suggestive to us of billiards): desire and reasoning may each expel or 'knock out' the other (*EE* 2.8.1224b21–4); one desire may conquer and drive out another, like one ball hitting another (*DA* 3.11.434a12–14).[39] I take such talk of desires in conflict to leave the interpretative options open. The traditionalist understands from *Nicomachean Ethics* 7.3 that when a choice is put out of action, it is also put out of mind. Yet it in no way follows that the agent never feels 'torn apart' (cf. 9.4.1166b19–22); for choice, and the sensitivity on which it rests, are not likely to volatize at the mere breath of unruly appetite, but will struggle for supremacy and survival. We may imagine an agent who strives to keep in mind the salient feature of the situation, but succumbs to temptation and fails to keep it in focus. There may be a real distinction between hard and soft acrasia, and Aristotle may usually exclude the former; but this is not the same distinction as that between cases of felt conflict and cases of unconscious myopia.

I am happy to interpret Aristotle according to the traditional and natural reading of *Nicomachean Ethics* 7.3 to the extent that I can fathom his grounds. My conception of them was very briefly as follows: a properly deliberated choice expresses a reflective grasp upon a context of action that brings to bear all an agent's motivations; if his choice is overridden in action by emotion or appetite, his grasp loosens, leaving only a wrack of words behind. Essential to Aristotle's conception is that choice is all-things-considered, and that it commits the agent to action (unless he is prevented). If we can separate out these features, we may hold that choice as all-in practical judgement can clash with choice as effective impulse. Aristotle has some notion of the second: the acratic seek (*haireisthai*, cf. n. 10) not what seems to them good, but pleasant things that are harmful (9.4.1166b8–10). Yet he does not allow that all-in practical judgement can remain sincere even if becomes detached from effective impulse. In criticism of Socrates (in Chapter 1 § 2) I in effect asserted that it can do so; but Aristotle's position is more complex and reflected, and cannot be dismissed on a presumption. I believe that his very notion of practical judgement contains an irresoluble tension: judgement that involves all-in evaluation must be intimately related to the totality of an agent's desires; and yet, if it is indeed to be judgement, it must achieve a reflective distance from them that frees it from dependence upon their fluctuating intensities. Practicality cannot, without equivocation, be at once a feature of the *content* of practical judgement, and a matter of its *effect*. Of course this comment is cryptic and not truistic; it can here only be a gesture towards an objection. Aristotle is a philosopher of common sense who unfailingly leads us into intellectual territory where common sense is no longer a competent guide.

4

THE STOICS

1

As we trace developments through Socrates, Plato, and Aristotle, we are exploring a tradition that never defined itself as a body of doctrine. When we come to the Stoics, we meet a different tradition that at once took on the discipline of a school. The Stoa was founded at Athens, not long after Aristotle's death, by Zeno of Citium, who was followed at its head by Cleanthes, and Chrysippus. My main concern is Chrysippus, both because he wrote a lost but lengthy treatise *On the Affections* (*Peri pathôn*), and because fragments of it survive within Galen's *De placitis Hippocratis et Platonis* (*PHP*), a polemical work which has, ironically, become invaluable for the evidence it contains of the theory it rebuts. When I speak of 'Stoic' views, I shall primarily mean those of Chrysippus. I shall also pay attention to another writer for whom Galen has become a major source, Posidonius, a contemporary of Cicero (who knew him well, *TD* 2.61); he counted as a Stoic even though, if Galen is to believed, he reverted in a book also called *On the Affections* to the views of Plato and Aristotle. Cicero testifies that the early Stoics denied any division of the mind along Plato's lines, whether into parts or powers:

> Whereas the ancients said that those affections [distress, desire, dread, pride] were natural and not sharing in reason, and placed desire and reason in different parts of the mind, he [Zeno] did not agree with these either; for he thought that even the affections were voluntary, and entered into by a judgement of opinion.
>
> (*Acad* 1.39)

Before we can consider what may have motivated orthodox Stoics in

145

rejecting even what Aristotle accepted from Plato, we need to sketch their conception of intention (as, in effect, it is), and their application of it even to emotion.

The Stoics posited a series of events within the mental process leading to action, conceiving of them within a materialist philosophy of mind, but a partly immaterialist logic. Firstly, there is an impression or presentation (*phantasia*), which is at once a physical alteration of the mind's matter (which they took to be a 'fiery stuff' or *pneuma*), and the presentation of an incorporeal proposition (an assertoric 'sayable' or *lekton*).[1] Secondly, comes an assent (*synkatathesis*) to the proposition that the presentation presents. Thirdly, in the case that the proposition is practical, presenting some attainable object as good and so 'to be taken' (*haireton*) or some practicable action as beneficial and so 'to be chosen' (*haireteon*, the same verb with a different termination, *SVF* 3.22.19–23), the assent yields an impulse (*hormê*), or 'motion of thought to something or away from something' (3.92.4–5). This accords with the assent, and may be thought of as a self-addressed command (3.42.4–6 = Plutarch, *DSR* 1037F): if the assent was to the proposition that it is appropriate to Φ, the command to oneself is to Φ, and the impulse is towards the predicatively identified attribute Φ-ing (*katêgorêma*, *SVF* 3.91, 3.398 = Cicero, *TD* 4.21). Finally, if there is no external obstacle (*SVF* 2.290.34–5), there ensues the action of Φ-ing. Some of these states are causally distinct. Thus a presentation is *a* cause, though not *the* cause, of an assent: in Stoic jargon, it is its 'proximate' but not its 'principal' cause, occasioning it like a blow that sets a cylinder rolling but only according to its own nature (2.283.16–24 = LS 62C8 = Cicero, *On Fate* 42). Others are only notionally different: thus an impulse can be identified with an assent (*SVF* 3.40.27–8 = LS 33I1). The whole sequence constitutes the *hêgemonikon* or 'commanding faculty' of a man in action; indeed, the Stoics identify the action either with the extension of the *hêgemonikon* into the limb that moves, or simply with the *hêgemonikon* itself (*SVF* 2.227.40–2 = LS 53L = Seneca, *Letters* 113.23).

In applying this account to *all* adult action, in a manner that might seem artificial and schematizing, the Stoics were making explicit what is virtually the concept of intention that is familiar in modern philosophy.[2] To grasp the originality of this aspect of their theory, one may recall its absence from the almost equally elaborated psychology of Aristotle. Aristotle has two concepts for mapping the same region of psychological space: choice (*prohairesis*), which is narrower, since it entails prior deliberation (*NE* 3.3.1113a9–12), and the voluntary (*hekousios*), which is wider, since it applies to all actions that issue from desire, even (as we would say) against the agent's will.[3] In anticipating us, the Stoics were capturing perennial reality (as it is already evidenced in, for example, the role of decision in the minds of Homeric heroes; cf. Sharples 1983, Williams 1993: ch. 2). Even irrational action that is contrary to deliberation accords with intention – or it would not be action. It does not issue according to a play of psychic forces from which the subject could stand back (perhaps discovering the relative strengths of his desires from the upshot). The Stoics recognized that reason constitutes no privileged standpoint within the soul in relation to which irrational behaviour consists not of acts that it performs but of happenings that it perceives. We may regret that, in deriving all actions from impulses initiated by acts of assent, they tried to capture the notion of agency by multiplying acts (as if all and only internal acts are no problem). Yet we should recognize that, in inventing the myth of an act of will preceding every action, they were articulating the reality of intention.

The Stoics departed further from common sense when they applied their framework not only to evident actions, but to affections or passions (*pathê*). Of the affections Zeno gave four genera: appetite (*epithymia*), fear (*phobos*), pleasure (*hêdonê*), and distress (*lypê*, *SVF* 1.211). Some interpreters propose a single structure to accommodate all four, but the evidence rather supports a pair of accounts.[4] Arius Didymus relates the four as follows (in a report preserved by Stobaeus, *SVF* 3.92.15–21 = LS 65A):

> Appetite and fear come first, the former in relation to what appears good, and the latter in relation to what appears bad. Pleasure and distress result from these: pleasure, whenever we secure the objects of our appetite or avoid the objects of our fear; distress, whenever we fail to get the objects of our appetite or experience the objects of our fear.

So we may call appetite and fear 'primary' affections, and pleasure and distress 'secondary' ones. Andronicus gives the following definitions (*SVF* 3.391 = LS 65B, rearranged):

> Appetite is an irrational stretching [desire], or pursuit of an expected good.
> Fear is an irrational shrinking [aversion], or flight from an expected danger.

Pleasure is an irrational swelling, or a fresh opinion that something good is present, at which people think it right to be swollen [i.e., elated].
Distress is an irrational contraction or fresh opinion that something bad is present, at which people think it right to be contracted [i.e., depressed].

The primary affections have internal and external aspects: within the soul, identified materially with the *pneuma* in the heart, appetite is an *orexis* (a term that conveys at once physical stretching and mental desire), while fear is an *ekklisis* (which conveys at once physical shrinking and mental aversion); within the world, appetite seeks a supposed good, while fear flees a supposed evil. The secondary affections are provoked by things external but directed at things internal: pleasure is a swelling, or a thought demanding a swelling, at the presence of some supposed good; distress is a contraction, or a thought demanding a contraction, at the presence of some supposed evil. Primary affections motivate actions that pursue a purpose, whereas secondary ones cause motions that express a reaction. Yet it seems that, despite their differences, the primary and secondary affections share three aspects:

(a)   There is a false judgement about some object that is indifferent (neither good nor bad), but preferred or rejected (such as health or sickness, cf. LS 58). This is an opinion that holds both that it is good or bad, indeed extremely so (cf. *PHP* 264.11–16 = LS 65L2), and also either – if the affection is primary – that it is to be intensely pursued or shunned (*SVF* 3.104.31–5 = Cicero, *TD* 4.26), or else – if the affection is secondary – that it is the right sort of thing about which to have a contraction or swelling of the soul (*SVF* 3.95.30–3 = Cicero, *TD* 4.14).[5]
(b)   There is an impulse that may be called 'excessive' (*pleonazousa hormê*).
(c)   There is a psychic motion of the soul (whether it be stretching, shrinking, swelling, or contraction) which is a physical change in its *pneuma*.

Of these, (b) supervenes on (a), while (c) depends on (b); all three arrive together. How does (b) occur even within a secondary affection, and (c) even within a primary affection? I conjecture that the stretching or shrinking of a primary affection *is* the impulse (cf. 'that kind of motion and the impulses according to it', *PHP*

256.11–12), while the swelling or contraction of a secondary affection *is initiated by* the impulse. Just as a thought approving an action produces that action through an impulse, so it must be through an impulse that a thought approving a swelling or contraction produces that motion; Chrysippus actually writes of 'the impulse towards the contraction' (284.9 = LS 65O2).[6] Within the primary affections, the internal motion of the *pneuma* is also an impulse aiming outside. Within the secondary affections, the impulse is towards the internal motion. This may well have external manifestations (such as the 'extravagant gaiety' that accompanies pleasure, *SVF* 3.93.6–7 = Cicero, *TD* 4.15, or weeping out of distress), which are themselves as voluntary as the motion itself; but it does not seem to constitute a further impulse towards external action securing a good or evading an evil.[7] We may suppose the initial impulse to be a mini-motion that is slight in itself and yet sufficient, since its object is only internal or symptomatic, to be excessive in its effect (though I know of no explicit evidence); if so, the secondary affections, too, may count as excessive impulses. Judgement, impulse, and psychic motion form a multiplicity that permitted a variety of emphases: Galen tells us that Chrysippus identified affections with 'judgements of a kind', while Zeno and others identified them with the psychic motions 'following on judgements' (*PHP* 246.38–248.3 = LS 65K1); yet affections are commonly identified with excessive impulses (*SVF* 1.205, 3.92.5, 3.92.11 = LS 65A1). Given that the three aspects are links in a single chain of determination, it is hard to see that this was an issue. So it seems that Chrysippus read Zeno as identifying affections with judgements (*SVF* 1.212 = Cicero, *TD* 3.74–5 and *PHP* 280.21–6), and yet was willing himself to identify the affection either with the impulse (240.13, 260.32), or with the psychic motion (240.3–5 = LS 65D4). As Aristotle might have put it, the three aspects are three in definition, but one in reality: one and the same psycho-physical entity may be indicated in any of these ways.

The excessive nature of the affection is conveyed in many phrases, which one must be careful not to interpret inappropriately. The impulse is 'carried away and disobedient to reason' (*SVF* 3.92.6) in that it disregards right reason from the first, and soon escapes recall by any reason (possibilities that I shall try to clarify later). It is not that a man's reason says one thing while his affections say another: rather, affections are 'perversions of reason and mistaken judgements of reason' (3.93.17–18). Making one blind to evident facts, they 'knock out' reasonings and opposite presentations (3.95.1–4 = Plutarch, *DVM*

450C), not in Aristotle's sense of defeating an opposing force (*EE* 2.8.1224b23–4), but in that of displacing them altogether. They exercise compulsion (*SVF* 3.93.25 = Plutarch, *DVM* 449C, *SVF* 3.94.27 = LS 65A6, *SVF* 3.95.12–13 = Plutarch, *DVM* 450C, *SVF* 3.95.26–7), 'forcibly propelling' the opposite acts (3.95.4–5 = Plutarch, *DVM* 450C) 'in a disorderly manner' (*SVF* 3.95.38), or 'throwing off the reins' (*PHP* 244.6, 262.26–7). Galen ascribes this last way of speaking, if only in indirect speech, to Chrysippus himself. This has been viewed sceptically, but one should not underestimate his willingness to take on board ways of speaking that threaten to sink his boat. We must suppose that he had in mind a perverted reason that throws off the restraints of reasonableness. It is thus that we also should understand a simile in Arius of the rider carried away by a disobedient horse (*SVF* 3.94.29 = LS 65A6). It marks their distance from Plato and Aristotle that most Stoics did not hesitate to deny affections, strictly so called, to animals and even to children (*PHP* 294.17–20): affections are deformations of reason, and belong within the repertory only of rational agents.

This account of the secondary affections at once raises two questions. Firstly, what are the content and application of the notion, mentioned by Andronicus, of a 'fresh opinion'? Cicero makes it clear that the freshness consists not, in itself, of a small elapse of time since the opinion's acquisition, but of a 'greenness' (*viriditas*) that can last: he cites the widow Artemisia, who lived and died in sorrow, so that her grief was 'fresh every day' (*TD* 3.75). The term 'fresh' is occasionally attached to the object of the affection instead of to the opinion that helps constitute it (*SVF* 3.95.42–3, 3.96.1; also *TD* 3.26 unless emended). This variation may be careless, but seems innocuous so long as it remains true that the freshness is a matter of subjectivity and selective attention, and not of objective timing. The term is always used only of the secondary affections (with one exception that seems to be a mistake); hence it can actually be glossed by Arius as 'stimulative of an irrational contraction or swelling' (*SVF* 3.92.23 = LS 65C).[8] The restriction seems artificial: precisely if what counts is the vividness and not the timing of the object, surely all affections are (and must be) 'fresh' in a natural sense, appetite and fear as well as pleasure and distress. However, this may depend on the terms of the comparison: any affection might count as 'fresh' compared to any dispassionate opinion, but, within the Andronican definitions (*SVF* 3.391 = LS 65B), pleasure and distress owe a special freshness to the 'presence' of their objects. Secondly, one must ask in what sense 'swellings' and 'contractions' can be ordinary objects of impulse. It may surprise us to find them figuring not just as postulates within a materialist metaphysic, but as intentional objects of common experience, so that emotive presentations both cause, and make us will, our souls to contract or expand. As objects of impulse, they presumably need to be understood impressionistically in a way that fits at once Stoic and folk psychology. One may recall familiar turns of phrase of our own such as 'feel elated' or 'feel depressed', which capture mental reality by physical metaphor. One may also compare Cicero's paraphrase of 'contract' by 'be cast down and shrunken in mind' ('demitti contrahique animo', *SVF* 3.95.31 = *TD* 4.14, where 'animo' implies a reading of 'demitti' and 'contrahi' that is at least in part metaphorical). Once one distinguishes the aspects, even without any metaphysical dualism, it becomes natural to suggest that the contraction that is a common intentional object of impulse is mental and metaphorical, even if the causal effect of the impulse is a literal and physical contraction. Yet the subject may count as being aware of the physical motion in the sense that it is felt and registered in his consciousness, even though he is not thereby aware what kind of thing he is aware of.

We have seen that there are two levels of misjudgement, the first (overestimating some object) common to all the affections, the second (inviting either external or internal motion) differentiating the primary from the secondary. It is true that the one level connects with the other through natural associations, and it might even be taken as criterial of really ascribing *extreme* value to a preferred indifferent that one supposes that its absence demands keen pursuit, and its presence a grateful swelling of the heart. And yet the distinction between the two levels invites the question whether a subject might not falsely judge an intense response, external or internal, appropriate in response to a real and so (according to the Stoics) moral good or evil. Cicero blames Cleanthes for overlooking that affections can be provoked by thoughts of virtue and vice, citing Alcibiades, who was thrown into tears by realizing that he lacked virtue (*TD* 3.77–8, cf. 4.61–2) and through failing to grasp that his evaluation of virtue was right but his contraction at the thought of lacking it wrong. As it happens, Cicero claims that philosophers are wiser than to be thrown into distress by the realization that they have yet to achieve wisdom (3.68–71), but a prentice philosopher might well need to be persuaded to desire wisdom without feeling pain. It may be that Chrysippus appreciated the point, for Cicero tells us that, while Cleanthes held that the only cure for distress was ceasing to believe in the presence of something bad, he thought that the first task was ceasing to believe that it made a contraction appropriate (3.76).

Is it an implication of the Stoic account that affections *are* actions? Suppose that we take as paradigmatic actions of the most familiar kind, for example, closing a door *post* and *propter* an appropriate sequence of presentation, assent, and impulse. Strictly analogous to this can only be a secondary affection (like pleasure and distress), and only if (as Chrysippus reports of Zeno, *PHP* 246.39–248.3 = LS 65K1) that is identified with the swelling or contraction to which there is an impulse consequent on a presentation and identical to an assent; then a secondary affection turns out to be an internal action in precisely the same sense in which closing a door is an external action. The analogy is weakened if it is really indifferent whether the secondary affection be identified with judgement, impulse, or swelling or contraction, and it is weaker still in the case of the primary affections (like appetite and fear). However, the thought of Zeno's from which I started, that even the emotions are voluntary, is associated by Cicero (*Acad* 1.39) not with his special view of the secondary affections, but with his general view that all affections depend on judgement. If we shift from the precise question whether affections are identical to actions to the vague one whether agents identify with their affections, we can see that the general view is enough to do a lot of work. Firstly, the agent is denied the option of retreating from his affections into his reason: affection is no less an activity of reason than reasoning is. Secondly, affection shares with all belief the element of an act of assent. While this internal act cannot, on pain of a regress, constitute an action in the manner of the external action of closing a door, that is through resulting from some previous act of assent, yet the element of assent remains the fulcrum of identification between agent and affection. On the Stoic account, affections cease to be passive: emotion is a field of free and fully human activity.

2

A philosophical theory is in some ways an artefact, an invented construct that accommodates the raw materials of experience in a manner that need not contradict alternatives. To understand such a theory is not just to articulate its structure, but to grasp why it might be preferred, or what, besides inventiveness, motivates it. Ideally, it may be possible to identify some actual point of disagreement, say some neutrally describable possibility that will be registered as a datum by one theory, and dismissed as a fiction by another. Alternatively, it may be that the theory's goal is less to hit the target of truth, to get things right, than to direct us in a new way, to put us right. I shall not be concerned with the practical moral that the Stoics drew from their remapping of the mind, almost all-important to them though it was, but rather with points that they might have put to Plato and Aristotle to persuade them of the faithfulness of Stoic psychology to psychic reality and moral practice as these already existed for all of them. What I am in search of is at once explanation and at least partial justification, for these are likely to go together within any philosophy that deserves to be remembered: an ostensible motivation that is in fact without ground may have been real, but risks showing up as rationalizing.

One possibility is that the Stoics wished to extend the area of human *rationality*. Various texts convey the thought that all the operations of the adult human mind are distinctively human, and so alien to any powers separate from reason that we might share with animals. Reason is a 'collection of certain conceptions and precon-ceptions' (*PHP* 304.35 = LS 53V; for the distinction, cf. LS 39E). Part of the force of likening the senses in relation to the commanding faculty to the tentacles of an octopus (*SVF* 2.227.25–7) must be that our perceptions are applications of concepts. All the presentations of rational animals are rational (2.24.21–2 = LS 39A6), and what they present are propositions (*lekta*). All their impulses are rational (*SVF* 3.42.4–6 = LS 53R = Plutarch, *DSR* 1037F), and they are directed at attributes identified by predicates. In Justin Gosling's paraphrase, an adult human impulse 'is directed at an objective in accordance with a conception of it' (1990: 52). Our intelligence permeates the whole of our mental life in a way that transforms it as we grow up into our humanity, grasping first concepts, then higher concepts.

Yet is this enough to identify a disagreement? Martha Nussbaum offers an argument from rationality against partition: complex emo-tions require the conceptual capacities of reason; but then, unless we are to redouble faculties, reason seems the place in which to house emotion (1987: 151–2); so Platonism must either deny the intelli-gence of emotion (which is false), or multiply faculties (which is extravagant). This has some force against a partition of the mind that locates its parts in different locations within the body: Plato would at least need to explain how rationality suffuses the whole body, to a greater or lesser extent, without there being three brains, in head, breast, and belly. (Possibly he could give an account analogous to his descriptions of how each sense-perception affects the soul as a whole: sound causes a motion that starts in the head, close to reason, and ends in the liver, close to appetite, *Tim* 67b2–5; likewise, our single brain might be a resource tapped by every part of the mind, if unequally.) Yet that parts can share faculties is not excluded but presupposed: conflict in belief or in desire implies not only that each part can form desires and beliefs, but that these share at least some concepts; for otherwise the kind of mental conflict that Plato and Aristotle describe – whether it takes the form of contrariety or of confrontation – would be impossible.[9]

To set Plato and Aristotle in relation to the early Stoics, it may help to draw on a later Stoic who resumed talk of tripartition of a kind within Stoic terminology. Galen relates Posidonius as follows to predecessors of other schools:

> Posidonius and Aristotle grant that the powers of the soul are three in number, and that by them we desire, feel anger, and reason; but that they are also spatially separate from each other, and that our soul not only contains many powers but is composed of parts that differ in kind and in substance, this is the doctrine of Hippocrates and Plato.
>
> (*PHP* 312.29–34)

Posidonius seems to have supposed that if reason can discourse with spirit they are two different things in a sense denied by Chrysippus (332.20–31 = LS 65I1–3). If even rational thinking can take the form of an internal dialogue (cf. Plato, *Theaet* 189e4–7, *Soph* 263e3–5), that yields indefinite division. Plato's criterion is more demanding, requiring a tendency to conflict and not just a capacity for conversation: if spirit becomes an 'ally' of reason against appetite, there are three interlocutors but only two factions (*Rep* 4.440a8–b4); it is only because reason and spirit have a natural tendency to be at odds that they count for Plato as two different parts (cf. 441a4–c2). Here Posidonius looks careless (or Galen unreliable). What is he unable reflectively to accept in Plato? At least, it appears, a spatial division of parts.[10] (I shall make a further suggestion in §5, and support it in an appendix.) About the motivations characteristic of the three parts or powers, Posidonius appears to have followed Plato and Aristotle. They had assigned different goals to different parts of the soul: reason aims primarily at truth, though also at the realization of what Aristotle calls practical truth; spirit tends to aggression and self-righteousness (making us angry and telling us that we *must* put up a fight); appetite aims at physical pleasure. Posidonius agrees that the affective soul has its own proper (*oikeios*) objects of desire (*PHP* 288.9 = LS 65P2): one of its powers aims at pleasure, the other at mastery and victory (*PHP* 288.14–16); the proper desirables of the animal-like soul are pleasure and mastery over one's neighbour, but of the rational and divine soul wisdom and all that is good and fine (330.2–6 = LS 65N). Using the Platonic language of 'parts' but the Stoic language of 'orientation' (*oikeiôsis*), Galen puts this as follows: 'There are these three things towards which we feel a natural orientation, corresponding to each form of the soul's parts: pleasure through the appetitive form, victory through the spirited form, and the fine through the rational form' (*PHP* 318.12–15 = LS 65M1; cf. Kidd 1988: ii. 574–6). The standard Stoic position was that such different mental sets are successive and not synchronous (cf. LS 57B3 = Seneca, *Letters* 121.15): as the individual develops, more primitive concepts or conceptions are subsumed under more sophisticated ones. Posidonius insists that the adult never wholly outgrows the child, alleging two ways in which the non-rational soul remains distinctive in its mode of operation: it is stimulated not by rational persuasion but by some graphic representation like a perception (*PHP* 330.25–31 = LS 65Q3–4), and it moves and rests within a cycle of pursuit and satiation (*PHP* 288.9–12 = LS 65P2). He thus extends throughout the affections paradigmatic features of the appetites.

This final point invites a contrast with Chrysippus that is at last concrete. It was problematic for him to explain how affections tend to abate with time: why should it be that, as time passes, the opinion loses its freshness so that the impulse towards the contraction falls away (*PHP* 284.8–9 = LS 65O2)? We may compare Aristotle, who, holding hatred to be a rational affection, claims that it differs from anger in not being cured by time (*Rhet* 2.4.1382a7–8). It fits the Stoic emphasis upon rational persuasion that Cicero insists that the cause is not the mere passage of time ('non ipsa diuturnitas') but continued reflection ('cogitatio diuturna', *TD* 3.74): reflection serves to place the object of the affection within a truer and wider perspective, so that it no longer appears either a proper goal of intense pursuit, or a proper occasion of a swelling or contraction. We may envisage that, even before reason can fully resume its reign, prudent presentations pave the way for its gradual restoration, and the eventual recovery of self-mastery. Posidonius, on the other hand, allows for a recovery from affection that is both more rapid, and independent of reflection (rather as I lose my hunger as I eat, without having to wait for the assessment 'That was a nourishing meal'). This looks like an empirical issue, if not one instantly resolved by appeal to experience. However, Chrysippus again eludes easy capture. He allows a simile of sating, 'In the case of distress some seem similarly to take leave of it as though sated', and illustrates it from Homer (*PHP* 286.12–16). What follows is more analytical: 'By this account a person would not give up hope that with the passage of time, when the inflammation of the affection has abated, reason will make its way in and find room, so to speak, and expose the irrationality of the affection' (286.18–21). Here the affection's importunacy is assigned a physical cause: 'the inflammation of the affection' is not a metaphor, but describes a state of the *pneuma*. Thus Chrysippus supposes the abating of a physical process with its own momentum where Posidonius alleges the sating of a mental drive with its own goals. Both can explain the different rhythms of rational and irrational desires in their own terms: within Posidonius, reason is the divinity in ourselves akin to the untiring divinity that rules the whole universe, while the non-rational soul shares the changing life of the beasts (326.20–7); within Chrysippus, it is the excessive motions of affection, and not the calmer motions of reason, that tend to cycles of 'stop–go'.

Posidonius is faithful both to Plato and to Aristotle when he remarks that our non-rational powers are 'clearly seen also' in the lower animals (288.14–17), and indeed that the lower element of the human soul shows up 'animal-like' (*zô(i)ôdês*) in comparison with the divine element (330.4–6 = LS 65N). This entails no denial that spirit and appetite take on within the human soul distinctively human forms. It is particularly clear of spirit that it ceases to be a mere instinct towards aggression, and takes on sophisticated goals (e.g., glory) and directives (e.g., universal, if too general, principles) which display an intelligence that, though not the highest of which men are capable, is yet peculiarly human. Intelligence does not permeate our souls uniformly, for reason has a richer logical and conceptual repertory than spirit, and a far richer one than appetite. We may speak equivalently either of a rational capacity which is variably realized within the three parts or powers, or of a capacity of reason's which spirit and appetite imperfectly incorporate for their own ends. The early Stoic account sounds very different – but is the difference substantial? It indiscriminately makes all practical thoughts judgements of what is right or appropriate; however, as I have argued, Plato and Aristotle can allow even appetite to aim at the good, so long as its conception of goodness identifies the good with pleasure. 'Good' and 'appropriate' label a goal that is only determinable, just as truth is the formal target of any belief, however ill-founded. Chrysippus insists more than anyone that affection is irrational: even though an affection is a judgement in a way, it is also, in another sense, without judgement, that is, without reasoning or circumspection (*PHP* 248.14–25), being an unreflective assent to a presentation that is vivid and fairly primitive. All these philosophers recognize in our passions and appetites thought-patterns that display, by reason's standards, varying degrees of stupidity. They theorize this recognition variously, but it does not itself explain the difference between their theories.

3

Mental conflict is so much part of our experience, and the Platonic picture of the mind as a field of warring factions can appear to do it so much justice, that denial of the picture may seem to us perverse (as it did to Plutarch and Galen). And yet it is worth exploring the possibility that the Stoics may have hoped to capture the *phenomenology* of a divided mind (that is, what it is like to be subject to mental division) in a way that would not imply that a mind has parts.[11] In this section, I shall reflect on the standard Stoic picture according to which desires conflict not at a time, but over time.

It is not evident how our shared phenomenology is to be investigated. One need not be a disciple of Wittgenstein to doubt whether the proper means is simply introspection: looking within oneself is in itself private, while what we are after must be applicable, and communicable, to others. Galen complains repeatedly that Chrysippus' fondness for literary quotation was unscientific (*PHP* 178.1–6, 192.3–6, 196.5–14, 198.23–5, 198.33–200.17), but we may suppose that he deliberately chose a form of confirmation that was at the same time a means of communication. He clearly cited widely, relevantly for us about characters in conflict: Odysseus in Homer, Menelaus and most famously Medea in Euripides (Odysseus: 184.14–23, 188.11–16, 190.12–14; Menelaus: 272.3–19; Medea: 188.17–18, 190.12–15, 274.10–17). The general pattern that he extracted to set against the Platonic picture of synchronous conflict between parts in confrontation was one of diachronous vacillation between conflicting

157

resolutions. Euripides' Menelaus, who draws his sword to kill Helen and kisses her instead, acts, by a nice paradox, at once rebelliously and yieldingly (272.10–18): through weakness of soul, and not after rational persuasion, he discards a previous judgement and adopts an external prompting. Our best evidence here comes from Plutarch's *De virtute morali*. According to his understanding of Stoic theory (of which he is as critical as Galen), weakness is manifested not in the defeat of reason at the hands of an irrational part of the soul, but in the inconstancy of a reason 'that wholly turns around and changes' (*DVM* 441C = *SVF* 3.111.17–20 = LS 61B9). He even reports, as what 'some say', an accelerated version of the same sequence: a turning of the same reason in each direction escapes our notice through the abruptness and swiftness of the change; they compared the sudden assaults of children who are violent out of weakness (*DVM* 446F-447A = *SVF* 3.111.27–38 = LS 65G). This nicely fits one distinctive term that Zeno applied to the affections, 'fluttering' (*ptoia*, *SVF* 1.51.2, 3.92.13–14 = LS 65A2, cf. *PHP* 260.16–18): one may compare a trill in music, which, if fast enough, would sound like a chord if it were not for a peculiar vibrancy. Plutarch objects that this contradicts the clear evidence of our perceptions (by which he has in mind our inner experience): reason does not disappear in the face of affection, but confronts it, so that the agent is carried back and forth from one to the other, lying between them and sharing in both (*DVM* 447A-B). But might it not be a rapid alternation between contraries that yields the experience of feeling torn apart (cf. Aristotle, *NE* 9.4.1166b18–25)? There might only be a difference in timing between cases in which one's own agency is so rapid as to escape one's notice, and more leisurely cases, like that of Menelaus, in which the agent is consciously active, 'without judgement or reasoning setting his course towards the very opposite of what he had originally decided on' (Chrysippus, *PHP* 272.16–17).[12]

The Stoics accordingly reconceived strength of will (*enkrateia*) as constancy over time: it is 'an unconquerable character [*diathesis*] in respect of what appears according to right reason' (*SVF* 3.67.20–1, cf. 3.67.45–68.1). Correspondingly, weakness of will (*acrasia*) is a close relation of what Epictetus calls folly (*aphrosynê*):

> At one time you think of these things as good, and then of the same things as bad, and later as neither; and, in general, you are subject to pain, fear, envy, turmoil, and change; this is why you admit you are foolish.
>
> (*Disc* 2.22.6–7, cf. 22.25)

More precisely, folly is classified among the 'primary' vices, consisting of a lack of knowledge or of expertise, while weakness of will counts as a 'secondary one' (*SVF* 3.23.32–5, 3.65.17–19): the weak man lacks the strength of soul, at once mental and physical, that consists of a tension (*tonos*) that is sufficient for correct judging and acting (3.68.30–1).[13] Like the angry or inconsolable Achilles, he frequently abandons his correct judgements according to circumstance (*PHP* 278.24–5). Beauty of soul is a harmony and constancy (*SVF* 3.68.41–3 = Cicero, *TD* 4.31, *SVF* 3.95.28–9) between the 'parts' or 'proper divisions' that constitute its reason (*PHP* 304.10–11, 19–21); that is, between the conceptions and preconceptions of which its reason is a collection (304.35). This beauty is lacking to a soul that vacillates in the manner that Epictetus describes. Logically, this picture of acrasia has its advantage: it hopes to elude Plato's principle for dividing the soul (*Rep* 4.436b8–9), which demands simultaneous conflict. Phenomenologically, it at once fits one prevalent pattern of weakness of mind, that of irresolution, and it can be made to fit others.

Right reason may be discarded blindly: as if he were no longer the same person, the agent becomes blind to what had previously weighed with him (*PHP* 280.6–9). More often, however, he is described not merely as disobeying but as rejecting reason, a complex attitude of denial towards the awareness of reason that it betrays. His irrationality means '"disobedient to reason" and "reason turned aside"' (240.23–4 = LS 65J4), a stance that combines an involuntary awareness with an intended blindness. Christopher Gill nicely compares the attitude of denial that Leontius (*Rep* 4.440a2–3) adopts towards his necrophilic desires, at the same time as he consents to them, in ascribing them to his eyes (1983: 147 n. 24). Precisely how to capture the state of mind of those who are consciously irrational becomes a fine point: it is difficult to deny that there can be a synchronous conflict between the biddings of reason and the impulses of affection, with the latter disobeying the former and the former confronting the latter. Loss of control may explain why reason loses, but does not explain away the confrontation. Yet presumably the rejection of reason has to be glossed not as disobedience to an occurrent command, with the agent simultaneously ruler and rebel, but as disregard of what the agent is aware he *would be* commanding if he were still rational. Thus Gill glosses rejection of reason as 'a recognition, but deliberate rejection, of what a reasonable human being would do in these circumstances' (1983: 141). In the case not of involuntary motion but of intentional action, one senses that one has lost control of oneself not by doing one thing while willing another, but by willing one thing with an awareness that willing something else would be more rational but is no longer an option. Vacillation permits a memory of a conflicting judgement, and even a recognition of its rationality. One's present self may remember a judgement of a past self, and respect it without being able to accept it (rather as, on the Platonic model, one part of the soul may register, and yet reject, the preference of another part). Through memory, the Stoics hoped to reconcile awareness of conflict with an absence of synchronous conflict.

This has been very abstract, and it may clarify the options to recall a particular example, that of Medea as presented within her monologue in Euripides' play (*Medea* 1021–80). As I observed in my Introduction, his presentation of most of her conflict as a series of shifts and turns is unsurprising: an actor has only a single voice, and synchronous conflict can only be communicated through translation into diachronous indecision or oscillation. And yet the effect must certainly have been sweet to Stoic ears. Medea's transitions are extreme and abrupt; except that each switch of mind has to last long enough to be communicated to an audience, her speech well exemplifies a sense of being torn apart arising from a rapid alternation between opposites. A Stoic account will take Medea to be rehearsing two sets of presentations, both equally rational up to a point, with no ability to integrate them into a reflective equilibrium. If she is merely oscillating, her mind is made up, and her assent fixed; yet she can still feel the pull of the presentations that she resists. If she is vacillating between alternative acts of assent, the conflicting presentations are also conflicting options. What, however, of her eventual state of mind (a termination that no Greek moralist would think rational enough to constitute any real resolution)? Galen had no doubt that it was a refutation of Chrysippus from experience, if only fictional (*PHP* 274.10–24). Yet might it lend itself to recognizably Stoic sense? Medea displays an intricate interplay of passivity and activity. Rival presentations come to her unchosen and yet invited. She herself has her children brought out to her (*Medea* 1019–20), and she freely feasts her eyes and other senses upon them (1069–72); at other times she calls them up in her imagination (as at 1065–6). Finally, she feels carried away – by herself. She recognizes the evil aspects of what she is resolved to do (which falls short of judging that it is evil overall), but is unable or unwilling to focus upon them in order to rethink her resolve. Her anger may be winning out in two ways, corresponding to the two readings of the ambiguous line 'My heart is master of my deliberations' (1079): these deliberations may be that subset of her reflections (those dwelling on the charms of her children) that has just preceded (1069–75), with the thought that they are losing out to those deliberations that demand revenge (as at 1062–4); or they may be her overall deliberations and eventual decision (as at 1044, 1048), with the thought that her anger is dictating her deliberations and intentions come what may. In either case, the anger is not an alien force within her: on the contrary, she has been stirring it up herself, combating, for instance, the sweet sight of her children with the still sweeter image of her murdered rival (1065–75). As Gill well observes, 'Medea, on these occasions, combines reasons and feelings in an attempt (partly by persuasive self-description) to make one of her possible selves the dominant one, and the one who takes effective action' (1983: 142). She is now like the runner carried away by the momentum of his own body (*PHP* 242.2–8 = LS 65J7–9, *PHP* 256.7–9, 276.34–278.2), for she cannot recall her anger, nor even sum up against it, however well she may remember that, in a different mood, she has just recoiled from its consequences. So elaborated, Chrysippus' account appears to do justice at once to Medea's directive intelligence and to her eventual impotence.

We may conclude that the Stoics cannot fairly be refuted by any easy appeal to experience, fictional or real. Nevertheless, it seems that they conceded that the appearances can be Platonic: as Plutarch records their view, mental conflict may apparently occur at a time, though in reality it takes place over a time that may be very brief. However, such refinements rather confirm Stoic ingenuity than explain Stoic motivation: why should they have rejected the appearances? If we are to understand why they say what they do, we have to look further.

4

A clearer gain in the Stoic account is an enlargement of the region of *responsibility*. If affections are internal activities (and some of them perhaps even internal actions), we can aptly hold individuals responsible both for the external actions that they cause, and for the internal states that they involve; and we do, pre-theoretically, commonly praise and blame one another for both (saying not only 'You ought not to have bitten the carpet', but also 'You ought not to have been upset'). Thus Cicero gives as the purpose of defining the affections as varieties of belief (which the Stoics held to involve an act of assent) that this should convey not only how faulty they are, but also how much they are under our control (*SVF* 3.92.32–93.3 = *TD* 4.14). All the elements in the sequence that produces visible action are ascribed to a single mental agency, the *hêgemonikon* or 'commanding faculty' of man, which possesses a single rational capacity whose exercise is multifarious. Simplicius records a Stoic definition of a 'power' or 'capacity' (*dynamis*) as 'that which brings on a plurality of occurrences and controls the activities subordinate to it' (*SVF* 3.49.16–18 = *CIAG* 8.224.27–8), and among the activities of the *hêgemonikon* are propositional presentation and assent, impulse, and action. We need not take their unification to be arbitrary: reflection and decision at least typically come together at one focal point where all practical considerations can be rationally registered and resolved. It was a bolder move to attach emotions to the same point, but one that fits at least one response to emotions, moral evaluation, that is otherwise problematic.

Of course there is a cost in plausibility: while not *all* affections are evidently passive, surely *some* are. The Stoics qualify their position by admitting an exception: 'preliminary affections' (*propatheiai*) are affections (*pathê*) only with a qualification, for they are unchosen responses, strictly belonging to the body (Seneca, *Letters* 71.29), to which even the sage remains liable, since it may not be in his power not to be 'bitten' by some presentation (Epictetus, *Disc* 3.24.108). Seneca reports already from Zeno that the mind of the wise man retains as it were a scar after the wound, so that he feels 'certain intimations and shadows of affections' ('suspiciones quasdam et umbras affectuum') though not the affections themselves (*SVF* 1.215 = *Ira* 1.16.7, cf. *Letters* 58.4). In an equally memorable phrase, Cicero concedes that, even after the 'invitation' to grief has been removed, there will still remain 'stings and certain slight contractions of soul' ('morsus tamen et contractiunculae quaedam animi', *TD* 3.83). Thus a Latin derivative from a lost book of Epictetus' *Discourses* (LS 65Y) describes how 'a frightening sound from the sky or from a falling building' will briefly trouble the mind of the sage with 'certain rapid and unreflective motions which forestall the proper function of mind and reason', until he reflects that he really has nothing to fear; however, only the fool additionally attaches assent (*prosepidoxazei*). Two examples from his surviving *Discourses* are sexual attraction (2.20.19), and an eagerness to address another (2.24.16). Chrysippus may aptly have cited laughing (cf. *PHP* 284.16 = LS 65O4); as Aristotle already noted (*NE* 7.7.1150b10–12), attempts to restrain laughter tend to produce an explosion (what the French call 'fou rire'). This concession about affection is the exact analogue of one that Aristotle makes about motion: 'involuntary' motions of the heart in fear, and of the penis in sexual arousal, are provoked by the appearance of some object before the mind without thought's 'commanding' any flight or pursuit (*DA* 3.9.432b29–433a1, *DMA* 11.703b4–8). The Stoics take most emotional responses to presentations to be voluntary, while Aristotle takes most motions following on desire to be voluntary, but both have to concede exceptions. For both, the gap between the standard cases and the exceptional ones is wide: within the soul as within the body, a motion does not amount to an action where there is no will or desire both directed towards it and causing it. However vivid their phenomenology, preliminary affections on their own are neither mental acts nor causes of external actions.

Aristotle can hope to make out a claim that the affections themselves are voluntary by a complication that he shares with the Stoics. In effect, his view is that they are indirectly voluntary: our characters constitute our susceptibility to the affections (*EE* 2.2.1220b7–20), and our past activities have determined our present characters (*NE* 3.5.1114a4–12). It does not follow that our present affections are within our present power: he compares the stone that leaves our control as we throw it (a17–19).[14] The Stoics shorten the relevant time-span: not only the general tendency, but each emotional occurrence, is voluntary in origin (cf. Cicero, *Acad* 1.39). Yet Chrysippus writes that emotions tend to become 'out of control' (literally, *akrateis* or 'acratic'), 'as if the men had no power over themselves but were carried away' (*PHP* 256.7–8). Love (276.7–25) and anger (278.32–280.6) make us resemble runners who continue moving even against their will.[15] Seneca compares those who plunge into anger or love to bodies cast from precipices (*Ira* 1.7.4, cf. Cicero, *TD* 4.41). Again, wittingly or not, the Stoics are applying a move of Aristotle's within a new context: in *On Memory*, he argues for a physical aspect to the operation of memory from the fact that an unsuccessful effort to recollect leaves a felt discomfort even after it has been renounced, again comparing one's inability to halt a stone after it has been thrown (2.453a14–23). He comes close to anticipating the Stoics when he adds: 'This is the reason why attacks of anger or fear also, when once they have begun a motion, do not settle down in the face of counter-motions, but press on in the same direction' (a26–8); what is lacking is precisely any claim that episodes of emotion are initiated by choice. The Stoics' general claim that emotion is a free activity permits a recognition that it tends to run out of control: if it is true of emotion, it is also true of action, that one may be unable to stop what one has once started.

There is more to be said about what it can come to in the Stoic view, cognitively, emotionally, and physically, for one's affections to become 'out of control' (*akrateis*, *PHP* 256.7). The expression is recurrent and not inadvertent, and etymology made inescapable the thought that 'acratic' states are those of agents who are no longer in control of themselves (256.7–8, 276.37–278.1). Affection is wilful in its origin: like a runaway horse, it 'throws off the reins and departs and disobeys the command' (244.6–7); Arius compares every affection to 'a disobedient horse' (*SVF* 3.94.29 = LS 65A6) – disobedient, I have suggested (in §4), to what reason would command if it were allowed a voice. Yet it is often involuntary in its continuation: those who indulge their affections resemble runners who cannot stop, while those who are guided by reason are like walkers who can stop as they choose (*PHP* 256.7–32). How is this to be explained without partition? Relevant up to a point, but then restricted, is a passage that Galen quotes from Chrysippus' *On the Affections*:

> Someone might inquire about how the abatement of distress comes about, whether because of the alteration of some opinion or in spite of the continuance of all opinions, and why this will be so. I think that this kind of opinion does persist – that what is actually present is an evil – but as it grows older the contraction and, as I take it, the impulse towards the contraction, lessen. But it may be that even when this persists the consequences will not correspond because a differently qualified disposition supervenes, which does not reason from those events. So it is that people cease weeping and people weep who do not want to, when different presentations are created by external objects, and something or nothing stands in the way.
> (*PHP* 284.5–13 = LS 65O2–4)

Here it appears to be Chrysippus' own preferred diagnosis that the evaluative opinion 'What is actually present is an evil' remains, while the practical opinion 'This merits a contraction' (which is identical to an impulse towards a contraction) falls away with time. However, he admits that he cannot exclude the possibility that the contraction and the weeping that betrays it may cease even though the impulse continues, through the intervention of quite other considerations (say, distractions that take my mind off my misfortune without persuading me that the contraction is inapposite).[16] Loss of self-control in the form of a stampede and not a stand-still is exemplified by the converse case: though my impulse is not to grieve, sad sights or imaginings may force my tears to flow. However, while we would count this as emotional acrasia, orthodox Stoics would deny that it is strictly an instance of grief, just because judgement constituting impulse is lacking; they would class weeping in response to some presentation but without any impulse to grieve as a 'preliminary affection' or *propatheia*. For a mismatch between negative impulse and actual affection we have rather to look to a passage in Arius which says that people continue to be grieved or afraid even after they have been persuaded that they ought not to be (*SVF* 3.94.39–41 = LS 65A8). Now it is highly unlikely that the Stoics envisaged a divorce between judgement and impulse: that would imply a need for ways of manipulating impulse even after judgement has been persuaded, whereas Stoic therapy was standardly by way of rational persuasion (cf., e.g., *PHP* 286.17–18).[17] (Here they reject a common opinion cited by Aristotle that the acratic are less curable than the wicked since they cannot be persuaded to act otherwise, for they act as they do despite being so persuaded; he nicely invokes a proverb, 'When water chokes, what must one drink to wash it down?', *NE* 7.2.1146a31-b2.) They would also insist that a swelling or contraction can only constitute an affection if it follows on judgement and impulse. Yet it would seem consistent for them to admit that judgement and impulse together may be unable to revoke a swelling or contraction that was once approved, and hence still amounts to an affection. This would make the running analogy very close: just as a runner's limbs continue to move (and he still counts as running) even after he has willed to stand still, so an angry man's heart may continue to swell even after he has willed to calm down.

In what other ways may an affection run 'out of control'? Galen quotes, also from *On the Affections*, a passage in which Chrysippus allows for an abatement of distress, whose irrationality can then, but only then, be appreciated:

> By this account a person would not give up hope that with the
> passage of time, when the inflammation of the affection has

slackened, reason will make its way in and find room, so to speak, and expose the irrationality of the affection.

(*PHP* 286.18–21)

Here the cause of the affection's obstinacy appears to be physical (an inflammation), and its effect to be the exclusion of rationality. Until the affection has weakened, reason must lose out not because its decisions are defeated in a conflict of forces, but because it is unable to decide intelligently. In this case, a better comparison than those with running or falling is one recorded by Plutarch (*DVM* 447A = *SVF* 3.111.36–8 = LS 65G3): affections resemble the unsteady and clumsy motions of a small child. Infants suffer less from a mismatch between desire and motion (as in the case of paralysis mentioned by Aristotle, *NE* 1.13.1102b18–20) than from a general lack of self-determination and co-ordination: they are equally unable to control what they want and what they do. We may compare a remark of Aristotle's: 'If appetites are strong and violent they even expel the power of calculation' (3.12.1119b10). Stoics can allow that affection may be out of the subject's control because it is in control of him: it can make him incapable of the reflection by which it would be dispelled. Chrysippus reads into absurd manifestations of anger (biting keys and beating against doors when they are not quickly opened, breaking stones and throwing them afar when we stumble on them) that it 'blinds' us as if we had become different people from when we were philosophizing (*PHP* 280.2–9). This is typical of his bland, or bold, treatment of language that seems to invite a different theory: instead of banishing it, he domesticates it within his own way of thinking.

Thus Aristotle and the Stoics share a structure of thinking about our responsibility for the affections: both count as voluntary what was voluntary in origin; Aristotle looks back to the origin of the general susceptibility, the Stoics to the origin of the particular emotion. Both allow responsibility to survive a loss of autonomy, so that I can be responsible for what I do though it is no longer within my control. Yet it would be misleading to play down the difference between them as merely one of degree. Firstly, Aristotle envisages, as the Stoics do not, that affection may not only become out of one's control, but be from the first against one's will: in his view, I may succumb to an affection at the same time as I wish neither to feel it nor to act on it. Secondly, he is willing to trace back the determinant acts to a distant former self: though their effects are part of me, I may

no longer be the sort of man to choose them, so that my responsibility, though real and remaining, is a matter of history. Thus we
are identified with our affections more intimately by the Stoics than
by Aristotle, and we need not doubt that this was part of their
motivation for attaching them so closely to acts of assent.

5

So far I have been looking in three areas for the motivation of the
Stoic doctrine of the affections: rationality, phenomenology, and
responsibility. In all three, the Stoics display as much perception as
prejudice, and yet only in the third does any clear gain emerge: by
making us responsible for each occurrence of an affection, the Stoics
do help out common moral attitudes (right or wrong). However, we
must doubt whether psychology should be led by ethics: it would
seem more just to accept the moral implications, radical or con-
servative, of whatever view best fits the psychological phenomena.
To do the Stoics fuller justice, I shall now pursue a different strategy:
as if within a Platonic perspective, I shall press them to make
concessions, testing their resistance until we come to a point where
they are able, and right, to stand firm.

We have seen (in §3) that the Stoics ascribe the appearance of
synchronous conflict to a reality of diachronous vacillation, so swift
that it yields an illusion of simultaneity. This clearly applies to beliefs
and desires as *occurrences*, that is, to acts of forming them or of
rehearsing them. But what of beliefs and desires as *dispositions*, that
is, underlying states that are manifested in thinking and acting? I shall
now argue that the Stoics do recognize these, and hence can be
pressed into recognizing patterns of synchronous conflict between
dispositions, and between occurrences and dispositions, if not between occurrences, that might turn out to fit the Platonic model.
Brad Inwood reports a dispute between interpreters of the early
Stoics: did they hold that the mind has no enduring differentiations,
so that all its motions are fleeting alternations and not activations of
lasting dispositions, or did they recognize that there are states that
endure between activations and partly determine them? He argues
for the second, more common-sensical, interpretation (1985: 34–41).
Memory, for instance, does not consist in a series of conscious acts
of recall unconnected by any underlying ties; if it did, there would
be no explanation of why memories agree – nor indeed of how they
are memories. Rather, memory endures unexercised as a 'storehouse

of presentations' (*SVF* 2.23.20), much as reason itself is a 'collection of conceptions and preconceptions' (*PHP* 304.35). The Stoics could hardly avoid conceding that the mind has dispositional qualities which are 'so constituted that they can remain on their own when inactive, since they provide stability from within themselves and their own definition' (*SVF* 2.130.21–3). Thus to an impulse (*hormê*) as a mental event corresponds a dispositional state of impulse (*hexis hormêtikê*) 'from which the action of impulse comes about' (3.40.15–16). What states correspond to those judgements or impulses that are affections? No doubt it is a precondition of susceptibility to affection that one should be in a state of vice (*kakia*). Vices are defined as the absence of virtues (*aretai*), that is, of the cognitive states that these are (3.65.20); more deeply, since knowledge is single and unitary, it constitutes a single state of virtue, as ignorance a single state of vice (*PHP* 436.13–14). Logically speaking, vice and virtue are both 'characters' (*diatheseis*) rather than mere 'tenors' (*hexeis*) in that they allow of no variations of degree (*SVF* 2.129.37–43 = LS 47S2): it is either simply true that one is virtuous, or simply true that one is vicious. However, tendencies to the affections do come in degrees, and so can be identified more closely with 'tenors' that are not 'characters' (*SVF* 3.25.15–18). Of these there is a plurality even of kinds, partly answering to the different aspects that constitute an affection. Just as each affection is centrally constituted by a faulty judgement, so the underlying state, though called a 'sickness' (*nosêma*), is centrally conceived as a disposition of belief: it is 'a belief of desire strengthened and hardened into a tenor according to which they take things which are not choiceworthy to be very choiceworthy' (3.102.37–9, cf. 104.31–3 = Cicero, *TD* 4.26), or else, that things which are to be pursued lightly ('leviter') should be pursued vigorously ('valde', *SVF* 3.105.1–3 = Seneca, *Letters* 75.11); of course strength and hardness come in degrees. Of such sicknesses there seem to be two kinds of cause. One is the force of the presentations:

> The magnitude of apparent goods or evils moves one to believe that it is proper and in accordance with one's estimate of them to be moved affectively when they are present or approaching and to accept no reasoning that says one should be moved by them in another way.

> (*PHP* 264.22–5, cf. 266.1)

Here the salient causes of going wrong are external and indefinite in number (272.18–19): for example, Helen's beauty for Menelaus, gold for Eriphyle (272.32–5). Such 'persuasive qualities of external things' may be seconded by 'the communications of companions' (*SVF* 3.228, cf. *PHP* 320.17–18 = LS 65M7); corruption is social as well as personal. Yet these are not causes that, as Aristotle put it, 'overstrain human nature and no one could resist' (*NE* 3.1.1110.a25–6), and it must be characteristic of certain agents that certain allurements loom large for them. Another kind of cause is the weakness (*astheneia*) that makes a sickness also an ailment (*arrôstêma*).[18] What differentiates ailment as a species of sickness? Ailment is associated with inferiority (*PHP* 264.30–266.5, 272.18–22), and so we can appeal to a later remark about 'inferior men' (*hoi phauloi*): 'Chrysippus says that their soul is analogous to a body which is apt to fall into fever or diarrhoea or something else of that kind from a small and chance cause' (294.33–6 = LS 65R1). While some men are liable to excessive presentations, others are liable to respond excessively even to modest ones; in either case, the effect is that their characters are marred by faulty standing opinions that show up in false practical judgements constituting affections.

Let us return to Epictetus' description of folly:

> At one time you think of these things as good, and then of the same things as bad, and later on as neither; and, in general, you are subject to pain, fear, envy, turmoil, and change; this is why you admit you are foolish.
>
> (*Disc* 2.22.6–7)

Take, for example, a man who is given both, out of a desire for women, to philogyny, and also, out of a fear of them, to misogyny (Greek terms that that I borrow from Cicero, *SVF* 3.103.39–104.3 = *TD* 4.25). Now it would be an obtuse oversight to suppose that he could never display both attitudes simultaneously (say by making love to a woman in ways that are at once exciting for him and humiliating to her). Yet suppose that he behaves as the Stoics describe, vacillating between the two. Even if the vacillation is unpredictable, its poles might be highly repetitious, revealing a restricted though irreconcilable repertory of beliefs. Compare Keith Campbell:

> The considerations which appeal to us fall into reasonably stable clusters, and our assenting responses take on recognizable patterns. These are our dispositions and habits, tendencies and cast of character . . . . Whole stable clusters of our personalities are at odds with one another.
>
> (1985: 331)

We would then have reason to ascribe to the man simultaneous dispositions of belief that contradict and even confront one another, even if there were no time at which both beliefs were occurrent: as a misogynist, he is likely to hold not only that women are of little value, but that loving them (and holding them to be of great value) is of little value also; when hating women he will recall that he often loves them, realize that it is in his nature to do so, and hate himself to a degree for that. Thus one set of his dispositions and activities will relate adversarily to another. Excluding any conflict between occurrent affections changes the style of confrontation without removing the fact. Now nothing that I have just said contradicts the characterization of a Stoic position in my Introduction. Indeed, it connects well with a Stoic idea that opposite sicknesses may arise through collision (*proskopê*): love of women or wine can lead to hatred of women or wine (*SVF* 3.102.39–103.1). Cicero explains that this comes of the mutual conflict of corrupt beliefs: when a 'changing and turbulent tossing of beliefs' becomes established, and settled as it were in our veins and marrow, there arise sicknesses together with their opposites (3.103.29–33 = *TD* 4.24). All that becomes clear is that there is an area of unclarity in the contrast between the Stoics and Plato. If strong contrariety and confrontation are the criteria of partition, so that (as I supposed) to allege partition *is* to speak of families of beliefs and desires with a tendency to be so related, only investigation can determine whether the soul, at least in its motivational aspect, divides into parts, and possibly even the parts distinguished, identified with different strata of the personality, and traced back to their instinctive origins, by Plato.

Another area in which the Stoics may have to retreat before a Platonic offensive is that of the 'preliminary affections' or *propatheiai*. As Gosling persuasively urges, they have good reason 'to try to portray them as mere blenchings and shiverings', though this is often implausible; for, if they are rather 'residual takings' of certain sights and sounds 'as signs of danger', they will threaten a dual level of judgement, one gradually acquired, the other never wholly discarded (1990: 66). Seneca remarks that they occur 'after the opinion that one has been injured' (*Ira* 2.2.2); if he really has in mind more than 'the presentation of an injury received', this suggests that they are more akin to thoughts than to reflexes – for how can a mere bodily reflex respond differentially to a presentation that wins assent? A Latin derivative of Epictetus (LS 65Y) gives as causes not only 'some frightening sound from the sky or from a falling building' but 'the sudden announcement of some danger'; it is perhaps particularly clear in the last case that an emotive response involves at least a moment of belief. Only theory prevents him from conceding this when he adds that such presentations prevent rational assent until the moment when the sage 'discards and rejects them and sees that there is nothing in them to be feared': if he needs to 'discard' them (the word is *abicere*), they were surely initially not only present but accepted. One may compare an episode in Saki: "'I ought to have told you that I'm a Food Reformer. I've ordered two bowls of bread-and-milk and some health biscuits. I hope you don't mind." Clovis pretended afterwards that he didn't go white above the collar-line for the fraction of a second' ('The Match-Maker'); for surely that was a symptom of his being momentarily taken in. The Stoics risk excluding a conflict of thoughts by the expedient of denying non-rational thought the status of 'thought'. The speed and spontaneity of the responses they describe reveal that, even in the souls of the wise, there survives a submerged mentality which mistakes preferred indifferents for goods. Wisdom may ensure that it only emerges briefly, and disappears again without having to be combated. This may seem a small concession: even the wise cannot escape moment-ary assents to overwhelming presentations. Yet this little fact evi-dences a reality that endures from moment to moment: the wise retain dispositions to unreasoning assent in exceptional circum-stances. Experience would further suggest – unless the Stoic sage is a character so extraordinary as to live beyond our horizon – that he will often feel drawn towards such assents even when he is not stampeded into them. He is likely to betray a dual level of judgement in the sense that he remains subject to temptations to irrational assent that are not dissolved by philosophical reflection. Of half-stoical minds we would expect a livelier conflict between spontaneous fears and philosophical consolations. Their inconsistencies may betray a pattern of disunity that is broadly Platonic: thus, as Galen reports Posidonius, 'Impulse is sometimes generated in the animal as a result of the judgement of the reasoning element, but often as a result of the motion of the affective element' (*PHP* 320.27–8 = LS 65M8).

So the Stoics need to make some concessions or accommodations if their view is to capture human nature as we know it, and not to transport it to the high ground of idealization. However, in one crucial respect they can claim to be champions of common sense.[19] Even if Platonic tripartition fitted the patterns of mental conflict, it would still be incredible if it had the effect of permitting one and the same person to subscribe consciously and simultaneously to beliefs or intentions of whose inconsistency he was aware. Plato attempts in a single passage (*Rep* 4.437b1-c10) both to embrace the paradox, and to disarm it: he compares conflicting occurrent desires to opposite acts both of assent and dissent, and of pulling and pushing. But while pushing and pulling are easily reconciled by qualification (as when the archer pushes the bow-tree as he pulls the bowstring), contradictory assent and dissent must be self-defeating. Looking around for psychic realities in respect of which it is intelligible to ascribe a conscious simultaneous contrariety that invites partition, I proposed wanting to do things in the sense of feeling set on them, and half-believing things. Thus I may feel set on two incompatible courses of action attractive in quite different ways (for example, relieving my thirst or preserving my health), or I may imaginatively half-believe what I yet, in a sense, know by calculation to be false (for example, that the rope-ladder, despite all tests, is unsafe). Plato is sensitive to such possibilities, but one strand of his thinking, which I denied to be central but must admit to be present, mislocates their possibility. If I want to drink at the same time as I refuse to drink because part of me desires and part of me refuses, where parts are distinct subjects of mental states, then it ought to be equally possible for me to believe that I shall drink at the same time as I believe that I shall not. (One aspect of appetite might be an incorrigible optimism about the satisfaction of its cravings.) I defended Plato's perceptive-ness by arguing that his central view is closer to common sense: parts are rather fields than subjects, and house desires and beliefs of which it is strictly always the person who is the subject. The Stoics add that what connects person to impulse or belief is an act of assent to a presentation which makes the person as a whole simply responsible. To this insight even Posidonius appears to have remained loyal: in the sentence just quoted (*PHP* 320.27–8 = LS 65M8), he avoids ascribing impulses to each of the three powers of the soul, which, in the Stoic sense of 'impulse', would make of each power a distinct subject of assent. To do the Stoics full justice we need to dwell on their insistence that each person is a single agent. It is evidence of the inescapability of this conception that it surfaces in Plato and Aristotle also, but with no secure resting-place.

Plato is recurrently inclined to analyse a human being into constituents, and then to speak of him as an agent who operates upon them as if from outside. Already in the *Gorgias*, the foolish man is said to place his soul (by which is meant his reason) at the service of his appetite (493b5–7). In the *Phaedo*, 'we' or the like can be spoken of as if we stood outside soul and body, opting between them (67e6–8, 78b9, 83a1–3, 107c6–8, 114d8–115a2). In the *Republic*, an active self is sometimes placed outside the tripartition in order to be able decisively to take sides: thus the psychic timarch is described as himself handing over the domination of reason to spirit (8.550a4–b7), and the oligarch as himself handing over the domination of spirit to appetite (553b8–c6); truthful and not Oedipal dreams come to the sleeper who has roused his reason, and soothed his spirit and appetite (9.571d6–572b1). In the *Laws*, every man is urged to keep hold of the leading-string of reasoning and counteract the pull of the other sinews (1.644e4–645a1). However, Plato has no theory that permits an agency in the soul external to his tripartition. Rather, it must be reason that balances conflicting claims within the soul; and yet reason is only one of three factions that may directly cause action. His alternative language testifies to the pull of unity, but reintroduces the single agent in a manner that reduces him to an extra element within his own soul.[20]

Some of the same uncertainties survive in Aristotle. On the one hand, there are factions within the soul that are conceived of as sources of agency producing action according to a play of forces – which suggests that in a case of conflict the subject could look on with curiosity, and infer the relative strength of the forces from the upshot. Thus, in a case of acrasia, appetite 'takes the lead, for each of the parts [sc., of the soul] can cause motion' (*NE* 7.3.1147a34–5). It does not wait for authorization; rather, 'Appetite, if reason or perception merely says that an object is pleasant, springs to the enjoyment of it' (7.6.1149a34–b1). The metaphor of appetite's leading the soul, or taking the lead, is recurrent (e.g., 7.7.1150a25–7, 7.9.1151b11–12). It is once specified that the leading is by force, not persuasion (*EE* 2.8.1224a38–b2): the agent as a whole acts voluntarily, for the appetite is *his* appetite, but his reason may be said to act (or be acted upon?) by compulsion (b28). And yet it appears that for Aristotle hard acrasia is an impossibility, so that wrong appetites and affections can only prevail through the means of misjudgement or misperception. In intemperance, appetite produces deception, decking out the pleasant in the guise of the good (*NE* 3.4.1113a33–b2); in acrasia, it produces a blind spot, detaching principles from particular instances (7.3.1147a31–b17). Thus reason is either seduced or silenced. Details are disputed, and (what is worse) the motivation is never explained. I speculated as follows. Aristotelian practical reason has no substantive goals of its own (only the formal one of 'truth in agreement with right desire', 6.2.1139a29–31). Its final end, *eudaimonia*, is nothing but the maximal reconciliation of all goals, practical and intellectual, divine and animal, over a lifetime. Even an adult male may on occasion fail to derive his effective desire from that sum of desires, and the resulting action will not be chosen; but once a focus has been achieved, then, so long as it is maintained, every desire is either endorsed or overridden. This places the person as a whole behind deliberate choice and action, but makes impulsive or acratic action an aberration on the side for which he has to bear responsibility rather like the parent of a delinquent child. It seems only fair of Aristotle to concede that such action is not 'especially' voluntary (9.8.1168b35–1169a1).

Thus it is in sympathy with aspects of Plato and Aristotle that the Stoics insist that each agent is a single agency who acts on his intentions, or not at all. Being in every way human, and in no way just animal, he will be drawn towards rationality, but not unfailingly. We can interpret the more paradoxical claim that even affections are internal acts as a corollary of a general assumption: affection directly causes not just symptoms but actions. As we have just seen, Plato and Aristotle fumble in reconciling that with a kind of unity in action. Chrysippus accommodates it unflinchingly by taking affection to be a kind of irrational intention, and so (if intentions are formed and do not just arise) a kind of internal activity. Tracing an action back to an affection becomes like following a chain of intentions: rather as (in Elizabeth Anscombe's famous example, 1963: 37) I infect a house's water-supply by pumping the water by moving my arm, so I may strike someone by getting angry by assenting to anger. Just as bodily action is action by means of one's body, so passionate action is action by means of an affection. It is not denied that affection, like action, tends to run out of control: Plutarch was not contradicting the Stoics, as he supposed, when he remarked, 'Nor does the lover cease loving when he reasons that he must restrain his love and fight against it' (*DVM* 447B). The Stoics shared some of Aristotle's concern to 'preserve the appearances'.

What, however, of their rejection of partition? In a way, this has turned out to be unsound. For even if we set aside conflicts between occurrent desires, there remain conflicts between occurrent desires and dispositions to desire, and between the dispositions themselves; and it is an empirical question about human nature whether these conflicts reveal desire-clusters that constitute a small number of fairly permanent parts, rooted in different strata of our make-up. Better grounded is the Stoic denial that such conflicts are resolved for one, as it were, through an observable play of internal forces. A satisfactory moral psychology needs to do justice at once to the intentional character of actions, and to the multiformity of motivations. Between the damaging disunity of Platonic and Aristotelian factions, and the deceptive unity of the Stoic *hêgemonikon*, a mean must be found.

BETWEEN PLATO AND THE STOA: APPENDIX ON POSIDONIUS

In interpreting Posidonius, I incline towards a mean between a Platonic reading, and the Stoic one of Cooper (unpublished), usefully summarized by Annas (1992: 118–20). If we trust Galen's statements and quotations, we may place Posidonius as at once Platonic in his location of the affections, and Stoic in his conception of impulse. I take these in turn. We may accept that he identified affections not with judgements, but with certain 'affective motions' that belong to spirit or appetite (cf. *PHP* 248.3–6 = LS 65K2, *PHP* 292.20–5, 312.29–31, 322.11–14 = LS 65M11, *PHP* 336.24–6, 348.17–19), and are shared with the lower animals (cf. 288.16–17, 294.16–19, 334.2–7).[21] Galen quotes him arguing that on Chrysippus' view there should be no slip between thinking that it is appropriate to be moved affectively, and being so moved; yet fine things do not cause wise men, who think them appropriate objects of pleasure or appetite, to be so moved (264.18–27). Himself identifying being moved affectively and having an affection (cf. 264.29, which evidently takes 'being carried away by fear' to be an instance of being moved affectively), and assuming the same identification in Chrysippus (not incorrectly, cf. 240.3–5), he would explain that affections belong apart from judgements within the affective soul, which lacks any orientation towards that which is fine. If we distinguish aspects within identities, we may count affective motions as the physical aspect of affections (cf. 322.3–4 = LS 65M10, *PHP* 322.12–13 = LS 65M11, *PHP* 322.21–3), and so as helping to explain them without being external to them. This is how I would read two passages that may otherwise appear to separate affections from affective motions: 322.17–19 say that affections are easier to cure when affective motions are not strong, and 286.22–6 that men who have got their fill of affective motions enjoy a respite from the affection.

Posidonius may still have taken a Stoic view of the nature of impulse itself. The evidence is against his counting affections as impulses: impulse is rather to be ascribed to the agent as a whole even when it is determined by his affective powers. In the absence of further indications, we may presume that he retained the Stoic identification of impulse, within adult humans, with a judgement of reason, reasonable or unreasonable. Thus the motion of the affective element of the soul may control the impulse *of the animal* (288.11, cf. 320.27–8 = LS 65M8 quoted in §5). This is also implicit when Galen reports, 'He says that is impossible that impulse be present, but activity in accordance with it be prevented by some other cause' (*PHP* 288.21–2); for that would be easy if each power had its own impulses as it has its own affections. Impulse is not identical to affection, and it is impulse that can be caused by affection, not affection by impulse: affections arise 'by' affective powers (*hypo*, 248.5 = LS 65K2, cf. *PHP* 286.8 = LS 65P1), whereas impulse may come 'out of' affection (*ek*, *PHP* 328.25–6 = LS 64I6, *PHP* 330.23–4 = LS 65Q2, which are actual quotations). It seems that Chrysippus called the excessive impulse 'according to the affection', which permits a closer connection (*kata*, *PHP* 242.17–18, 254.24); what Posidonius calls 'according to affection' is not impulses, but affective motions (268.16–18, 282.9–10, 322.21–2, 25). We must suppose that the affective soul contains presentations (e.g., of goals or of principles), and passive inclinations inspired by them that fall short of full or active assent; through these presentations affections can, to a limited extent, be aroused by reason and rational desire (cf. 288.29–30, 330.28–31 = LS 65Q4).[22] If this is right, Posidonius differs from Plato, Aristotle, and Chrysippus in denying what (towards the end of §5) I called a general assumption, that affection can directly cause action. Impulse becomes a mediator or censor that may translate affection into action, or bar it from action.

The best reason for supposing, instead, that Posidonius retained the standard Stoic conception of affections as false judgements or excessive impulses (apart from the general fact, stressed by Cooper, that he counted as a Stoic) is his low view of them (which itself, however, helps to explain that fact): they constitute 'discord and the unhappy life' (*PHP* 326.20–1), and it is 'unwise men' who fall into them (266.9–10, cf. 296.3–4 = LS 65R4). Yet this evidence is indecisive (and cannot safely override Galen's plain statements that he ascribed affections to animals). It may rather be that he restricts the term 'affection' to what Aristotle had called 'disturbances' (*tarachê*, e.g., *Rhet* 2.5.1382a21) and Hume would class as 'violent' rather than 'calm' passions, that is, to emotional transports with which one can become sated (*PHP* 288.9–12 = LS 65P2, *PHP* 290.8–19). These are the affections relevant to the question that Galen says he keeps asking (248.7–8 = LS 65K3): what is the cause of excessive impulse? Such affections frustrate rational guidance, and so manifest in an unregenerate form 'the irrational, unhappy, and godless element of the soul' (*PHP* 326.27). With training, he actually agrees with Plato, the affective element of the soul can be prepared in childhood to accept the rule of the rational element (324.9–11, cf. 290.5–7 = LS 65P4): he has in mind the use of music (*PHP* 330.8–21), and, in a term from Aristotle, 'habituation' (*ethismos*, 324.22, cf. *NE* 1.7.1098b4, *Pol* 8.5.1340a23). Yet it is unsurprising if the term 'affection' retained for him a Stoic colouring, and applied only to mental turmoil unbefitting a Stoic sage (or, indeed, an Aristotelian gentleman).

An important passage in Galen (*PHP* 320.23–8 = LS 65M8) is probably corrupt, and certainly problematic; I tentatively understand it as follows. In the practical sphere, a weak reason abandons its own judgement, and falls into false opinions that permit an 'affective pull' to produce false suppositions. For example, if reason holds, through weakness, the false evaluation that that one's bereavement is an evil, it becomes liable to succumb, through the pull of the affections, to the irrational practical judgement or conclusion, identical to an excessive impulse, that the loss demands a mausoleum. I would therefore paraphrase:

> False practical judgements arise in the practical sphere through the pull of the affections. But before this come false evaluations, because the rational element is weak in its own judgement. For impulse is sometimes generated in the animal as a result of rational judgement, but often as a result of affective motion.[23]

On this reading, Posidonius stands between partition and monism. He departs from the Stoa in identifying affections not with impulses, but with inclinations towards impulses. He keeps his distance from Plato in two ways, not only denying spatially separate parts of the soul, speaking instead of 'powers of a single substance which stems from the heart' (*PHP* 368.23–4), but also conceiving of these as sources of motivation but not as alternative loci of practical judgements that may issue in action.[24] He may thus turn out the implicit hero of this book, reconciling unity in intention with variety in inclination, in a way that also constitutes a middle path in the area of responsibility: the Stoics may have objected that he relieves us of responsibility for our own affections, but Plato and Aristotle would have to concede that he keeps us unequivocally responsible for our actions.

NOTES

INTRODUCTION

1 This paragraph displays the allegedly sexist usage of 'he', 'him', and 'his' that will be recurrent throughout this book. I believe that, in the interests of free speech, there is a moral obligation to be politically incorrect whenever, as in this matter, it is perfectly harmless to be so.

2 In pursuit of a consistency more philosophical than poetic, Diggle (1984) doubts the authenticity of *Medea* 1056–80, following Reeve (1972). Contrast Lloyd-Jones (1980): he suspects only 1059–63, which contain two lines that reoccur later (1062–3 = 1240–1). What matters most for us is that our text was already familiar to the Stoic Chrysippus about two centuries later; Diggle provides a long list of later authors who cite 1078 ('I understand what ills I am about to dare').

3 Thus Eustratius, in his commentary on Aristotle's *NE*: 'So Medea, knowing from her reasoning that what she was about to do was wrong, but overcome by her angry desire, performed those things that her reasoning showed to be wrong' (*CIAG* 20.279.36–280.2).

1 SOCRATES

1 A number of transitions between the strictly Socratic and the sheerly Platonic may be marked by a sequence of styles of assent by the young Socrates to Diotima. He firmly or emphatically agrees (*alêthê* or *alêthestata legeis*) that all desire is for the good and for happiness (*Symp* 205a4, a13 – as he has always thought, 206a2), that true opinion falls between the opposites wisdom and ignorance (202a10), and that *poiêtês* can widely mean 'craftsman' (cf. *Euthyphro* 3b2) but narrowly only 'poet' (205c3, c10). By contrast, he only tentatively agrees that *erôs* can be generic or specific (205d9), and that the object of specific *erôs* is generation in beauty (206e6). Thereafter, he only feels or expresses puzzlement (207c1, 208b7), and a desire to be enlightened (207c5–7, 208b8–9), before falling wholly silent. Though Plato's style is more often easy than rigid, he may be conveying by his wording that some theses (most importantly, that all desire is for the good, i.e., happiness) are

179

strictly Socratic, others (as that specific *erôs* is for generation in beauty) only loosely Socratic, others again only distantly Socratic (the elaboration of the notion of generation in beauty for body and soul) or downright Platonic.

2　The fact is obvious, but I owe my grasp of its significance to Ferrari (1991: 175–6). In Price (1989) a realization that the psychology of the Socrates of the *Symposium* is Socratic occurs as an afterthought in introductory note and index (xi n. 3, 259). Had I reached it sooner, I would not have left it so open whether the deficiencies of his account arose 'from a simplicity of thought, or a simplification of presentation' on the part of Plato (ibid.: 58).

3　I write 'presumably', because Socrates does not explain. Xenophon has Socrates warning him that one kiss can at once make him a 'slave' instead of a free man (*Memorabilia* 1.3.11), and the same would hold, *a fortiori*, of making love. Such language of mental slavery was commonplace (cf. Dover 1974: 208); yet, as we shall see, it is actually inconsistent with Socratic psychology.

4　In thinking along these lines, Plato's Socrates pushes to an extreme a tendency to collapse any contrast between *agatha* (good or beneficial things) and *kala* (beautiful, fine, or admirable things) that was already present in oratory; cf. Dover (1974: 70–2).

5　If one is familiar with Aristotle, it may help one to think this through within the context of his own similar but more developed conception of *eudaimonia*. In his ethics, *eudaimonia* is both the goal of all rational (though not of all) desire, and a whole containing disparate elements. So we should expect – though Aristotle himself does not make the point, and may not have seen it – that if, say, I have to sacrifice some piece of contemplation to the demands of justice, I shall feel some rational regret in relation to the contemplation I am forgoing; for it would have contributed to my *eudaimonia* in a special, though less imperative, way. Yet, to the extent that I am rational, I shall not feel torn or distressed, since *eudaimonia* is *all* that I am rationally after, and it requires me to make the sacrifice.

6　This conclusion would be strengthened if Socrates were not only ascribing to us (a) a single conception of the good which is the focus of all our desires, but also both ascribing and approving (b) a conception of goods as all being of the same kind. For (b) implies that, whether I realize it or not, I have *no reason* at all for drinking when it is not best to drink. Thus there is point in Martha Nussbaum's attempt to make out that Socrates is inviting us to consider all beauties and even goods to be homogeneous as a sure prescription for the avoidance of mental conflict (1986: 178–81). However, I believe that she lacks textual warrant (cf. Price 1989: 207–14, 1991: 287–9). I also doubt whether (b) on its own, without (a), has the further implication that, if I know that I should not drink, I shall have *no desire* to do so; cf. §2.

7　A more sophisticated view than is evidenced in the *Symposium* would distinguish the goal of appetite (which may just be the pleasure of the moment) from the teleological ground of having appetites: by their brute importunity these may generally serve our survival, and so happiness, better than they would do if they were less insistent; yet our happiness may not be their object, and they may trouble us even when that is not well served by their satisfaction.

8 Taylor (1991) has Socrates actually say that a bad pleasure deprives '*one* of other pleasures' (*Prot* 353e7–354a1), or '*you* of greater pleasures than it has in itself' (354c7–8). The 'one' and 'you' are his additions, but implicit in the Greek.

9 Here I follow Vlastos (1991: 204–5, 209–11, 300–2), and others, against Gosling and Taylor (1982: 59–68).

10 Taylor rests his equation of 'good' with 'contributing to a life in which pleasure predominates over pain' (1991: 180) especially upon 355a2–5, which he translates as follows: 'Or are you content to say that it [namely, the good] is a pleasant life without pains? Now if you are content with that, and aren't able to call anything good or bad except what results in that, listen to what follows.' I would prefer a more literal 'what results in these', namely, enjoying pleasure and avoiding pain. However, Taylor's equation is better supported at 354d5–e2.

11 Of course, if we wish to make it true by definition that a person tries to do what he thinks best, we can rewrite inertia and inhibition not as obstacles to achievement (except when incapacitating), but as things we think it good to give in to. On our ordinary conception, however, inhibitions, for example, can operate neither by incapacitating, nor by penalizing, but (how one can put it?) by inhibiting.

12 Aristotle recognizes this divergence as to time between judgement and a kind of desire that he calls 'appetite' as a source of conflict between desires, and evidence that motion has multiple causes (*DA* 3.10.433b5–10, quoted at the start of Chapter 3 §2).

13 Socrates hardly escapes a suspicion that his loyalty to the equation of thinking best with effectively desiring in disregard of the phenomena, and his further view that it is the thinking that wears the trousers, betray a prejudice on behalf of the power of reason. This prejudice is an occupational hazard of doing philosophy, as David Pears beautifully diagnoses:

> When philosophers set up their examples, it is only too easy for them to project their own assumptions into the characters that they create. Of course, their thought-experiments are supposed to be controlled by what they find it natural to say when they are describing human agents and their vicissitudes. But there are so many opportunities to idealize, and even to idealize consciously, thus providing an example of the very irrationality about which they are so sceptical. The motive is the glorification of reason, which does not encounter much opposition, because reason itself is being used by the philosopher who is presenting his characters in *akrasia*. His reason is quietly projected into them and he feels that he is talking about himself.
>
> (1984: 247–8)

14 As I noted above (n. 6), Nussbaum reads part of the *Symposium* in a

similar way: on her interpretation, Socrates and Diotima would have us take all beauty to be homogeneous, whether or not that is true, in order to relieve our lives of tension and vulnerability. However, we can now see that the homogeneity thesis that she reads into the *Protagoras* is more startling than that which she finds in the *Symposium*: there was no call there to suppose that beauty *and ugliness* belong together on a single scale.

15 One might yet be inclined to buy homogeneity, despite Socrates' omitting to try to sell it, if its purchase was all that was needed to make it practicable to apply an exact art of measurement, within practical deliberation, to pleasures and pains. But even this is not so: Taylor carefully exposes a nest of problems most of which would be untouched, and none of which would be removed, by a thesis of homogeneity (1991: 195–9). They mostly concern comparison between mental states, actual or only possible, of which no one person is simultaneously conscious: how can their phenomenology (i.e., what it is or would be like to experience them) be compared with any great specificity?

16 Eudaimonism can, if it wishes, differ from impartiality within a lifetime in valuing a life not as a ragbag of goods but as a temporal structure, within which, for example, progress from a low is preferable to decline from a high, and one's deathbed matters more than any other bed. Cf. Bradley (1927: 241–2); also Price (1980) – though I there draw some inferences from Aristotle's text that he is unlikely to have intended. In the *Protagoras*, Socrates clearly excludes such extra considerations (355d6–356c3), but I do not know whether this is because the hedonist is less likely to give them weight than the moralist.

17 The *Euthyphro* contrasts questions about numerical quantities, which are settled by calculation (*logismos*), with questions about right and wrong, which are controversial (7b7–d7); there is no inference to moral scepticism. The *Euthydemus* differentiates making discoveries, which is a task of 'geometers, astronomers, and calculators', from knowing how to use them, which is the task of dialecticians (290b10–c6). It then distinguishes similarly between making captures of armies and cities, which is the task of generals, and making use of those captures, which is the task of politicians, who need the 'royal art' (*basilikê technê*), at once the art of kings and the king of arts, that provides happiness (290c9–291b7). If dialectic is also practical (cf. 292b1–c1), we can connect the two distinctions; and then we have a contrast between calculation, which produces the instruments of happiness, and dialectic, which produces happiness itself and its constituents. A Socrates who identified the art of living with an art of measurement would be conflating these. Mathematics was to loom larger for the mature Plato (cf. Vlastos 1991: ch. 4), and we should not view that 'art of measurement' in the *Politicus*, essential to the political art as to all others, which aims at 'precision' in relating the greater and the less to the 'mean' of 'the moderate, the fitting, the timely, the necessary' (284a1–e8), as a Socratic aspiration.

2 PLATO

1 It is likely that this is also the distinction between 'wishing' and 'desiring' that Socrates alludes to in the *Protagoras* and ascribes to Prodicus (340a8–b1), whose pupil he claims to be (341a4, cf. *Meno* 96d7). If so, it mirrors his distinction between intellectual and sensual enjoyment: 'One derives enjoyment from learning or the exercise of intelligence purely in the mind, but pleasure from eating or some other pleasant, purely physical experience' (*Prot* 337c2–4). By contrast, in the *Meno* Socrates allows Meno no distinction between desiring and wishing (compare 77b4–5 with 78b3–4); hence he presents desiring only what one thinks to be good as a corollary of wishing to be happy (cf. 77d7–78b2). Thus Plato's use of 'desire' (*epithymia*) and its derivatives is variable: they may signify desire of any kind (even one for wisdom, *Pdo* 66e2–3), or those desires, centrally for food, drink, or sex, traditionally labelled 'appetites'. We may find this variation illuminating (as suggesting a kind of primacy of appetites over other desires that invites Freudian if not Platonic speculation); we must find it inconvenient. Aristotle was to escape it by inventing the term *orexis* for the genus, and restricting *epithymia* to the species. In discussing Plato, I variously render *epithymia* by 'desire' or by 'appetite'; in discussing Aristotle, I render *epithymia* by 'appetite' and *orexis* by 'desire'.

2 Socrates says that phrases like 'master of oneself' (*kreittôn hautou*) were familiar (*Rep* 4.430e7–9), and K.J. Dover confirms it (1974: 126). Non-lovers are said to be 'masters of themselves' in the commonplace speech that Plato either borrows from Lysias or invents for him in the *Phaedrus* (232a4–5). The element of paradox becomes eloquent in a line of *Paradise Lost*, 'Thy self not free, but to thy self enthrall'd', and comical in an exchange in Ivy Compton-Burnett that Gosling (1990) aptly takes as its epigraph: '"I must try to conquer myself", said his wife, with the sigh natural to this purpose. "As you only have your own power to do it with, it sounds as if it would be an equal struggle"' (*Parents and Children*).

3 Cf., again, Dover (1974: 208). He cites Lysias as speaking of not being 'worsted by pleasure' (21.19), Demosthenes of not being 'so completely conquered by his desire' for his mistress (40.9), and Xenophon of being 'a slave to the desires of the body' (*Apology* 16). In *Republic* Book 1, Cephalus remembers hearing Sophocles characterize sexual desire as 'a raging and savage master' (329c1–4).

4 I take the Socrates of the *Republic* (after Book 1) and the Athenian Stranger of the *Laws* to be speaking for Plato, and shall allow myself to treat their assertions as his.

5 I was alerted to this distinction by a passage in an exchange between Allen Ginsberg and John Lofton in *Harper's*, vol. 280, no. 1676 (January 1990), p. 16. Ginsberg admitted, 'I like younger boys and I think that probably almost everybody has an inclination that is erotic towards younger people, including younger boys.' When Lofton objected, 'I think it's a rotten preference to want to have sex with young boys, and I don't think it's true that most people want to have sex with younger

people', Ginsberg corrected him: 'I didn't say that. You're putting words in my mouth. What I said was that most people have erotic *desires* for young people.' Note, however, that the act of *forming a desire* is likely, when it involves deliberating between alternatives and not just idly imagining one of them, to result in the state not just of having a desire, but of wanting.

6 Perhaps we get close to Plato's way of thinking if we express Gosling's case as follows: the man believes reflectively that the bridge is safe – where this does not entail that he does believe it, on reflection. 'Reflectively' must then be a qualification and not an explanation, rather as 'in respect of its circumference' qualifies, and does not explain, 'The top is moving' (cf. *Rep* 4.436d4–e4). However, the qualification is misapplied: it is better to say, 'Reflectively, he would believe it', i.e., 'He would believe it, so far as his reflection goes.'

7 Plato might well have introduced partition, and even a partition that imports homunculi (cf. the end of §5), through an insistence that appetite *does* pursue the good: if appetite is implicitly asserting that it is good to drink (i.e., better than not to) when it disregards reason's judgement that it is bad to do so (and so better not to), a reason and an appetite in open conflict are openly contradicting one another in a manner that constitutes them as two sub-persons; for openly contradicting oneself (unless one is changing one's mind) is unintelligible. This would have been the simplest way to press partition upon Socrates, who never doubted (as I complained in Chapter 1 §2) that desiring a thing is wedded to thinking it good. Hence the claim common to Cornford and Irwin (and others) that this linkage excludes mental conflict is not only false in fact, but false to an aspect (one which imports homunculi) of Plato's way of thinking.

8 Plato actually writes indifferently of a displacement of quantity between desires, and a redirection of the desires themselves (*Rep* 6.485d1–12). Though similar or worse problems arise, we may be able to make sense of the redirection and sublimation of desire if we allow the relation between a desire and its object to be loose (cf. Price 1990: 255–8).

9 On this reading, Plato comes close to Sebastian Gardner's 'compartmental thesis', which he states as follows: 'The mind has aspectual parts, which are internally cohesive sets of propositional attitudes, structured by non-propositional mental characteristics, which can be thought of as rational goal-structures, and are realised in phenomenological sets' (1993: 63). His label for these subsystems, 'characterised compartments', could aptly gloss Platonic 'parts', though appetite fails to fit his definition in lacking internal cohesion. In this it resembles Freud's id, which is also, in a colloquialism, 'all to pieces' (*PFL* xv. 296), but differs in being all unconscious. The least Freudian limitation of Plato's picture of the mind is that it focuses largely upon conscious mental states (with the notable exception of certain 'lawless desires' revealed in sleep, *Rep* 9.571b4–572b7), and conscious contrariety.

10 I illustrate how the mind may come to function according to its own models of its workings in Price (1990: 267–70). I also suggest there that an unexpected degree of accord between Plato and Freud in partitioning

the mind indicates that they are perceptive of perennial psychic reality. I do not think that that suggestion is undermined by my fuller realization now (see §7) that Plato is less successful than Freud, for to register reality is not to get it right.

11 We are told that philosophers rule by 'necessity' or 'compulsion' (*anankê* or cognates, *Rep* 6.500d4–6, 7.519e4, 520a8–9, e2–3, 540a7–b1); but this cannot of itself imply any sacrifice of their utility, for they are also 'compelled' to gain a vision of the Form of the Good (519c8–d1, 540a7–9; cf., of the prisoners in the Cave, 515c6, e1, e6). We also read that they practise ruling 'not as something fine but as something necessary' (540b3–5); but this had better mean not that they find no intrinsic value in acting justly (a conclusion that would disappoint Glaucon, cf. 2.358d1–2), but that what differentiates it for them from practising philosophy, when both are valuable, is that it precisely fulfils an *obligation* (as was argued at 520a6–e3). We should not infer that philosopher-kings are rationally conflicted.

12 Plato supplements this logical ground for the tendency of rational desires to achieve consensus with a metaphysical one. The ultimate object of reason is Goodness itself (*Rep* 7.532a5–b2), and the dialectician is the man who can at once abstract the idea of the Good (534b8–c1), and see things in their interconnections (his vision is 'synoptic', 537c7). So the perfected reason of the dialectician achieves a world-view, both of the world as it is and of the world as it should be, that accommodates all facts and values within the unifying framework of a single teleology.

13 In the notes to his Loeb translation of the *Republic*, Paul Shorey nicely illustrates 8.553d3–4 from a *Times* obituary notice, 'Money-making is an art by itself; it demands for success the devotion of the whole man' (ii. 273).

14 Plato evidently presumes that basic human appetites, such as hunger and thirst, have two aspects that are conjoined: they arise physiologically (cf. *Rep* 4.439d1–2, 442a7–8, 9.585a8–b1), and aim at bodily pleasure (cf. 4.436a10–11, 442a7–8). However, the two aspects may on occasion come apart: if, say, I am desperately thirsty, I may have an appetite to drink even though I know (and my appetite knows – for it also recoils) that the only drink available, say salt-water, will be no pleasure *at all*.

15 I owe this point to Bobonich (forthcoming).

16 More problematic is the mixed characterization of spirit as 'lion-like and snake-like' at *Rep* 9.590a9–b1. The conjunction of lion and snake surprises: Aristotle contrasts them (*Hist an* 1.1.488b16–17), and one might suppose that 'snake-like' better fits appetite, especially if we think of a hydra (cf. 'many-headed', *Rep* 588c7–8, 589b1, and 'mob-like beast', 590b7). Yet the context precludes taking 'lion-like and snake-like' as a description of spirit-cum-appetite (cf. especially 'this same high-spirited element', 590b5–6). Perhaps the term 'peevishness' (*dyskolia*) provides a clue: it characterizes spirit elsewhere in the *Republic* (3.411c2, 9.586c9), but a mean-minded spirit that indeed, within Aristotle's contrast, characterizes a snake rather than a lion. Thus spirit is protean: it may resemble lion, or snake, or ape.

17 John Ferrari puts to me that, if the democratic man of the *Republic* can

have an appetite for philosophy (8.561d2), we need not be surprised if there can be an appetitive sort of courage also. However, while it is easy to understand from that passage how a desire to philosophize can become appetitive in style (pursuing the pleasure of the moment with no real interest in achieving truth), we are given no indication in the *Phaedrus* of how appetite's own anger differs from spirit's anger on its behalf. (For an inapposite possibility, cf. Chapter 3 n. 7.)

18 Malcolm Schofield pointed this out to me.

19 Irwin extends the domain of spirit to include attitudes to the good that fail to relate goods to an overall good, and are not wholly responsive to an overall view. This attractively fills the logical space that he finds between appetite's indifference to goodness, and reason's ability to weigh up goods (1977: 192–5). Yet he concedes that much of what Plato says is less conveniently general, and seems to be replacing a rich empirical picture by an abstract logical schema (which is fine in its way, but different). I have already discussed, and doubted, whether 'good' must fall outside appetite's vocabulary. I have also dissented from Irwin's conception of the desires of reason. On my view, a desire to master some body of knowledge is already to be ascribed to reason if its goal is cognitive, and not competitive or frivolous (cf. *Rep* 9.581b5–7). On his view, as I understand it, it only counts as being reason's if it either derives from desire for the overall good, or else (more weakly) depends upon all-in reflection in that it would automatically wither without its approval (cf., perhaps, 5.475b11–c2).

20 For later confirmation of the familiarity of the topos of the three lives, cf. Aristotle, *NE* 1.5.1095b14–19, *EE* 1.4.1215a32–b5; Cicero, *TD* 5.9; Plutarch, *DLE* 8A; Iamblichus, *De vita Pythagorica* 58.

21 However, when Plato does turn his mind to the training of appetite, he only explicitly envisages habituation in pleasure or pain, i.e., within appetite itself: cf. Price (1989: 82–4) on *Phaedrus* 254e5–255a, and Gill (1985: 11–12) on the *Laws*.

22 However, an earlier contrast becomes awkward:

> The other virtues that are called the soul's look like being close to those of the body – for in reality they are not present in it earlier, but are later instilled by habit and practice – but the virtue of intelligence, it seems, is most assuredly of something more divine, which never loses its power.
>
> (*Rep* 7.518d9–e4)

Either this contradicts 10.611c4–5 (which is quite possible, given the speculative character of the later passage), or Socrates meant not that intelligence alone is prenatal, but that, in the form of a capacity for recollection (implicit for a Platonist at 518b6–d7, and alluded to later at 10.621a7–8), it is the one quality of incarnate mind that is innate.

23 Christopher Rowe has pointed out to me how artfully here, and untranslatably, Plato teases his reader's expectations: the abrupt addition of a single word at the end of the sentence (*poiei to meta touto tachu tauta*, *Phdr* 255e4) converts conventional climax ('and indeed, as is likely, he accomplishes what comes next quickly', namely, making love) into

unexpected suspense ('and indeed, as is likely, he accomplishes next quickly – these things', namely, nothing yet beyond sharing a couch). The climax that Plato is preparing is neither facile nor familiar.

24 It should be noted that neither here, nor elsewhere in the *Timaeus*, does Plato apply the term *meros* ('part') to the soul; instead, he uses *eidos* or *genos* ('kind'). However, the *Republic* alternates indifferently between the three terms, and here even *genos* appears only twice in this sense (69c7, e4), if we understand 73c4 otherwise, and *eidos* only once (69d5).

25 Already in the *Republic*, ignorance or *amathia* was once characterized not as a state of reason, but as a 'disturbance and wandering' of the parts of the soul in relation to one another (4.444b6–8). A slightly different but related gloss upon *amathia* is needed for a preceding passage: Socrates identified just action as whatever action produces and preserves a unified soul, and wisdom as the knowledge that is set over it, unjust action as whatever action dissolves this condition, and ignorance as the opinion that is set over that (443e5–444a2). If ignorance there is to be parallel to wisdom, conceived of as a directive state of reason (cf. 442c5–7), it cannot be identical to the psychic discord which is an effect of unjust action and prevents the whole man counting as wise in virtue of the wisdom of his reason, but must be some system of belief upon which the unjust man acts. This may be a subservient state of reason itself (as within oligarchic and democratic souls, cf. 8.553d1–4, 560b7–c3), or an opinionated state of spirit or appetite that resists reason. There need be no implication that all immorality is caused by ignorance in a manner that would imply the impossibility of acrasia.

26 I am persuaded by Bobonich (forthcoming) to be sceptical of the syncretism of Saunders (1962).

27 Within hard acrasia one can distinguish further. Gosling focuses on acrasia in relation to decision: 'The strain is ... between seriously declared intent and intentional action' (1990: 125); 'The air of irrationality ... is that the agent seems decided in favour of one side of the dispute but mysteriously chooses the other .... The puzzlement about *akrasia* arises from the contrast between apparently sincere declaration of intent and actual performance' (ibid.: 152). David Pears has a phrase 'conscious last-ditch acrasia', which sounds the same, but is glossed as acrasia in relation to judgement:

> The test is to take a case in which an agent makes a strong value-judgement, which stands unrevised, and yet acts against it, and to ask whether the explanation has to be one of the following three: he did not really mean the value-judgement, or he did not know that he was acting against it, or his action was, by ordinary criteria, unavoidable. If the explanation need not be any of these three, it may be conscious last-ditch acrasia.
>
> (1984: 233)

I do not think that this case needs to be difficult enough to count as last-ditch: as I observed in Chapter 1 §2, decision and desire can be affected by proximity, so as to prefer the nearer to the greater good, even when judgement is unaffected, since there is no error of perspective or discounting over time. However, no more than Socrates does Plato allow decision to divorce itself from judgement; so such distinctions within hard acrasia are unreal to him.

28 Freud's imagery of horse and rider may derive, directly or ultimately, from the *Phaedrus*, for one-horse variants of Plato's chariot of the soul were common in late antiquity (cf. Inwood 1985: 295 n. 63).

29 If we separate judgement from decision (or deciding *that* from deciding *to*), there is a further ambiguity within (a):

(a(i))   Leontius impulsively changes his mind about *how to act* without changing his judgement about *how he should act*; he acts irresponsibly and with a bad conscience, but not out of what ought to count as last-ditch acrasia (cf. n. 27).

(a(ii)) Without changing his mind in any way, and with his conscientious decision how to act still intact, he ceases to resist temptation and acts against his own will.

Some may suggest that (a(ii)) is what (a(i)) looks like to an introspection that is self-deceived. (Consciously acting badly while pretending to oneself to be decided to act well would be appearance without reality, like performing a dirty deed with gloves on.) Yet we may be able to justify the distinction by relating judgement, decision, and action as follows: I can freely decide to act in disregard of a current rational judgement of what action is best or of how I ought to act (so acrasia in relation to judgement can be free); I can also act in disregard of a current decision, but this must be involuntarily and under psychological compulsion (so acrasia in relation to decision cannot be free). Of course this demands work on how appropriately to distinguish intentional action – which may be neither deliberate nor voluntary – from action in accordance with a decision.

30 It is true that the Stranger remarks that the case exemplifies the greatest 'ignorance' (*amathia*, *Laws* 3.689a1); I explained how this does *not* exclude its being an example of hard acrasia in §10, where I also discussed 1.644d7–645b1. An interesting development from the *Republic* is that while that only allowed executive sophistication to be applied to bad ends after a general corruption of reason (cf. 8.553d1–4), the *Laws* concedes an 'agility of soul' to the strictly acratic (3.689c7–d3). On the other hand, a new pessimism about the autocrat applies to his understanding, and so denies him hard acrasia: even if he recognizes in the abstract that the civic art should pursue the public interest, 'his mortal nature will always urge him on to grasping and self-interested action, irrationally avoiding pain and pursuing pleasure ... causing darkness within itself' (9.875b6–c2) – which I take to mean that his whole sould is clouded by its mortal aspect, losing any clear sight of what the public interest demands.

31 Alternatively, it might be suggested that the man who is only convinced rationally that injustice is a disaster, while his unreason believes otherwise, fails to count as knowing *as a whole man* that it is so (cf. *Laws* 3.689a1–b2, 696c8–10, discussed in §10). However, I have doubted, in discussion of the *Republic* (cf. §6), whether appetite is capable of taking

a view about its long-term self-interest; so I take reason to enjoy a monopoly of the knowledge here taken to suffice for excluding injustice. We must now suppose that the man who 'does not love but hates what he believes to be noble and good' (689a5–6) fails fully to appreciate the ruinous effect upon his own life of the evil and injustice that he loves.

3 ARISTOTLE

1 On the terminology, cf. Chapter 2 n. 1. 'Desire' translates Aristotle's invented term *orexis*, literally 'reaching out for'. Martha Nussbaum well notes the felicity of the coinage, conveying at once that desire is directed at an object, and is a source of activity (1986: 273–5). 'The desiderative faculty' translates *to orektikon*, a derivation from *orexis*. 'Reasoning' translates *logos*, which can mean a piece of reasoning, or reasoning in general (so that to have a rational capacity is to 'possess reasoning', e.g., *NE* 1.13.1102b15). 'Appetite' translates *epithymia*, which in Plato can signify desire of any kind, or appetites such as hunger and thirst, but in Aristotle is restricted to the latter.

2 The places where Aristotle gives wish, anger, and appetite as the three species of desire (*orexis*) are these: *DA* 2.3.414b2, 3.9.432b3–6, *DMA* 6.700b22, *EE* 2.7.1223a26–7, b26–7, 2.10.1225b25–6, *Rhet* 1.10.1369a1–4; also *DMA* 7.701a36–b1 (as emended in Nussbaum 1978). There is nothing equally explicit in the *Nicomachean Ethics*, but cf. 3.2.1111b10–30, which argue that choice is to be identified neither with appetite, nor anger, nor wish before proceeding, clearly on the assumption that all the species of desire have been covered, to deny that it can be identified with opinion either. Altogether more dubious is a passage in the *Politics* (7.15.1334b18–25), which may be identifying anger, wish, and appetite as three species of desire belonging to the non-rational soul, but is more likely corrupt. If we delete the mention of wish (= rational desire) in order to avoid having it ascribed, alongside anger and appetite, even to the newly-born (cf. Vander Waerdt 1987: 639), we are left only with 'anger and appetite'. The most one could then say of these is that they *may* exhaust irrational desire, just as 'reasoning and intelligence' (*logismos* and *nous*) exhaust the rational soul if *nous* here signifies intuition in contrast to demonstration (as at *NE* 6.8.1142a25–6, 6.11.1143a36–b1), which are the two types of cognition.

3 In Plato, I discussed whether 'good' belongs to appetite's vocabulary above (Chapter 2 §4). In Aristotle, one might argue that it does from *DA* 3.7.431a10–11, 'To feel pleasure or pain is to be active with the perceptual mean towards the good or bad as such'; however, it may be that 'as such' should be glossed not by '*qua* good or bad' but by '*qua* perceptible'. Or one might cite *NE* 3.4.1113a33–b2; but the victim of the deception that mistakes pleasure for the good may be reason, not appetite. Or *DA* 3.10.433b7–10, where it cannot easily be intellect (*nous*), and may well be appetite, that mistakes immediate pleasure for unqualified goodness 'because of not seeing the future'; but one might paraphrase, 'What appetite pursues as pleasant presents itself to reason as good, but reason

may reject it.' More decisive may be *EE* 7.2.1235b26–9: the pleasant may appear good in one part of the soul even if it is not thought to be good in another. In Aristotle as in Plato, it seems innocuous to allow appetite the use of 'good' so long as it can only conceive of goodness in its own way, as identical to pleasure. A separate point is that, according to Aristotle, pleasure is intimately and internally connected to goodness, supervening upon it (*NE* 10.4.1174b20–33), and varying with it (10.5.1175a21–8); so when they target pleasure, creatures are in fact – whether they realize it or not – targeting goodness also. A further point is that, to the extent that animal natures are to be explained teleologically, we would expect their pursuit of pleasure to serve their attainment of the good. Yet neither of these points bears on the intentionality of appetite – neither defines how *it* conceives its objects (i.e., how a man conceives them *qua* creature of appetite).

4 'Appearance' translates *phantasia*, which covers the perceiving or imagining of a gestalt, that is, of an image taken a certain way in a compound of sensing and associating; for example, a man prone to anger receives the impression of an insult when someone else might, as we say, *see* the incident quite differently. Within the phrase 'reasoning as it were that anything like this must be fought against' (*NE* 7.6.1149a33–4), 'reasoning' is equivalent not to 'inferring' but to 'premissing', for even unreason can hardly attempt to infer 'Anything like this must be fought against' from 'This is an insult or slight.' We must rather suppose a pair of premises: 'Any insult or slight must be fought against', and 'This is an insult or slight'; cf. Müller (1982: 36–9).

5 This is also implicit in the *Nicomachean Ethics*, though only in a statement of common opinion: courage and temperance 'are taken to be the virtues of the non-rational parts', presumably because one relates to spirit, the other to appetite (3.10.1117b23–4).

6 This passage (*Pol* 7.7.1327b40–1328a5) follows immediately on a precise reminiscence of the *Republic*, recalling Socrates' requirement that guardians (like dogs) should be gentle to those they know, and harsh to those they do not (2.375c1–e8). Aristotle then makes a point against this which he couches in terms of Plato's subsequent tripartition: a sign that spirit is the seat of affection is that it is more excited against intimates and friends than against strangers when it thinks it has been slighted. Curiously, this implicitly treats spirit as a homunculus: the line of thought appears to be that, since any person (or quasi-person) is only especially angered when slighted by his (or its) own friends, and one is angry by one's spirit, which means that it is one's spirit that is angry, my friends must be my spirit's friends also. However, in Aristotle's own account of friendship, the occurence of 'wish' in the definition of loving (as at *Rhet* 2.4.1380b36–7) implies that it is at least in part a rational attitude; and he elsewhere recognizes that, while we are indeed angrier with friends who maltreat us than with others (2.2.1379b2–4), anger is provoked as much by the frustration of appetite as by that of other desires (2.2.1379a12–24).

7 Yet the reason that Plutarch gives for Aristotle's change of mind (a recognition that 'anger is a kind of appetite, namely, a desire to cause

pain in requital') is surprising. He is quoting the *De anima* definition of anger (1.1.403a30–1), but essentially the same definition already occurs in the *Topics* also (8.1.156a32–3), and it in no way tells against placing anger outside Aristotle's conception of appetite. What might lead Aristotle to subsume anger under appetite would be if its object were desired as being pleasant; but even the *Rhetoric*, after slightly expanding the *Topics* definition (2.2.1378a31–3), only makes the converse point that revenge, because desired, is anticipated with pleasure (b1–9). However, it may be that Plutarch is taking over the Stoic extension of 'appetite' to cover all irrational desire (cf. *SVF* 3.95.20, 96.22), so that anger could be defined as an appetite for revenge in someone who thinks that he has been wronged (3.96.27–8, 37). If so, he has in mind not that all passions are desires for pleasure, but that they should not be classified under two headings according as to whether pleasure is their object or not.

8 The wider sense of 'to possess reason' was already anticipated at *NE* 1.7.1098a3–5: 'There remains the active life of the part that possesses reasoning (of this, one part does so as being obedient to reasoning, the other as possessing it in the manner of exercising thought).' However, D.J. Allan may have been right, within his copy of the *Nicomachean Ethics*, to mark what I have translated between brackets as an editor's proleptic gloss.

9 Michael Frede puts to me that *orexis* or *orektikos* may be used either specifically or generically, and that here, within the phrase 'the appetitive and (to generalize) desiderative part' (*to d'epithymêtikon kai holôs orektikon*, *NE* 1.13.1102b30), 'desiderative' covers anger but not wish. Now there is a little evidence elsewhere that *orexis* can be used to signify irrational desire. One may cite *DA* 3.9.433a7–8, 'The encratic, when they are desiring and having appetites [*oregomenoi kai epithymountes*] do not do that of which they have the desire [*orexis*].' (But the phrase *kai epithymountes* may be a corrective gloss to *oregomenoi* and *orexis*, which is easy with the Greek *kai* as it is not with the English 'and'.) One may also cite *EE* 2.8.1224b21–4, which oppose *orexis* to calculation (*logismos*) as two factions within the encratic and acratic soul. However, if *orexis* is usually generic – as the references within n. 2 above go to confirm – how can *orektikos* be specific after the words *kai holôs*? Cf. 'appetite and wish and desires generally' (*kai holôs hai orexeis*, *DA* 1.5.411a28). And *NE* 1.13 supplies two further arguments. Firstly, we read that the non-rational soul of the encratic man 'obeys' reasoning (1102b26–7), even though his appetites are bad (cf. 7.1.1145b13, 7.2.1146a10, 7.9.1152a1–2). This would seem to imply that his non-rational soul houses his wishes, which are good; for to obey is not simply to be overpowered, and when Aristotle writes 'The many obey necessity rather than argument' (10.9.1180a4–5) he has in mind penalties, not *force majeure*. Buridan offers a nice illustration: 'If anyone, conquered in war, was being led forcibly into prison ... we would not say that he was obeying the man who led him' (*QEAN* 1.21). Further, Aristotle's remark that a temperate non-rational soul 'accords with reasoning in all respects' (1.13.1102b28) implies in context that an encratic one does so in some respect, presumably in respect of its wishes. (There is a possible answer to both

these points: appetite is not the only irrational desire, and an encratic non-rational soul whose appetites disobey reasoning may still be obedient in respect of its anger. But does Aristotle really hold that, in instances of encrasia when wish is good but appetite is bad, some other non-rational desire will *always* be good? He certainly does not make that possibility a condition of encratic action: 'The encratic man, knowing that his appetites are bad, does not follow them because of his reasoning', 7.1.1145b13–14.) Secondly, we are told that 'all censure and encouragement' act on the non-rational soul (1.13.1102b33–1103a1), and yet they may, on occasion, be directed at wish alone.

10 Cf. *NE* 5.11.1138b8–13, which assign desires to the rational part in the narrow sense in which that stands to other desires as ruler to ruled; also 3.3.1113a6–7, which identify 'the ruling part' of a person with 'that which chooses' (given that choice or *prohairesis* falls within desire or *orexis*, a10–12); also 9.8.1169a17–18, which identify the *nous* that a good man obeys with a *nous* that seeks (*haireitai*) what is best for itself. (Note that *haireisthai* is not a technical term in Aristotle: equivalent to 'pursue', *diôkein*, cf. 7.9.1151b1, and opposed to 'flee', *pheugein*, cf. 3.4.1113b1–2, it signifies effective desire of any kind, whether rational, cf. 1.2.1094a18–20, or contrary to reason, cf. 9.4.1166b8–10.)

11 Franz Brentano (1977: 100–3) argues that reason has its own desires on two grounds: firstly, because it has its own goals (e.g., *NE* 10.7.1177b19–20), and secondly, because it has its own pleasures (*Met* 12.7.1072b24, *NE* 3.10.1117b27–31, 10.4.1174b20–3, 10.7.1177b20–1), and any pleasure must entail appropriate desire, as sensory pleasure entails sensory desire (*DA* 2.2.413b23–4, 3.11.434a2–3).

12 It is broadly true that Plato thinks of partition in terms of (a) factions, Aristotle in terms of (b) capacities. Thus in *Nicomachean Ethics* 6.1 Aristotle recalls the division between two 'parts' of the soul, 'that which possesses reason' and 'the non-rational' (1139a3–5, referring back either to 1.13.1102a27–8 or to *EE* 2.1.1220a8–11), and then subdivides 'that which possesses reason' according to the principle that different things are grasped by different 'parts' of the soul, since knowledge is 'in virtue of a certain likeness and kinship' (1139a6–11). Plato used the same principle to distinguish capacities (*dynameis*) in *Republic* Book 5 (477c9–d5), but with no implications for partition or sub-partition. However, it complicates my contrast between (a) and (b), and does a little to excuse Aristotle, that Plato's parts do differ in their rational capacities: reason has a richer logical and conceptual repertory than spirit, and a far richer one than appetite. (Or we may speak of a single rational capacity that is variably realized within the three parts.) However, (a) and (b) remain different: the unequal capacities of Plato's parts help explain, but do not themselves constitute, what indeed makes them different parts by his criterion.

13 *Chôristos* ('separate') and its cognates are chameleons, ranging in signification from conceptual distinction to spatial separation; cf. Morrison (1985: 102–5). 'Separate' at *DA* 3.9.432a27 may mean no more than 'differentiate' (cf. 'separate . . . in definition', a20); but 'tear apart' at b5 implies a stronger sense for 'separated' at b2.

14 There are traces in the *De anima* (cf. 2.2.413b13–16, 3.4.429a10–13, 3.9.432a18–20) of a concern about the spatial separation of parts such as we found elaborated in the *Timaeus*, where Plato apportions the three parts of the soul to parts of the body, reason to head, spirit to breast, and appetite to belly (69d6–70a4, 70d7–e2). It is thus that Simplicius understands Aristotle (*CIAG* 9.288.17–18): 'He fights ... against the torn-apart and spatially partitioned.' So also Galen (*PHP* 212.34–214.1): 'Aristotle ... agrees that we have in our souls a plurality of powers differing in kind, but not that they reside in different organs; he wants the heart to be the source of all' (cf. 368.22–4). As I noted earlier (in Chapter 2 §9), spatial partition makes a particular problem of the efficient causation of agency. In the *De anima* Aristotle indicates a single type of mechanism, on the model of the ball-and-socket joint (3.10.433b21–7), without stating whether it is realized only once in each animal. However, he may well be assuming, as he makes explicit in the *De motu animalium* (7.701b28–32), that motion originates in a single place, the area around the heart, where even the smallest change may have great repercussions; and the heart is the seat of perception, thought, and desire. But how, within Plato's account, is desire to effect motion? As I complained, the *Timaeus* offers no answer. If there is some central organ of desire (analogous to Aristotle's central sense-organ), within which desires join or 'knock out' one another (cf. *EE* 2.8.1224b24) and then act upon the body, that organ would be the seat of desire, and of all the soul's parts. This is a better point against the *Timaeus* than any that *DA* 3.9 may be making against the *Republic*.

15 To suit the interests of the orator, the focus of the *Rhetoric*'s treatment of the affections is further selective. We should not congratulate Aristotle on anticipating our concept of emotion (even though we shall find that emotions are among the things he has much to teach us about), for appetite, which is not an emotion, is eventually mentioned as an affection alongside anger (2.12.1388b33); it falls easily enough under the earlier characterization (2.1.1378a19–21), since the expectation of pleasure, which is appetite's object, also works deceptively upon judgement (*NE* 3.4.1113a33–b2). Yet appetite is neglected, presumably because the orator is not expected to excite it: when the courtesan Phryne won her case by exposing her charms to the jury, she was achieving the goal of oratory by a different means. Neglected too is grief at loss or parting, as also in the *Ethics*, perhaps here because Aristotle's topic is forensic, political, and (to a lesser degree) epideictic oratory (cf. *Rhet* 1.3), and not obsequies or valedictions.

16 It is indicative that the *Topics* says indifferently, in different places, that anger presupposes the supposition (4.5.127b30–1, 6.13.151a15–16), and the appearance (8.1.156a32–3), of an injury. So when we meet one term without the other, we cannot safely infer anything more than a shifting focus.

17 A paper by John Cooper (Cooper 1993), and a brief conversation with him and Myles Burnyeat, inspired a late rewriting of this paragraph, albeit only some way in the direction in which they pointed me. I owe the anagram to Christopher Ricks.

18 When Nussbaum ascribes to the Stoics a 'cognitive view, according to which all passions are false judgments' (1993: 101 n. 5), she follows a multitude of the illatinate to do evil to etymology (Latin *cognosco*, 'to recognize'). Anyone who finds in Aristotle a cognitive view of the passions aptly so called (e.g., Sherman 1989: 170–1) owes us an Aristotelian account, preferably evidenced in Aristotle, of the perceptual mechanism through which affections (as distinct from perceptions suffused by reason, cf. *Pol* 1.2.1253a14–18) register value-laden aspects of reality or objective demands. Presumably it would be a kind of 'incidental' perception, resembling that in which we see not colours and shapes but men and trees, but distinctive in that it essentially involves non-rational desire. Aristotle conceivably invites such an account at *DA* 3.7.431a8–14; but, to take appetite as an example, I do not know that he ever counts a reliable perception that a thing is pleasant as an expression rather than a stimulant of appetite (cf. *NE* 7.6.1149a34–b1). We shall find that he holds that within the mature soul affection serves not as reason's informant but as its servant.

19 It is extraordinary, but not really contradictory, that in one place (*Rhet* 1.11.1370a18–27) Aristotle distinguishes appetites (i.e., desires for pleasure) that are natural (or by *physis*) from others that are rational (or with *logos*). Natural appetites may originate in the body (like hunger and thirst), while rational ones are inspired by information. As he has just repeated his standard view that appetite is a desire for the pleasant (a17–18), the information is that some things are pleasant (cf. *NE* 7.6.1149a35), not that they are good (as the Revised Oxford Translation still misleadingly has it). There is then only a verbal inconsistency: desires that are irrational in one way (since they are unreflective responses to the prospect of pleasure) may yet be rational in another (in that they are responsive to propositional inputs).

20 However, this contrast between rational and non-rational affections has its problems: if friendly feeling and even hatred are classified as kinds of wish, how is Aristotle to allow, as surely he should, that they can be causes of conflict and acrasia? Cf. the case that I discuss at the end of §7.

21 While Aristotle no more reduces emotions to feelings than to beliefs (which are the two reductions that have tempted oversimplifying theorists), he rather suggests than excludes that different feelings are characteristic of different emotions: fear involves 'a certain' pain or disturbance (*Rhet* 2.5.1382a21), as does shame (2.6.1383b12–13); 'a certain pain' is also an aspect of pity (2.8.1385b13), envy (2.10.1387b23), and emulation (2.11.1388a32). This may be explained in two ways, material and dialectical. Physiologically, one would not expect the pain of blood boiling in anger (*DA* 1.1.403a31) to be the same as that of blood cooling in fear (*Rhet* 2.13.1389b32). Psychologically, one would expect the pain to vary with the object that it is 'because of' (*dia*, 2.2.1378a30–1), 'concerning' (*peri*, 2.6.1383b12–13), or simply 'at' (*epi*, 2.8.1385b13, 2.9.1386b9, 2.10.1387b23, 2.11.1388a32). Aristotle does not know how to connect the two aspects intelligibly; nor do we.

22 On the text and interpretation of *EE* 2.1.1219b37–8, cf. Woods (1992: 95, 188).

23 For further confirmation, cf. *EE* 3.1.1228b4–38, which permit the brave man to be 'gently' or 'mildly' afraid (*êrema*, b29, 38). Most suggestive is a remark that fearful things will appear fearful to him *qua* man, but either not fearful at all or only 'mildly' so to him *qua* brave (b27–9). Parallels elsewhere (*NE* 8.11.1161b5–6; Plato, *Rep* 1.345c1–d1) show that this means not that men fear these things while brave men do so hardly or not at all (which is incoherent anyway), but that brave men fear them because they are men, but do so only slightly because they are brave men; in short, they are 'dauntless as men may be' (*NE* 3.7.1115b11). It is a typical example of a commonplace that only needs refining to achieve truth that 'everyone actually defines virtues in an off-hand manner as being insusceptibility or mildness [*apatheia kai êremia*] in the sphere of pleasures and pains, vices in opposite terms' (*EE* 2.4.1222a3–5); so a quasi-Aristotelian definition of courage runs 'a mildness of soul concerning things that cause fear or confidence as they appear according to the correct reasoning' (Pseudo-Plato, *Definitions* 412a8–9).

24 This passage (*DA* 3.3.428A20–4) is naturally taken to be decisive against allowing beliefs to non-human animals by Irwin (1988: §§168–71) and Sorabji (1992: 198–208). Yet it might not be Aristotle's last word, if one could compare the way in which he can both ascribe action (*praxis*) to them (*NE* 3.1.1111a24–6), and deny it to them (6.2.1139a31, *EE* 2.8.1224a28–9): belief and action might be distinctively human in narrow but not in wider senses. And when he later writes, 'The reason why they [sc., the lower animals] are thought [*dokein*] not to possess belief is that they lack reasoned belief' (*DA* 3.11.434a10–11), it is ambiguous whether he is giving a justification or diagnosing a mistake. However, in the absence of any clear contrary evidence, 424a20–4 have to stand. I do not know why he should allow non-human animals desires, but not beliefs, of a kind; it would seem more consistent to allow them not desires, but only attractive or repellent *phantasiai*.

25 It is true that Aristotle can call one part of the strictly rational soul 'the opining' one (*to doxastikon*, *NE* 6.5.1140b26), but this may distinguish it within the rational soul and not from the non-rational soul. Later he distinguishes 'the opining' part or capacity, whose virtues are cleverness and practical wisdom, from the 'the ethical' one (so called from *êthê* or qualities of character, which are closely connected to affections or *pathê*, cf. 8.2.1155b9–10, *Rhet* 1.10.1369a18, and best displayed in choice, *NE* 3.2.1111b5–6), whose virtues are natural or developed (6.13.1144b14–16). However, since practical wisdom is not only a rational state (for it cannot be forgotten, 6.5.1140b28–30), nor virtue proper only an ethical one (for it involves practical wisdom, 6.13.1144b16–17), we should think of the opining and the ethical soul as two aspects of the composite soul, both spanning its rational and non-rational capacities, and differing in definition but not separable (which is how Aristotle speaks of 'being opining' and 'being perceptive', *DA* 2.2.413b27–32). It is true that the virtues of the opining soul *as such* are purely intellectual, for though some beliefs *are* formed without the assent of reason, no beliefs *should be*.

26 How may this carry over to conflict in belief? Where belief is practical

or evaluative, and so the propositional partner of desire, it is easy to translate what I have said about desire into the language of belief. In the rare example that Aristotle provides, anger pronounces 'Anything like this must be fought against' (*NE* 7.6.1149a33–4). Reason would like to disagree, but will lose hold of its contrary judgement (or at least be unable honestly to apply it) if anger prevails. By contrast, anger has the privilege that it may retain its view even if reason wins, for that view depended upon anger alone. More generally, we may learn something from a sentence in the *De anima* about action and appearance (*phantasia*): 'Because appearances remain and are similar to perception, animals do many things in accordance with them, some through lacking intelligence, namely, beasts, other through their intelligence being sometimes clouded by passion or illness or sleep, namely, men' (3.4.429a4–8). *On Dreams* supplies many examples, of which these are two: the coward phantasizes and believes that he sees his enemies, the lover that he sees his beloved (2.460b5–7). If they act on the delusion, they must lose hold of any corrective beliefs, which can no longer rest upon a co-operation between appearance and reflection. If they rationally detect the delusion, but continue to experience a surge of fear or love, this would evidence that the irrational belief remains in the soul, disowned and disregarded by reason but conniving with appearance and passion. However, this is speculation not by, but after, Aristotle. I pursue it a little just to show how it can fit within his framework.

27 For related diagnoses of Aristotle's motivation, cf. Dahl (1984: 184, 188, 207–10), and Wiggins (1991b: §5).

28 I add this caveat to make explicit that I remain neutral about the best location of the books common to the *Nicomachean* and *Eudemian Ethics* (*NE* 5–7 = *EE* 4–6) as we have them. Anyone who finds them inconsistent with the remaining books of either the one or the other (but not both) has a reason to place them elsewhere. Some have found their treatment of acrasia inconsistent with briefer characterizations in other books; I admit that to a small degree in §8.

29 Of all the previous discussions of *Nicomachean Ethics* 7.3 I know, the two I like most are Kenny (1973), and Dahl (1984: 139–224).

30 In so translating *NE* 7.3.1147b15–16 (after Jonathan Barnes), I am accepting an emendation, of *periginetai* for *parousês ginetai*, proposed by Stewart (1892: ii. 163–4). As Dick Hare pointed out to me many years ago, the manuscript text permits the same interpretation: 'For it is not the presence of so-called knowledge proper that is affected by the passion.' However, Stewart's emendation makes the text easier, and more reminiscent of Plato. 'Overcome', 'drag about', and 'as if a slave' are taken from the *Protagoras*: all three occur at 1145b24 and in *Protagoras* 352c1–5; with Stewart's emendation, 'drag about' occurs also at 1147b16. These verbal borrowings make it certain that the Socrates with whom Aristotle is agreeing and disagreeing is the protagonist of the *Protagoras*.

31 Some have suggested that to exercise knowledge of a proposition is not just to have it in mind and to mean it, but also to put it to some further use; cf. Kenny (1979: 161) and Gosling (1990: 29–30, 32–7). This would

allow one to say that not to exercise 'the last premiss' (*NE* 7.3.1147b9) is to fail to draw the conclusion or to keep it in mind; then the apparently very implausible denial that the last premiss is exercised is simply an automatic corollary of a less implausible denial that a conclusion is drawn and maintained. So just as incapacity or interference can get in the way between drawing a practical conclusion and enacting it (1147a29–31), so acrasia can get in the way between grasping the premisses of a practical syllogism and drawing or maintaining its conclusion. However, no Aristotelian passage that anyone has cited in this connection does actually show that a man who fully assents to a proposition without putting it to further use does *not* count as 'contemplating' it (cf. 1146b33–5, *theôrein*), 'using' it (cf. 1146b32, 1147a12, *chrêsthai*), or 'exercising' or 'actualizing' it (cf. a7, *energein*). Here and (I think) elsewhere, Aristotle makes no distinction between these terms when he is contrasting any of them with merely 'possessing' knowledge (*echein*), and it is implausible to say that, when I can get no further in a train of thought (say because my relevant knowledge runs out), I am not 'contemplating' or 'actualizing' my knowledge of the last point I get to.

32 I take from Kenny (1973: 44–6) that *NE* 7.3.1147a31–4 present a pair of premisses ('the universal opinion . . . and the other opinion', cf. a25 'the one opinion is universal, while the other . . .'), and not a pair of syllogisms. What Aristotle equivalently calls 'the last premiss' (*hê teleutaia protasis*, b9) or 'the ultimate premiss' (*ho eschatos horos*, b14) will be the final element (here, 'Tasting this would be excessive') within a conjunctive minor premiss. It is a slight awkwardness that the clause 'The one tells him to avoid this' (a34), which could be an exact statement of the conclusion, has to be taken as an inexact restatement of the universal premiss; but this is at once possible (cf. Dahl 1984: 178), and inevitable (since 'the one' can only have that reference). It would make no significant difference if we had a pair of syllogisms, one proscribing the tasting as excessive, the other describing it as pleasant. Aristotle's point would then become that only the first is practical in itself, while the second is non-practical in form (containing only indicative premisses), and only causes action because it is exploited by an overriding appetite, namely, desire for pleasure. Alternatively, if there were a pair of syllogisms, the prescriptive syllogism might be something like 'No one with diabetes should taste anything sweet, I have diabetes and this is sweet; so I should not taste this'; this would give point to Aristotle's preliminary distinction (a4–7) between the subject and predicate of the universal principle.

33 Kenny translates not 'the last premiss' (*NE* 7.3.1147b9) but 'the last proposition', identifying this with whatever proposition it is (premiss or conclusion) 'whose absence, or whose ineffectiveness, is the cause of the incontinence' (1979: 164). But it is implausible that, in the syllogistic context emphatically set by 1147a25–8, Aristotle should be applying indifferently to premiss or conclusion not one but two terms, *protasis* (b9) and *horos* (b14), that the *Prior Analytics* applies only to premisses.

34 Others have offered other explanations of Aristotle's view that it is 'the

last premiss' (*NE* 7.3.1147b9) that is the weak point of the practical syllogism. There is value in this observation by Kenny:

> A man, we might say, has a whole lifetime to show in his behaviour whether or not he believes in a universal proposition of the kind which figures in Aristotelian practical reasonings: as the propositions become more particular and more immediately concerned with present action, it is current behaviour which becomes more and more central as criterial evidence for the acceptance of the proposition.
>
> (1979: 165–6)

Yet it is not safe to assume that, if a man generally acts on a prohibition, he never loses his grasp of it. Sarah Broadie tries to justify Aristotle differently: the universal premiss may occur 'in other practical arguments whose conclusions the agent uses by acting on them even while he fails to use' the conclusion he disregards, as when the prohibition is on eating unhealthily and the sweet-toothed man remains careful during the same meal to avoid unhealthy food so long as it is not sweet (1991: 302). This is a nice comment, where it applies. Yet in other cases it may be the particular premiss that continues to do work even through the acrasia: 'It is now between meals' might well play two roles within a greedy child, initially invoking the prohibition but then, after occlusion of the prohibiting principle 'Nothing pleasant should be tasted between meals', increasing the pleasure; and even 'This is unhealthy' might connect first with a rational recognition of the importance of health, and then with a dare-devil sense of bravado. A more general explanation that Broadie proposes applies more widely:

> The particular premiss represents that sentient side of the ethical soul through which appetitive affections . . . can attack . . . the whole set of premisses so as to render it null and void in incontinence. The part that has to do with particulars is uniquely the part through which the whole is subverted, and so it might easily come to be talked about as if it, uniquely, is subverted.
>
> (ibid.: 303)

A related thought occurs in Buridan:

> The affections of the sensitive appetite involve the motion of the blood, or of other humours or spirits, and if this motion is great it disturbs sense and prevents it from duly reporting to the intellect . . . . For if sense (which we have determined to be not other than the sensitive appetite) has been passively distracted, it will not show to the intellect anything except the affection.
>
> (*QEAN* 7.7)

On this diagnosis Aristotle exemplifies that theory, as well as passion, can blind one to particulars. However, we need it to tell against yet another possible cause of acrasia. Why does he appear to envisage motivated misperception, but not motivated irrationality? He allows that a perception that a tasting is unhealthy may be subverted, but not the subversion of an inference to the same effect, perhaps through the eclipse of a generalization about kinds of food (cf. *NE* 6.7.1141b20–1). Here my suggestion does no work: if the agent knows that unhealthy eating is wrong, he knows in a sense that he is tasting wrongly whether it be the particular perception (say, that this is venison) or the intermediate generalization (that venison is heavy and so unhealthy) that is subverted. The Buridan–Broadie line, if I may amalgamate their proposals, then does necessary work in pointing the finger always at the perception.

35 Thus an interpretation of *NE* 7.3 that opposes a bad syllogism of appetite (prescribing indulgence) to a good syllogism of reason (forbidding it) is not only implausible of 1147a31–4, but contradicts the distinction between the workings of appetite and anger in 7.6; while the same interpretation, applied to anger and not to appetite, is confirmed by 7.6. The difference is significant, for it has the corollary that anger permits a simpler argument against hard acrasia than appetite does: since anger is opinionated, to act on anger is to act on a proposition like 'This must be fought against', which reason often denies; unless reason is blinded, the man who acts acratically on anger will simultaneously be judging 'This must be fought against' and 'This must not be fought against', which may well be thought impossible. Thus it may indeed seem 'necessary' that, when rage or a similar passion masters a man, the effect should be to corrupt his judgement (*Pol* 3.15.1286a33–5). No such argument is applicable to appetite; cf. Buridan, *QEAN* 7.6–7.7. I face the issue of self-contradiction in Chapter 4 §5.

36 The sagest discussion is a brief one by Ackrill (1980: §9). He persuasively diagnoses Aristotle's inability to indicate how the rival claims of contemplating and acting are to be weighed, but does not infer any implausible thesis that they are incommensurable in the strong sense that any possibility of contemplating (however brief) 'trumps' any possibility of acting (however beneficial).

37 I owe my grasp of the analogy to Robert Gay.

38 Also awkward, but more equivocal, is a sentence in the *De anima*: 'Further, even when intellect commands and thought tells one to shun or to pursue something, one is not moved but acts according to appetite, like the acratic man' (3.9.433a1–3). 'Something' certainly suggests a particular prescription or prohibition, but it is not excluded that this may have been occluded by the time of action.

39 *DA* 3.11.434a12–15 are difficult to interpret in detail; for a full and fine discussion, cf. Dahl (1984: 237–46).

4 THE STOICS

1 Not even all complete *lekta* are propositions, since they include commands, questions, and the like, which cannot be true or false (*SVF* 2.186–8, 2.192). However, it seems that only propositions are objects of Stoic assent.

2 I write 'virtually' for two tentative reasons: firstly, I have said

(Chapter 2 §4) that intending entails predicting, that is, that I cannot intend to do what I do not predict I shall do (though this has been debated), and I do not know whether the Stoics held that I can only have an impulse to do what I expect to succeed in doing; secondly, it might be maintained that to have a distinct concept of intention is to have the concept of a state of will that may diverge from practical judgement (cf. Chapter 1 §2), whereas all the Greeks assumed that I (or a part of me) must pursue what I (or the same part of me) think appropriate or best.

3 It is true that Aristotle has a conception of psychological compulsion that operates upon the agent's desires (perhaps through severe torture), and counts as causing involuntary action if *no man* could have resisted it (*NE* 3.1.1110a23–6); it is less clear how he can justify that conception, limited though it is, in his own terms. The distance between Aristotle and the Stoics becomes evident if one reflects, however anachronistically, upon Freud's parapraxes (e.g., the speaker of the Austrian parliament who declared at the start of a session he expected to be difficult, 'I herewith declare the sitting closed', *PFL* i. 59–60): precisely on Freud's account, which reveals them as both object and effect of wishes (even though either the causation, or the wish itself, is unconscious), these come out as voluntary for Aristotle, although they are not the product of any Stoic assent.

4 Here I follow Inwood (1985: Chapter 5, which corrects his p. 100) and Long and Sedley (1987: i. 421) against Arius Didymus (*apud* Stobaeus, *SVF* 3.378 and 389 = LS 65A and 65C, *SVF* 3.394) and Engberg-Pedersen (1990: Chapter 8). As I see it, Arius assimilates appetite and fear too much to pleasure and distress (by implying that all four involve impulses towards internal motion), while Engberg-Pedersen assimilates pleasure and distress too much to appetite and fear (by asserting that all four involve impulses towards external action). Arius' evidence is still invaluable, and I have learnt greatly from all the rest.

5 This is another application (cf. Chapter 3 §6) of David Wiggins' important distinction between evaluations and practical judgements (1991a: 95–6).

6 Actually, this is controversial: some follow De Lacy and translate 'the impulse that follows on the contraction'. I think that that sense would have been conveyed not by *epi* with the accusative (cf. *SVF* 3.92.4–5), but by *epigignomenos* with the dative (cf. *PHP* 292.19, *SVF* 3.95.3 = Plutarch, *DVM* 450C).

7 It may often be that a secondary affection is accompanied by a primary one, as in Chrysippus' characterization of envy: 'In the second book concerning Good, he explains envy as distress at another's goods, taking it to be felt by people who wish their neighbours' abasement in order to be superior themselves' (Plutarch, *DSR* 1046B–C) – where 'wish' (*boulesthai*) must unusually signify appetite (*epithymia*). Cicero sensibly observes that pity or 'misericordia', though a species of distress, usefully motivates us to give help (*TD* 4.46). Thus secondary affections may well generate primary affections in cases where there is something to be done. This even holds of impracticable affections like distress at bereavement, as in the instance (deplored by the Stoics) of Artemisia, who grieved to

death for the loss of her husband Mausolus, but not without acting on a desire to build him the Mausoleum (*TD* 3.75).

8 Arius is himself the exception (*SVF* 3.95.39–41), when he writes that fear, which is a primary affection, involves a 'fresh' opinion that its object is 'really' (*ontôs*) to be feared. But this is untrustworthy: his account is only consistent if we infer from 3.92.23 (= LS 65C) that what makes this opinion fresh is that (as within a secondary affection) it is stimulative of a contraction or swelling, while it is hard not to read him here as erroneously relating the freshness to the opinion's being that the object is *really* to be feared. Brad Inwood is typically judicious (1985: 147 n. 85), though I think that he is wrong to find some support for Arius in a phrase that Cicero applies to fear, *recessus quidam animi et fuga* (*SVF* 3.93.6 = *TD* 4.15), for this seems rather a precise Latin version of the Andronican definition that I quoted in my text (*SVF* 3.95.19 = LS 65B2).

9 This is not to deny that mental conflict may take a different form: for example, a felt ambivalence about an action may disclose a conflict between one tendency constituted by a complex of desires and beliefs, and another consisting of an instinct (very likely unconscious) untouched by conceptualization. But even appetite, as it appears in Plato and Aristotle, is less primitive than that: it has at least the concept of the pleasant, and this may constitute a conception of the good; hence reason can contradict it (denying that a thing really is pleasant or good), or confront it (disparaging the pursuit of bodily pleasure).

10 Galen testifies that Aristotle and Posidonius reject any spatial separation of parts, insisting that 'these are powers of a single substance which stems from the heart' (*PHP* 368.23–4); it is obscure what it would be for parts to differ 'in substance' (or 'essence', *ousia*), though Galen repeatedly alludes to this as a distinct claim (cf. also 338.4–5, 368.20–4). He comes closest to clarifying what suffices for a power but not a part when he complains that *Republic* Book 4 proves three powers but not parts (336.16–23, 338.9–14). A promise (336.26–32) to show that they are parts and not just powers 'in the next book' (i.e., Galen's Book 6) is apparently redeemed in a long argument that, just as it has already been shown that two parts are separately located in the head and the heart, so the appetite is located in the liver (373.16–19). It seems to be the question of spatial location that he takes as decisive.

11 I owe this thought to a helpful conversation with Tony Long (who might develop it differently).

12 However, as Stephen White has pointed out to me, it is not unproblematic to ascribe to agency mental acts about whose timing the subject is continually in error. It is not as if the speed of his alternations of will comes of practice, as with keyboard ornaments.

13 Unfortunately (as Malcolm Schofield points out to me), our sources, who are chiefly Stobaeus and Diogenes Laertius, offer us what look like inconsistent glosses upon the distinction between 'primary' and 'secondary' virtues and vices. Stobaeus lacks this terminology, but reports that some virtues and vices (four of each – wisdom, temperance, justice, courage, and folly, intemperance, injustice, cowardice) are states of knowledge or ignorance, while others are not (*SVF* 3.95). Diogenes

classifies the same eight virtues or vices as 'primary', and mentions weakness of will (*akrasia*) as 'secondary'; yet he adds unqualifiedly that vices are states of ignorance (*agnoia*, 3.265). In my text, I suppose that all virtue involves knowledge, and all vice ignorance, with the qualification that primary virtues or vices simply consist of fields of knowledge or ignorance, while secondary virtues or vices are either species of primary ones, or consist of sufficient causes of knowledge or ignorance in the face of various trials and temptations. Thus, whereas courage is simply 'knowledge of what is fearful and not fearful and in between', greatness of soul (*megalopsychia*) is 'knowledge that makes one rise above contingencies' (*SVF* 3.67.26–9). Whereas temperance is simply 'a tenor (*hexis*) that preserves the judgements of wisdom in pursuit and avoidance' (3.67.35–6), strength of will (*enkrateia*) is 'an unconquerable character in respect of what appears according to right reason, or a virtue that raises one above things that seem hard to refrain from' (3.67.20–2), or, more succinctly, 'a tenor invincible by pleasures' (3.66.40). I touch on the distinction between *hexis* or 'tenor', and *diathesis* or 'character' (translations that I take from LS) in §5; it was evidently not always respected.

14   It is striking that Aristotle and Chrysippus use almost the same example to exactly opposite effect: Aristotle uses the example of a stone that one throws to show that one remains responsible, Chrysippus that of a cylindrical stone that fate sets rolling downhill but which thereafter moves according to its own nature to make out that fate is not primarily responsible (*SVF* 2.294.15–23 = LS 62D4). However, the implication in both cases is to confirm *our* responsibility. The difference is that the stone is thrown contrary to its natural motion, while the cylinder is rolled according to its natural motion.

15   Gosling complains that this move cannot accommodate Plutarch's case (*DVM* 447B) of the lover who remains in love even when he has reasoned that his love must be restrained (1990: 60). Here each man had better speak for himself: in my experience, it fits at least the phenomenology of falling in love that it is a moment of freedom, less of falling than of letting oneself go, however impossible it may be to retrieve oneself thereafter.

16   Over how to interpret this passage (*PHP* 284.5–13 = LS 65O2–4), Malcolm Schofield persuades me to follow Long and Sedley (1987: ii. 413) rather than Inwood (1985: 149–51).

17   Posidonius is a natural exception, agreeing with Plato about the effect of music upon the irrational soul (*PHP* 330.6–21); yet it is probable, as I argue in Chapter 4, appendix, that even he attaches impulse to judgement.

18   Cf. *SVF* 3.103.1–2 = LS 65S3, *SVF* 3.103.5–6, 3.104.9. When Posidonius wishes to complain that Chrysippus cannot in fact explain the variety of people's reactions, he lets him appeal to two different variables, 'the magnitude of what is presented', and 'weakness of soul' (*PHP* 266.1, cf. 266.15). Since the kernel of every ailment (*arrôstêma*) is a sickness (*nosêma*), so that they differ in conception but are linked in actuality (*SVF* 3.103.30–4 = Cicero, *TD* 4.24, cf. *SVF* 3.104.13–14 = *TD* 4.29), it

is unsurprising that sometimes ailments are defined in a way that fits sicknesses; for example, 'Ailments arise in the soul not simply from the false supposition about something that it is good or evil, but from the supposition that it is the greatest [good or evil]' (*PHP* 262.11–13; cf. 262.34–264.1 = LS 65L1, *SVF* 3.104.31–3 = *TD* 4.26).

19 Malcolm Schofield focused my mind on this point.

20 The same tendency reappears, as if inescapably, in Galen, who adopts Plato's tripartition. He describes Medea as torn between two factions, with neither of which she is to be identified, and concludes, 'Then spirit again exerted an opposite pull, and then again reason .... Being repeatedly driven up and down by the two of them ... she yielded to anger' (*PHP* 188.23–5). In reference to Odysseus's self-addressed injunction in the *Odyssey*, 'Endure, my heart' (20.18), Galen allows himself as many modes of description as Plato: Odysseus is addressing himself (*PHP* 184.20); he is mastering spirit with reasoning (186.6, cf. 188.32); he is drawn forcibly by spirit but checked by reasoning (188.6–7); his reasoning is addressing his spirit (188.8–11).

21 It is true that I was sceptical, in §1, of Galen's claim that Chrysippus contradicted Zeno in identifying affections with judgements, and not with motions following on judgements (*PHP* 246.39–248.3 = LS 65K1). However, it looks as if his authority there was none other than Posidonius himself (cf. *PHP* 248.3–5 = LS 65K2), who also wished to make out that Chrysippus was at odds both with Zeno (*PHP* 258.22–3, 332.20–2), and with Cleanthes (332.29–31, 484.3–4).

22 It is compatibly with this that I would make sense, if we have to, of an unreliable and now corrupt passage of Plutarch or Pseudo-Plutarch: *if* Posidonius really identified 'strictly psychic' affections such as appetite, fear, and anger as being 'those in judgements and suppositions' (*DLA* 6, with 'those in', *ta en*, dubiously supplied), he may only have meant that, unlike affections of the other kinds listed (in a wide sense of 'affection'), they are intentional states that fuel, and are fuelled by, judgements and suppositions as well as presentations.

23 Long and Sedley (1987: ii. 412) may be wiser to despair of making sense of most of this passage (*PHP* 320.23–8 = LS 65M8). I follow De Lacy (after Pohlenz and Edelstein) in supplying the words 'in the practical sphere'. My understanding of 'judgement' (*krisis*) here as what reason ought, but ceases, to exercise in forming its practical conclusions (*hypolêpseis*), fits one Chrysippean usage (as when, to Galen's bafflement, he calls excessive impulse 'without reason and judgement', *PHP* 240.14); and false evaluations (e.g., that bereavement is an evil) are often ascribed to weakness (*astheneia*, 266.26, 268.3, 268.20). However, my distinction between 'opinion' (*doxa*) as initial evaluation and 'supposition' (*hypolêpsis*) as practical conclusion is strained, for it does not rest on any difference in meaning (cf. 286.23).

24 We can speculate that the two issues that divide Posidonius from Plato connect, as is explicit in Buridan: in *QEAN* 7.6, he denies that a man can simultaneously accept two opposite judgements, partly on the ground that 'There is a single soul in us, as I think, intellectual, sensitive, appetitive, locomotive, and vegetative, and it is not extended with the

extension of the body, but exists as a whole everywhere'; again, 'Our soul exists indivisibly in the whole body, and in each part of it, and the judgements which it pronounces are not only in the qualitative and quantitative dispositions of the organs subjectively, but in the substance of the soul.'

PRIMARY SOURCES

ANCIENT

Aristotle (fourth century BC)

De anima (*On the Soul*)	*DA*
De motu animalium (*On the Movement of Animals*)	*DMA*
Eudemian Ethics	*EE*
Historia animalium (*Animal Investigations*)	*Hist an*
Metaphysics	*Met*
Nicomachean Ethics	*NE*
On Dreams	
On Memory	*Mem*
On the Parts of Animals	*PA*
Physics	
Politics	*Pol*
Posterior Analytics	*Post Anal*
Prior Analytics	
Protrepticus (*Exhortation to Philosophy*)	
Rhetoric	*Rhet*
Topics	*Top*

Aristotle's commentators

Commentaria in Aristotelem Graeca (*Greek Commentaries on Aristotle*)	*CIAG*

Cicero (first century BC)

Academica (*Academic Discussions*)	Acad
On Fate	
Tusculan Disputations	TD

Demosthenes (fourth century BC)

Speeches

Epictetus (first/second century AD)

Discourses	Disc

Euripides (fifth century BC)

Medea

Galen (second century AD)

De placitis Hippocratis et Platonis (*On the Doctrines of Hippocrates and Plato*)	PHP

(My references to *PHP* are to page and line in
De Lacy's edition.)

Homer (? eighth century BC)

Odyssey

Iamblichus (fourth century AD)

De vita Pythagorica (*On the Pythagorean Life*)

Lysias (fifth/fourth century BC)

Speeches

Plato (fifth/fourth century BC)

Apology (*The Defence of Socrates*)	Apol
Charmides	Charm
Cratylus	

Crito	
Epinomis	
Euthydemus	
Euthyphro	
Gorgias	*Gorg*
Laches	*Lach*
Laws	
Lysis	
Meno	
Phaedo	*Pdo*
Phaedrus	*Phdr*
Philebus	*Phil*
Politicus (The Statesman)	*Polit*
Protagoras	*Prot*
Republic	*Rep*
Seventh Letter	*7th Letter*
Sophist	*Soph*
Symposium	*Symp*
Theaetetus	*Theaet*
Timaeus	*Tim*

Plutarch (first/second century AD)

De liberis educandis (On the Education of Children)	*DLE*
De Stoicorum repugnantiis (On Stoic Self-Contradictions)	*DSR*
De virtute morali (On Moral Virtue)	*DVM*

Plutarch or Pseudo-Plutarch (? first/second century AD)

De libidine et aegritudine (On Desire and Distress)	*DLA*

Pseudo-Plato

Definitions

Seneca (first century AD)

Letters
De ira (On Anger)   *Ira*

Xenophon (fifth/fourth century BC)

Apology (The Defence of Socrates)
Memorabilia (Recollections of Socrates)

MEDIEVAL

Jean Buridan (fourteenth century AD)

Quaestiones in decem libros ethicorum Aristotelis
ad Nicomachum (Investigations into Aristotle's
Nicomachean Ethics)   *QEAN*

MODERN

Johannes Von Arnim

Stoicorum veterum fragmenta (Fragments of the
Early Stoics), 4 vols, Leipzig: Teubner, 1906–24   *SVF*
(In my references to *SVF*, a pair of numbers
indicates volume and section, a trio of numbers volume,
page, and line.)

A.A. Long and D.N. Sedley

The Hellenistic Philosophers, 2 vols, Cambridge:
Cambridge University Press, 1987.   LS

NOTE ON TRANSLATIONS

In quotations I commonly make use of the following translations, with modifications:

ARISTOTLE

The Revised Oxford Translation, ed. Jonathan Barnes, 2 vols, Princeton: Princeton University Press, 1984.

Eudemian Ethics Books 1, 2, and 8, by Michael Woods, 2nd edn, Oxford: Clarendon Press, 1992.

GALEN

De placitis Hippocratis et Platonis (*On the Doctrines of Hippocrates and Plato*), by Phillip De Lacy, 2nd edn, 3 vols, Berlin: Akademie-Verlag, 1980–4.

PLATO

Gorgias, by Terence Irwin, Oxford: Clarendon Press, 1979.

Laws, by R.G. Bury, 2 vols, London: Heinemann, 1926.

Phaedo, by David Gallop, Oxford: Clarendon Press, 1975.

Phaedrus, by C.J. Rowe, Warminster: Aris & Phillips, 1986.

Protagoras, by C.C.W. Taylor, rev. edn, Oxford: Clarendon Press, 1991.

Republic, by Paul Shorey, 2 vols, London: Heinemann, 1930.

Timaeus, by F.M. Cornford, *Plato's Cosmology*, London: Routledge & Kegan Paul, 1937.

MENTAL CONFLICT

PLUTARCH

De Stoicorum repugnantiis (*On Stoic Self-Contradictions*), by Harold Cherniss, *Moralia* XIII part II, London: Heinemann, 1976.

THE STOICS

A.A. Long and D.N. Sedley, *The Hellenistic Philosophers*, 2 vols, Cambridge: Cambridge University Press, 1987.

SECONDARY CITATIONS

Ackrill, J.L. (1980) 'Aristotle on *Eudaimonia*', in A.O. Rorty (ed.) *Essays on Aristotle's Ethics*, Berkeley and Los Angeles, Calif.: University of California Press.

Adam, J. (1902) *The Republic of Plato*, 2 vols, Cambridge: Cambridge University Press.

Annas, J.E. (1992) *Hellenistic Philosophy of Mind*, Berkeley and Los Angeles, Calif.: University of California Press.

Anscombe, G.E.M. (1963) *Intention*, 2nd edn, Oxford: Basil Blackwell.

Bobonich, C. (forthcoming) 'Akrasia and Agency in Plato's *Laws* and *Republic*', *Archiv für Geschichte der Philosophie*.

Bosanquet, B. (1895) *A Companion to Plato's Republic*, 2nd edn, London: Rivington, Percival & Co.

Bradley, F.H. (1927) *Ethical Studies*, 2nd edn, Oxford: Clarendon Press.

—— (1935) 'On Pleasure, Pain, Desire, and Volition', in his *Collected Essays*, 2 vols, Oxford: Clarendon Press.

Brentano, F. (1977) *The Psychology of Aristotle*, trans. R. George, Berkeley and Los Angeles, Calif.: University of California Press.

Broadie, S. (1991) *Ethics with Aristotle*, New York: Oxford University Press.

Campbell, K. (1985) 'Self-Mastery and Stoic Ethics', *Philosophy* 60: 327–40.

Cooper, J. (1989) 'Some Remarks on Aristotle's Moral Psychology', in T.D. Roche (ed.) *Aristotle's Ethics*, *Southern Journal of Philosophy* 27 supplement: 25–42.

—— (1993) 'Rhetoric, Dialectic and the Passions', *Oxford Studies in Ancient Philosophy* 11: 175–98.

—— (unpublished) 'Posidonius on Emotions', available from the author.

Cornford, F.M. (1912) 'Psychology and Social Structure in the *Republic* of Plato', *Classical Quarterly* 6: 246–65.

Dahl, N.O. (1984) *Practical Reason, Aristotle, and Weakness of Will*, Minneapolis, Minn.: University of Minnesota Press.

Diggle, J. (ed.) (1984) *Euripidis Fabulae: Tomus I*, Oxford: Clarendon Press.

Dover, K.J. (1974) *Greek Popular Morality in the Time of Plato and Aristotle*, Oxford: Basil Blackwell.

Engberg-Pedersen, T. (1990) *The Stoic Theory of Oikeiosis*, Aarhus: Aarhus University Press.

211

Ferrari, G.R.F. (1991) 'Moral Fecundity: A Discussion of A.W. Price, *Love and Friendship in Plato and Aristotle*', *Oxford Studies in Ancient Philosophy* 9: 169–84.

Frankfurt, H. (1988a), 'Coercion and Moral Responsibility', in *The Importance of What We Care About: Philosophical Essays*, Cambridge: Cambridge University Press.

—— (1988b) 'Freedom of the Will and the Concept of a Person', in *The Importance of What We Care About: Philosophical Essays*, Cambridge: Cambridge University Press.

Freud, S. (1973–86) *The Pelican Freud Library (PFL)*, ed. A. Richards, 15 vols, Harmondsworth: Penguin Books.

Gardner, S. (1993) *Irrationality and the Philosophy of Psychoanalysis*, Cambridge: Cambridge University Press.

Gill, C. (1983) 'Did Chrysippus Understand Medea?', *Phronesis* 28: 136–49.

—— (1985) 'Plato and the Education of Character', *Archiv für Geschichte der Philosophie* 67: 1–26.

—— (1987) 'Two Monologues of Self-Division: Euripides, *Medea* 1021–80 and Seneca, *Medea* 893–977', in M. and M. Whitby, and P. Hardie (eds) *Homo Viator: Classical Essays for John Bramble*, Bristol: Bristol Classical Press.

Gosling, J.C.B. (1990) *Weakness of the Will*, London: Routledge.

Gosling, J.C.B. and Taylor, C.C.W. (1982) *The Greeks on Pleasure*, Oxford: Clarendon Press.

Groag, E. (1915) 'Zur Lehre vom Wesen der Seele in Platons *Phaedrus* und im zehnten Buch der *Republik*', *Wiener Studien* 37: 189–222.

Inwood, B. (1985) *Ethics and Human Action in Early Stoicism*, Oxford: Clarendon Press.

Irwin, T.H. (1977) *Plato's Moral Theory*, Oxford: Clarendon Press.

—— (1988) *Aristotle's First Principles*, Oxford: Clarendon Press.

Kahn, C.H. (1987–8) 'Plato's Theory of Desire', *Review of Metaphysics* 41: 77–103.

Kenny, A. (1973) 'The Practical Syllogism and Incontinence', in his *The Anatomy of the Soul*, Oxford: Basil Blackwell.

—— (1979) *Aristotle's Theory of the Will*, London: Duckworth.

Kidd, I.G. (1988) *Posidonius: II The Commentary*, 2 vols, Cambridge: Cambridge University Press.

Lloyd-Jones, H. (1980) 'Euripides, *Medea* 1056–80', *Würzburger Jahrbücher für die Altertumswissenschaft* 6a: 51–9.

Loening, R. (1903) *Die Zurechnungslehre des Aristoteles*, Stuttgart: Gustav Fischer; repr. Hildesheim: Georg Olms, 1967.

Long, A.A. and Sedley, D.N. (1987) *The Hellenistic Philosophers*, 2 vols, Cambridge: Cambridge University Press.

Moline, J. (1981) *Plato's Theory of Undertanding*, Madison, Wisc.: University of Wisconsin Press.

Morrison, D. (1985) '*Chôristos* in Aristotle', *Harvard Studies in Classical Philology* 89: 89–105.

Müller, A.W. (1982) *Praktisches Folgern und Selbstgestaltung nach Aristoteles*, Freiburg and Munich: Karl Alber.

Newman, W.L. (1887–1902) *The Politics of Aristotle*, 4 vols, Oxford: Clarendon Press.

Nussbaum, M.C. (1978) *Aristotle's De motu animalium*, Princeton, NJ: Princeton University Press.

—— (1986) *The Fragility of Goodness: Luck and Ethics in Greek Tragedy and Philosophy*, Cambridge: Cambridge University Press.

—— (1987) 'The Stoics on the Extirpation of the Passions', *Apeiron* 22: 129–76.

—— (1993) 'Poetry and the Passions: Two Stoic Views', in J. Brunschwig and M.C. Nussbaum (eds) *Passions and Perceptions: Studies in Hellenistic Philosophy of Mind*, Cambridge: Cambridge University Press.

Pears, D. (1984) *Motivated Irrationality*, Oxford: Clarendon Press.

Penner, T. (1971) 'Thought and Desire in Plato', in G. Vlastos (ed.) *Plato II: Ethics, Politics, and Philosophy of Art and Religion*, New York: Doubleday & Co.

Price, A.W. (1980) 'Aristotle's Ethical Holism', *Mind* 89: 338–52.

—— (1989) *Love and Friendship in Plato and Aristotle*, Oxford: Clarendon Press.

—— (1990) 'Plato and Freud', in C. Gill (ed.) *The Person and the Human Mind: Issues in Ancient and Modern Philosophy*, Oxford: Clarendon Press.

—— (1991) 'Martha Nussbaum's *Symposium*', *Ancient Philosophy* 11: 285–99.

Reeve, M. (1972) 'Euripides, *Medea* 1021–1080', *Classical Quarterly* 22: 51–61.

Roberts, J. (1987) 'Plato on the Causes of Wrongdoing in the *Laws*', *Ancient Philosophy* 7: 23–37.

Rowe, C.J. (1990) 'Philosophy, Love, and Madness', in C. Gill (ed.) *The Person and the Human Mind: Issues in Ancient and Modern Philosophy*, Oxford: Clarendon Press.

Saunders, T.J. (1962) 'The Structure of the Soul and the State in Plato's Laws', *Eranos* 60: 37–55.

—— (1991) *Plato's Penal Code*, Oxford: Clarendon Press.

Schiffer, S. (1976) 'A Paradox of Desire', *American Philosophical Quarterly* 13: 195–203.

Sharples, R.W. (1983) '"But Why Has My Spirit Spoken With Me Thus?": Homeric Decision-Making', *Greece and Rome* 30: 1–7.

Sherman, N. (1989) *The Fabric of Character: Aristotle's Theory of Virtue*, Oxford: Clarendon Press.

Slote, M. (1986) *Common-Sense Morality and Consequentialism*, London: Routledge & Kegan Paul.

Sorabji, R. (1992) 'Intentionality and Physiological Processes: Aristotle's Theory of Sense-Perception', in M.C. Nussbaum and A.O. Rorty (eds) *Essays on Aristotle's De anima*, Oxford: Clarendon Press.

Stewart, J.A. (1892) *Notes on the Nicomachean Ethics of Aristotle*, 2 vols, Oxford: Clarendon Press.

Taylor, C.C.W. (1991) *Plato: Protagoras*, rev. edn, Oxford: Clarendon Press.

Tracy, T.J. (1969) *Physiological Theory and the Doctrine of the Mean in Plato and Aristotle*, The Hague: Mouton.

Vander Waerdt, P.A. (1987) 'Aristotle's Criticism of Soul Division', *American Journal of Philology* 108: 627–43.

Vlastos, G. (1991) *Socrates: Ironist and Moral Philosopher*, Cambridge: Cambridge University Press.

Wiggins, D. (1991a) 'Truth, Invention and the Meaning of Life', in his *Needs, Values, Truth*, 2nd edn, Oxford: Blackwell.

—— (1991b) 'Weakness of Will, Commensurability, and the Objects of Deliberation and Desire', in his *Needs, Values, Truth*; also in A. Rorty (ed.) (1980) *Essays on Aristotle's Ethics*, Berkeley and Los Angeles, Calif.: University of California Press.

Williams, B. (1993) *Shame and Necessity*, Berkeley and Los Angeles, Calif.: University of California Press.

Woods, M.J. (1986) 'Intuition and Perception in Aristotle's Ethics', *Oxford Studies in Ancient Philosophy* 4: 145–66.

—— (1992) *Aristotle Eudemian Ethics Books 1, 2, & 8*, 2nd edn, Oxford: Clarendon Press.

INDEX

Ackrill, J.L. 199n36
acrasia 23–5, 94–103, 129–44,
    158–9, 163–6, 173–4; hard 18, 22,
    95, 97–8, 99–100, 142–3,
    187–8n27; soft 95, 100–2; weak
    or impetuous 139–40
Adam, J. 53
affective soul 118; beliefs of 125–9
Allan, D.J. 191n8
Andronicus 147, 150, 201n8
anger 52–3, 78, 101–2, 106–7, 115,
    116–17, 121, 190n6–191n7,
    193n16; how acratic 140–1,
    199n35; in children 53, 65, 121
Annas, J. 175
Anscombe, G.E.M. 174
appetite (to epithymêtikon) 35,
    45–6, 51–2, 59–65, 84–6, 186n21;
    and anger 78, 108, 190–1n7; in
    Aristotle 106–7; faults of 77–8,
    86–7; how acratic 132–9;
    typically insatiable 35, 60, 62, 85
appetites 13, 185n14, 186n21,
    194n19; and goodness 34–5,
    48–51, 63, 189–90n3; for money
    62; for philosophy 62–3; and
    pleasure 30–3, 37, 60, 61–2, 106;
    see also epithymia
Aristotle: De anima (1.1) 115; (3.9)
    112–14; (3.10) 104–5, 112;
    Nicomachean Ethics (1.13)
    105–6, 108–11, 113, 191–2n9;
    (7.3) 132–9, 196n29–199n35;
    Rhetoric 115–18, 193n15, 194n21

Arius Didymus 147, 150, 164, 165,
    200n4, 201n8

Barnes, J. 209; uneccentric 196n30
Bobonich, C. 185n15, 187n26
body and soul 36–9, 115, 121–3
Bosanquet, B. 50
Bradley, F.H. 61, 182n16
Brentano, F. 192n11
Broadie, S. 198–9n34
Buridan, J. 191n9, 198–9n34–5,
    203–4n24
Burnyeat, M. 193n17
Bury, R.G. 209

Campbell, K. 169
causation of action 89, 146, 174,
    193n14
Cherniss, H. 210
choice (prohairesis) 106, 146–7,
    189n2, 192n10
Chrysippus ch. 4 passim
Cicero ch. 4 passim, 186n20
Cleanthes 145, 151–2, 203n21
confrontation of beliefs or desires
    46–8, 52, 54, 68, 159–60, 169–70;
    within spirit 66–7
contrariety of appetites 45–6, 55,
    107; of beliefs 43–5, 49–50, 71–2,
    128–9, 158–9, 169–70, 171–2,
    195–6n26, 199n35; of desires
    41–2, 72, 90–1, 104–5; strong or
    weak 42–3, 46, 55, 123
Cooper, J. 107, 175, 176, 193n17

215

Cornford, F.M. 49, 70, 184n7, 209

Dahl, N.O. 196n27, 196n29, 197n32, 199n39
De Lacy, P. 200n6, 203n23, 209
Demosthenes 183n3
desire: and beauty 9–10, 32–3; and goodness 9–11; and pleasure 14–27, 32–3, 37–8; a physical or quasi-physical force 33, 88–9, 90–2, 104–5; rechannelled 55, 184n8; sexual 12–13 (*see also* erotic love); varieties of 30–1, 106, 189n2; *see also epithymia; orexis*
Diggle, J. 179n2
Diogenes Laertius 201–2n13
Dover, K.J. 180n3–4, 183n2–3

Engberg-Pedersen, T. 200n4
Epictetus 158–9, 162, 169, 170
epithymia (desire or appetite) 30–2, 59, 93, 106, 147, 183n1, 189n1, 200n7
erotic love 8–10, 12, 31–3; conflicted 77–80, 93, 98–9, 174
Euripides: *Medea* 2–5, 157–8, 169, 179n2
Eustratius 179n3

Ferrari, G.R.F. 180n2, 185–6n17
Forms: of Beauty 70–1, 78; of Goodness 129, 185n12; of Temperance 78–9
Frankfurt, H. 23, 98
Frede, M. 191n9
Freud, S. 34, 70, 80, 98, 184n9–185n10, 188n28, 200n3

Galen ch. 4 *passim*
Gallop, D. 209
Gardner, S. 184n9
Gay, R. 199n37
Gill, C. 6, 66, 102, 129, 159, 161, 186n21
Ginsberg, A. 183–4n5
Gosling, J.C.B. 153, 170, 181n9, 183n2, 184n6, 187n27, 196n31, 202n15
Groag, E. 75

happiness (*eudaimonia*): Socratic object of all desire 9–11, 27–9, 179n1; Aristotelian object of rational desire 106, 130, 180n5
Hare, R.M. 196n30
Homer 40, 147, 156, 157
homogeneity, mooted: of beauties 180n6, 181–2n14; of pleasures and pains 23–6, 182n15
Hume, D. 37, 80, 128, 177
hybris (outrage or excess) 31, 77

Iamblichus 186n20
ignorance as a cause or aspect of acting wrongly: general 86–7, 92–3, 95, 101, 159, 168, 187n25, 188n30–1, 201–2n13; particular 136–9
intention 42, 146–7, 199–200n2
Inwood, B. 167, 188n28, 200n4, 201n8, 202n16
Irwin, T.H. 30, 32, 49, 184n7, 186n19, 195n24, 209

Kahn, C.H. 70
Kenny, A. 196n29, 196n31–198n34
Kidd, I.G. 155

Lloyd-Jones, H. 3, 179n2
Long, A.A. 201n11; and Sedley, D.N. 200n4, 202n16, 203n23, 210
love and hate 190n6, 194n20
lovemaking: idyllic but second-rate 80; pleasant rather than beautiful 10, 32–3; tempts but fails to occur 78–9
Lysias 183n2–3

mental conflict, examples of: drinking 41–2, 46–7, 172; fear of the rope bridge 44–5, 172, 184n6; Leontius 52–3, 97–8, 159, 188n29; making love 98–9; Medea 2–5, 157, 160–1, 179n3, 203n20; Menelaus 157–8, 168; Odysseus 40, 47, 157, 203n20; trying out the echo in the reading-room of the British Museum 95–7

Moline, J. 114
Morrison, D. 192n13
Müller, A. 115, 190n4

Newman, W.L. 52
Nussbaum, M.C. 23–5, 80, 153,
    180n6, 181–2n14, 189n1–2,
    194n18

orexis (desire) 106, 116, 148, 183n1,
    189n1–2, 191n9–192n10
oscillation of mind 3–4, 160

parts of the soul 6–7, 53–5, 70–2,
    84–5, 92–4, 102–3, 105–8, 118,
    154–5, 171–3, 177, 184n7, 184n9,
    187n24, 190n5, 195n25; and
    capacities 111–14, 192n12;
    defined 53; and homunculi 56–7,
    184n7, 190n6; localized 84–9,
    193n14, 201n10; subject to
    persuasion 35, 50, 63–5, 85–6,
    101, 120–3; *see also* appetite;
    reason; spirit
pathos (affection or passion)
    114–25, 131, 147–52, 175–8;
    and emotion 193n15; and
    emotional disturbance (*tarachê*)
    116, 125, 176–7; and feelings
    119–20, 194n21; likened to a
    runaway horse 78–9, 150, 164;
    primary and secondary 147–9,
    150, 200–1n7; propositional
    but not cognitive 117–18,
    194n18
Pears, D. 181n13, 187n27
Penner, T. 61
perception 36–7, 70–1
person placed outside his physical
    and psychological make-up
    38–9, 91–2, 172–3
phantasia: appearance or
    imagination (Aristotle) 114,
    116–17, 122–3, 126–8, 190n4,
    195–6n26; impression or
    presentation (Stoics) 146
philosopher-kings 185n11
Plato: *Gorgias* 33–6; *Laws* 90–4,
    99–102, 187n26, 188n30–189n31;

Phaedo 36–40, 70; *Phaedrus* 30–3,
    66–7, 70–1, 74–81, 98–9, 186–7n23;
    Protagoras 14–27, 181n8–182n17;
    Republic 40–76, 96–8, 102–3,
    183n3–186n22, 187n25, 188n29;
    Symposium 8–14, 27–9, 69,
    179n1–181n7; *Timaeus* 82–9,
    102, 187n24
Plutarch 107, 146, 149–50, 153,
    157, 158, 166, 174, 186n20,
    190–1n7, 200n6–7, 202n15,
    203n22
Posidonius 145, 154–6, 171, 172,
    175–8, 202n17–18, 203n21–4
principle of non-contrariety 40–1,
    57, 68, 88, 90

reason: in Aristotle (*to logon
    echon*) 108–11, 192n10–11,
    195n25; in Plato (usually *to
    logistikon*) 51–2, 57–9, 81, 84–6,
    153–4, 186n19; in the Stoics 153,
    159; theoretical and practical
    129–31
Reeve, M. 179n2
responsibility 138–9, 161–7
Ricks, C. 193n17
Roberts, J. 101
Rowe, C.J. 80, 186n23, 209

Saunders, T. 93, 101, 187n26
Schiffer, S. 63
Schofield, M. 27–8, 186n18,
    201n13, 202n16, 203n19
self-mastery 31, 34, 94, 183n2; lack
    of 5
Seneca 146, 155, 162, 163, 168, 170
sexual arousal: caused by beauty
    12; escapes comprehension and
    control 79; not a remedy for the
    human condition 81–2; occurs
    involuntarily without thought's
    command 163
Sharples, R. 147
Sherman, N. 194n18
Shorey, P. 185n13, 209
Simplicius 162, 193n14
Slote, M. 22
Sorabji, R. 195n24

soul: and body 13–14; divine
74–5; imaged as winged and
feathered charioteer and horses
74–9, 81, 188n28, or as rider and
horse 150, 164, 188n28;
incarnation of 76–7, 82–3;
original nature of 73–6, 186n22;
sick 33, 168–9, 202–3n18; and
society 1–2, 56, 69; *see also*
affective soul; parts of the soul
spirit (*to thymoeides*) 52–3, 65–7,
84–8, 185n16, 186n19; in
Aristotle 106–8, 190n6; and the
emotions 68–70, 87–8; and
shame 66–7, 77–80
Stewart, J.A. 196n30
Stobaeus 147, 200n4, 201n13
Stoic jargon: *hêgemonikon*
(commanding faculty) 146, 162;
hormê (impulse) to an action
146, 148–9, 168, or to a swelling
or contraction 149, 151; *lekton*
(proposition) 146, 153, 199n1;
oikeiôsis (orientation) 155;
pneuma (fiery stuff) 146, 148–9,
156; *propatheia* (preliminary
affection) 162–3, 165, 170–1;
proskopê (collision) 170; *ptoia*
(fluttering) 158; *synkatathesis*
(assent) 146

Taylor, C.C.W. 18–19, 21, 22,
181n8–10, 182n15
temperance 33, 64; *see also* Forms
Tracy, T.J. 87, 122

vacillation of mind 4–6, 21, 157–60
Vander Waerdt, P.A. 189n2
Vlastos, G. 181n9, 182n17

White, S. 201n12
Wiggins, D. 24, 137, 196n27, 200n5
Williams, B. 147
wish (*boulêsis*) 30, 32, 106, 110,
113, 117, 189n2, 190n6, 191–2n9,
194n20, 200n7
Woods, M.J. 132, 194n22, 209

Xenophon 12, 180n3, 183n3

Zeno (the Stoic) 145, 147, 149, 152,
158, 162, 203n21